The Official Fan's Guide to
THE FUGITIVE

The Official Fan's Guide to
THE FUGITIVE

Mel Proctor

LONGMEADOW PRESS

Stamford, Connecticut

Cover and interior design by Pamela C. Pia.

Photo Credits
Muffett Martin Bowie: 9, 85, 87, 89 (left) Dave Brown: 47 (bottom left and right), 66 Kim Carlsberg: 9 (top right) Roy Huggins: 3 Frank Liberman Collection: 38 (all), 39 Kay Mcafee: v, 35, 40 (all), 41, 42 (left), 43, 44, 47 (top), 90 MPTVPA/David Sutton: 32, 59 MPTVPA, Warner Bros./Stephen Vaughan: 95, 96 Barry Morse: xiv, Jerry Ohlinger: 93, 94 (right) Mel Proctor: 5, 13 (left), 17 (left), 27, 43, 46 (right), 69 Worldvision Enterprises, Inc.: 6, 10, 11 (all), 12 (all), 13 (right), 14, 17 (right), 18 (all), 19, 20, 22 (all), 23, 24, 28, 29 (all), 30, 31, 36, 37, 42 (right), 46 (left), 48, 51, 52 (all), 53, 54, 56, 60, 62, 69 (right), 70 (all), 72 (all) 73 (all), 74, 75, 76 (all), 79 (all), 80 (all), 81, 82, 86, 89, 94, 99, 100, 101 (all), 103, 104, 105, 106 (all), 107, 108, 109, 110, 111, 112 (all), 114, 115, 117, 118 (all), 120, 122 (all), 124, 125, 127, 128, 129, 131, 133, 136, 137, 138, 139, 140, 141, 143, 144.

This Longmeadow Press edition is printed on archival quality paper. It is acid-free and conforms to the guidelines established for permanence and durability by the Council of Library Resources and the American National Standards Institute.∞™

Library of Congress Cataloging-in-Publication Data

Proctor, Mel.
    The official fan's guide to The Fugitive / Mel Proctor.
        p. cm.
    Includes bibliographical references.
    ISBN 0-681-00754-0
    1. Fugitive (Television program)   I. Title.
PN1992.77.F79P76   1995
791.45'72–dc20   94-44236
                                                                          CIP

Printed and bound in the United States of America.
First Longmeadow Press edition.
0 9 8 7 6 5 4 3 2 1

DEDICATION

This book is dedicated to the memory of David Janssen, a talented actor and warm, wonderful man, whose love, friendship, and humor touched the lives of all who knew him.

Mel Proctor
May, 1994

CONTENTS

ACKNOWLEDGMENTS

I am indebted to all of the talented actors, writers, producers, directors, and others who shared their *Fugitive* memories with me. Special thanks to: Barry Morse and his wife Sydney, Alan Armer, Roy Huggins, John Conwell, Walter Grauman, George Eckstein, Carol Rossen, Don Medford, Stanford Whitmore, Richard Anderson, Ed Asner, Jacqueline Scott, William Conrad, Muffet Martin Bowie, Berniece Janssen, Ellie Janssen, Dani Janssen, Suzanne Pleshette, Tom Gallagher and Diane Baker.

Thanks also to Angela Wright, David Hoff, Ken Levine, Neil Issacs, Don Wear, Jimmy Borges, Joe Moore, Kimo McVay and Tim Tindall.

Thanks to The Academy of Television Arts and Sciences Library, The University of Southern California's Cinema-TV Library, and the Columbia, Maryland public library.

Thanks also to fellow "Fugitive Fanatics," Rusty Pollard and his wonderful "On The Run" newsletter and Dave Brown. Without the help of Kay McAfee, this book wouldn't have been possible. Thank you so much, Kay, for your research, and for your love of David Janssen and *The Fugitive*.

A special thank-you to my good friend Chris Grant for patiently taking my countless phone calls regarding the use of a computer and for providing emotional support.

I owe a debt of gratitude to my agent Mark Joly of the Scott Meredith Literary Agency. Thank you Mark for your persistance and belief in this project. Thanks also to Arthur Klebanoff, President of the Scott Meredith Literary Agency, for believing in my abilities.

I appreciate the cooperation of Monique Reid-Berryhill of Worldvision and Lisa Berlin of Hamilton Projects.

I feel grateful that I found a kindred spirit in my editor Pam Pia from Long-meadow Press. Thank you Pam for your love of *The Fugitive* and for your guidance in getting this book published.

Above all, thanks to my wife Julie, my daughter Maile, and my son Billy, for providing love and support during this project. You can have your Dad and the computer back now.

Foreword

FOREWORD

I plunge my hand into the lucky dip which is the average old actor's memory bank, and out comes 1963 and *The Fugitive*.

I've never been one to collect archival material: For one thing, my favorite part is never the last one but always the next one; and for another, the sweet lady whom I call the Management (that's my wife Sydney) has always gently reminded me that if we started collecting professional memorabilia, we'd have to move out of our home and go live in the park. (We've been married almost fifty-five years and in our profession for almost sixty!)

So, my own remembrances of those times and that project are filtered through the last thirty years, and are inevitably what we call in the movie trade my "POV." (point of view).

Anyone who has spent time in a court of law and heard accounts of the same event from a succession of witnesses will know that such recollections can vary widely, even when those giving the evidence are honestly convinced that their version of events is the only accurate one.

In assembling such a volume and such a range of information and recollection about the making of this substantial piece of television history, Mel Proctor gives all those who down the years have fallen under the fascination of what has become known as "Fugitive fever" the opportunity to sift for themselves the thoughts and feelings of a number of us who can say, "I was there."

As so often happens in life, I was there through a succession of flukes. The theater tour of Harold Pinter's play *The Caretaker*, in which I played the eponymous character, had just closed in Los Angeles at the very time when Quinn Martin was putting together the unit to produce *The Fugitive* pilot.

I soon became aware that our project was viewed with considerable misgiving by most of the so-called "experts." Now, of course, one of the many peculiarities of our trade is that everybody is an expert in it. People who would never dream of offering advice to their dentist on how to fill teeth or to a roadworker on how to fill a hole will readily give omniscient guidance to those of us who labor down the movie mines.

Such people (bless their sweet, foolish hearts) never seem to realize that anybody who could infallibly predict the degree of success of entertainment projects would swiftly become one of the richest and most powerful people on this planet, without even getting out of bed. The fact that no one in the whole history of mankind has yet elected to grasp the opportunity shows remarkable restraint.

Despite all the gloomy predictions of the "experts," *The Fugitive* rapidly became one of the most popular dramas on television all over the world and, even more remarkable, has remained so for the last thirty years.

In fact today's younger generation of viewers, who weren't even born when we were making the series, prefer it to most of today's offerings.

All of which is very gratifying to those of us who had a hand in it, and leads to the show beginning to be called a "classic," which simply means, in my view, something that succeeding generations have continued to admire and enjoy.

Meanwhile, of course, those same "experts"

who long since foretold our failure have now joined the ranks of the "hindsighters," crying, "I told you so."

And so, the whirligig of time brings its revenges.

The joy of remembering that brave band of artists and craftsmen whose contributions have made *The Fugitive* a classic is darkened somewhat by the realization that all too many are no longer with us.

Most memorably, of course, our hero, David Janssen. David's early death was tragically wasteful in many ways. Not least in the sense of so much talent unused and unfulfilled.

Among all his other gifts and accomplishments, one that could never be adequately recognized and admired was that he was what we call in our trade "a real pro." All through the months and years when he was probably the most hard-worked actor in the history of television — he was

in almost every shot of every scene in the series — he never failed to be scrupulously prepared for everything he was called upon to do, and to extend total courtesy and consideration to the whole cast and crew.

And among all the parts he played, no one ever adequately captured and displayed what I always felt was one of the most valuable of his gifts: that dry, wry, whimsical sense of humor which colored his view of life in general and himself in particular, and which could have made him a superb romantic light comedian.

The Fugitive is a treasured memory in my life and career. To Mel Proctor and his record of those great years *The Official Fan's Guide to The Fugitive*, I can wish no warmer wish than: "Keep Running!"

Barry Morse
May 1994

Introduction

In 1963, when I first watched *The Fugitive*, it grabbed my attention like no other television show ever had. As a teenager searching for my own identity, I empathized with the loneliness and isolation of Dr. Richard Kimble. Sure, I knew *The Fugitive* was only a television show and David Janssen just an actor who played Kimble, but Kimble and his weekly predicaments became alluringly real.

As much as I loved Kimble, I hated his pursuer, Lieutenant Philip Gerard, portrayed so adroitly by Barry Morse. I hoped that Kimble would elude Gerard, find the one-armed man who killed his wife, and prove his innocence.

I was part of the record television audience which watched the final episode, "The Judgment," Part II, on August 29, 1967, which answered the question of who really killed Helen Kimble.

When *The Fugitive* went off the air, there was a void in my life. I would occasionally watch other shows, but none held my interest like *The Fugitive*.

Some twenty-five years later I rediscovered *The Fugitive* on A&E, the Arts and Entertainment Network. As I watched, I still found myself identifying with Richard Kimble, but discovered new levels of appreciation. I became intrigued by the show's terrific writing, and I smiled warmly as I saw guest stars like Telly Savalas, Ed Asner, and Carroll O'Connor, who in the 1960s were merely young actors building careers in television.

I decided it would be fun to research the show and possibly write a book.

I began by locating *The Fugitive*'s longtime producer Alan Armer and we agreed to meet at Nate 'n Al's delicatessen in Beverly Hills. Over the clatter of dishes, I listened in awe as Armer detailed the series' history and talked fondly of David Janssen.

Then I met with *The Fugitive*'s creator Roy Huggins. As we sat in the wood-paneled den where he had once played poker with David Janssen, Huggins regaled me with the story of *The Fugitive*'s conception and the obstacles he overcame in gaining acceptance for his idea.

As my magical trip through "Fugitiveland" continued, I listened as George Eckstein, *Fugitive* writer and associate producer, reminisced about writing the show's dramatic final episode.

In Santa Barbara I lunched with John Conwell, *The Fugitive*'s casting director and later vice president of QM Productions, which produced the show. Conwell opened a treasure chest full of anecdotes about the guest stars who appeared on the show and spoke fondly of his twenty-five-year friendship with Quinn Martin, the show's executive producer.

Over coffee and doughnuts in Tarzana, California, David Janssen's mother Berniece recalled her son's childhood and his beginnings in show business.

During my visit to Walter Grauman's, the veteran director talked of his friendship with David Janssen and recalled the difficulties in directing *The Fugitive*'s pilot.

At Grauman's suggestion, I lunched at the Formosa Cafe, one of David Janssen's favorite hangouts, across from the old Goldwyn Studios where *The Fugitive* was filmed. A waitress who had worked there for over thirty years pointed to Janssen's favorite bar stool and talked of the actor's visits. As I listened to her, I looked at the black and white photos of television and movie stars that adorned the walls, got caught up in the nostalgia, and half expected Janssen to walk through the front door.

While in Los Angeles, I also spoke with two of David Janssen's closest friends, actress Suzanne Pleshette and her husband Tom Gallagher, and with Jacqueline Scott, who played Richard Kimble's sister, Donna Taft.

Several weeks later in New York, I met with actress Carol Rossen, a frequent *Fugitive* guest star. And over the next few months I talked with David Janssen's two wives, Ellie and Dani; with Richard Anderson, who played Kimble's brother-in-law, Leonard Taft; and with Diane Baker, who played Jean Carlisle, Kimble's love interest in the final episode. I also visited with Don Medford, who directed the final episode of *The Fugitive*, Stanford Whitmore, who wrote the show's pilot, and Ed Asner, one of the many guest stars who graced *The Fugitive*. I enjoyed a wonderful conversation with the show's narrator, William Conrad, who in that thunderous voice recalled his work on *The Fugitive* and his relationship with Quinn Martin.

In Toronto I dined with Barry Morse and his lovely wife Sydney, and sat entranced as Morse reminisced about his sixty years in show business and recalled his fatherly relationship with David Janssen. Over a bottle of wine and a night full of wonderful conversation, Morse convinced me that I no longer hated Lieutenant Gerard.

As I researched this book, I became aware of the tremendous resurgence of interest in *The Fugitive*. There are at least two *Fugitive* fan clubs in the United States and one in France, and several *Fugitive* newsletters. I learned that writer Stephen King regarded *The Fugitive* as the best television show of all time, and that the late comic Sam Kinison would unwind from a concert by watching *Fugitive* episodes all night long.

My faith in this project was strengthened when *TV Guide*'s editors selected *The Fugitive* as the best dramatic show of the 1960s and *Entertainment Weekly* named *The Fugitive* the sixth best television show of all time, with the five shows ahead of it all situation comedies.

The release of *The Fugitive* movie in August 1993, touched off a whole new wave of *Fugitive* mania. WJBK-TV, Channel 2 in Detroit, aired a *Fugitive* marathon, hosted by Barry Morse, which dominated the ratings on a Sunday night. And NBC purchased three hours of *The Fugitive*, including the two-part conclusion, for airing on network television.

As this book began to take shape, I realized that in addition to trying to provide a good read, I also felt a tremendous obligation to accurately document the story of the truly wonderful and talented people who contributed to *The Fugitive*. I hope I have succeeded on both counts.

My trip back to *The Fugitive* was a marvelous journey. I hope yours will be too.

Mel Proctor
Baltimore, Maryland

The Official Fan's Guide to
THE FUGITIVE

Chapter 1

The Creator and the Creation – Roy Huggins

They thought it was tasteless. All they could see was that it was a series about a man who had been accused of killing his wife, had been found guilty and escaped, and is now on the loose. They just thought it was a dreadful idea.

—Roy Huggins, on his friends' reaction to The Fugitive

September 19, 1960, Los Angeles.

Blue sky. Bright sunshine. A perfect Southern California afternoon. Dressed only in swim trunks, Roy Huggins relaxed in a chaise lounge in his backyard.

The 46-year-old Huggins had just left Warner Bros., where he had made his mark in television as creator and/or producer of hit series like *Maverick, Cheyenne, Colt .45*, and *77 Sunset Strip*. Known primarily for his work in westerns, Huggins needed a new challenge.

Sitting at poolside, Huggins thought, "Westerns were all over the air, and I didn't want to do another western, but I knew there was something magical about westerns. I decided it was the character of the lead, it was the existential situation of the lead in a western. He was utterly free, he never had to answer to anyone, he never worked, it was never clear what he did for a living. He drifted and no one really knew why. How do you achieve that kind of mythic freedom in a contemporary setting?"

"I really went over every possibility. If a man is just a drifter in the 1960s, the audience isn't going to like him, they're going to say he's irresponsible, he's a bum. Then, it suddenly occurred to me that it had to be forced on him, and the only way it could be forced on him would be that he is wanted for a crime. And it had to be a capital crime, otherwise he wouldn't drift, he would fight it. But if it's a capital crime and all of his appeals have been exhausted and then he gets a chance to run, there's no question what he's going to do . . . he's going to run and he's going to be, in the existential sense, a western hero. So, that's how it happened."

Excited by his idea, Huggins rushed into his house, returning with a yellow legal pad and a pen. Leaning back in the chaise lounge, he began to write a six-page treatment that became the basis for one of the most popular and enduring television dramas of all time, *The Fugitive.*

Huggins described Dr. Richard Kimble, a physician found guilty of murdering his wife Helen. Despite Kimble's protestations that he had seen "a gaunt and red-haired man" running from his house the night of the murder, the real killer was never found. As Kimble was being transported to prison for execution, a train wreck occurred and Kimble escaped. The story dealt with what happened to Kimble as he moved around, trying to avoid capture and seeking to find his wife's real murderer.

In his treatment, Huggins mentioned that *The Fugitive* contained "the element of absolute freedom" found in the classic western movie *Shane.* He also referred to Victor Hugo's nineteenth-century novel *Les Misérables*, which depicted an incorruptible policeman, Inspector Javert, who spent his life tracking down a fugitive, Jean Valjean. Huggins described Kimble's pursuer as a man from the state's attorney's office and said the chase would embody the characteristics of Javert's pursuit of Jean Valjean.

After completing *The Fugitive* treatment, Huggins was contacted by ABC executive Ollie Treyz, who told him, "Roy, you're going to be getting two calls, one from MGM and one from Twentieth Century-Fox. They will both be offering you the job of running their television department. We don't care which one you take, but we hope to hell you take one of them."

In October 1960 Huggins accepted Fox's offer to become vice president in charge of television production. While flying from New York to California with his new boss, Peter Levathes, president of Fox Television, Huggins tried out his *Fugitive* idea. "You know, I already have a show that I have tremendous confidence in," Huggins told Levathes. "I think it should be our first at bat."

As Huggins described his idea, he sensed he was in trouble. "Levathes's eyes went blank, he turned pale, and I'm not kidding, the guy looked

Roy Huggins, creator of The Fugitive.

sick, absolutely sick," said Huggins, "and he didn't respond." As Levathes attempted to change the subject, Huggins thought, "This is the best idea I've ever come up with. I'll never have a more surefire concept in my life than *The Fugitive,* and he thinks I'm an idiot."

"When we landed in California," continued Huggins, "Levathes had already made up his mind that hiring me was the biggest mistake he'd ever made in his life. I was unhappy from the first day at Fox, because I knew Levathes thought I was a fake, that I had gotten this great reputation based on the work of others, not my own. And he couldn't have been farther from the truth." Levathes banished Huggins to a tiny back office, and Huggins immediately called his lawyer in an attempt to escape from his contract with Fox.

When Huggins's attorney Ed Erkle told him "Jesus, Roy, give it time, you're overreacting," he decided to stay at Fox and attempt to make the best of a bleak situation. Erkle also added that he didn't like *The Fugitive* either, saying it was an unsavory concept that the networks would hate.

Despite Levathes's reaction, Huggins still believed in the *Fugitive* concept and sought out others for reinforcement. "I told my closest friends, my agent, people in the business, and they all hated it," said Huggins. "They not only hated it, but they reacted just the way Levathes did."

Huggins's best friend, writer-novelist Howard Browne, told him, "Roy, you've got a great reputation in television. Take my advice. Don't tell that idea to anybody because that idea is so bad, your reputation can be blown in one moment."

In April 1962 Huggins reached a settlement on his contract and left Fox. "I quit television because of *The Fugitive,*" said Huggins. "When I took that job at Twentieth Century-Fox, running television, I decided that the job was so important and meant so much to me to succeed, because I also had an option to run the entire studio if I succeeded. Within a year or two, Spyros Skouras (president of Twentieth Century-Fox), had the right to pick up my option and put me in charge of the entire studio — television, films, everything. For that reason I decided it would be in my interest to give them *The Fugitive.* And Peter Levathes hated it so much, he never changed his mind. He thought he had hired an absolute idiot. As a result, instead of my running the television department, he ran it, and it failed. And here was this guy, me, who had come from Warner Bros., with this enormous reputation and that reputation was in shreds. And that was why I decided to enroll in graduate school at UCLA and quit television. I decided to go back, get my Ph.D.,

and go on with the career I had originally planned, which was being a college professor."

With plenty of money and time, Huggins decided to fulfill his dream of completing the doctoral program in political theory he had begun at UCLA years earlier.

In the summer of 1962, shortly after enrolling in graduate school, Huggins received a phone call from Dan Melnick, vice president in charge of programming at ABC. Melnick informed Huggins that ABC president Leonard Goldenson was headed west and wanted to meet with him. Huggins tried to beg off, telling Melnick he was no longer in television and was intent on finishing his work at UCLA. But Melnick was insistent. "Roy, don't ask me to tell Leonard Goldenson that you won't meet with him," said Melnick. "I don't want to be in that position."

"But, Dan," Huggins answered, "I haven't anything to talk to Goldenson about. I'm not in television. I have left television, possibly forever, but certainly I'm not in it now and can't be until I finish what I'm doing at UCLA."

"Roy, you must have some ideas you can discuss with Leonard," countered Melnick.

"I've got one idea that everybody in the world absolutely hates, it's called *The Fugitive.* It's about a man who is accused and found guilty of murdering his wife and when he's transported to death row, there is a train wreck and he escapes. It's about his life as a fugitive."

"Great, Roy, tell it to him."

Huggins knew Melnick said "great" only because the ABC executive wanted him to meet with Goldenson, but he thanked Melnick anyway, adding, "Dan, you are the first person who has ever reacted positively to that idea." So, Huggins decided to meet with Goldenson.

The meeting was held in a suite at the Beverly Hills Hotel. Present with Huggins were ABC executives Dan Melnick, Julius Barnathan, Ev Erlick, Burt Nodella, Tom Moore, and network president, Leonard Goldenson.

Huggins began his presentation explaining that each episode of *The Fugitive* would begin with "a signature," a short narrated piece dramatizing Richard Kimble's plight. "Then I gave them every detail, every reason why it was a good idea," said Huggins. "Tom Moore, who was in charge of programming at ABC, left the room, came back with a suitcase, and said, 'Sorry Roy, I've got a plane to catch.' He walked out and he made it very clear that his distaste for this idea knew no bounds."

Nearing the end of his pitch Huggins said, "That's the series and Kimble will find the man that he sought after and we can have an end to a show . . . to a series . . . something never done before."

As Huggins completed his thoughts, quiet settled over the room and the ABC executives all waited for Leonard Goldenson's reaction.

Looking straight at Huggins, Goldenson announced, "Roy, that's the best idea I've ever heard for a television series."

After hearing his idea laughed at, scorned, and ridiculed, Huggins had finally found a believer. He quietly answered, "Well, thank you, Leonard." Goldenson said, "Really Roy, it's absolutely a godsend. We'll buy it."

But Tom Moore wasn't the only voice of dissent. ABC's Julius Barnathan stood up, saying, "Well, I don't agree. I'm sorry, Leonard, but I think it's a terrible idea. It's a slap in the face of American justice every week . . . it's un-American."

"Well, Mr. Barnathan, that's why we have appeals courts," answered Huggins, "because courts do make mistakes. I don't think it's a slap in the face of justice, because sometimes justice isn't done."

"How do we know Kimble didn't kill his wife?" asked Barnathan, raising his voice.

Thinking this was the wildest question in television history, an incredulous Huggins patiently explained, "Because that voice I told you about who narrates the signature tells you Kimble didn't murder his wife. That voice is the all-knowing voice of God, if you want."

When Leonard Goldenson asked Huggins if he wanted to produce *The Fugitive* Huggins answered, "No. First of all, I suspected that the only two people in the world who liked the idea would be Leonard Goldenson and me," said Huggins. "I knew the guy I was going to have to work with, Tom Moore, didn't like it. So, no, I wasn't anxious to do it, nor could I. I couldn't take a spot in the UCLA program and then walk out, so I said, 'I can't do it.' "

When Goldenson asked Huggins if he would at least produce the pilot for *The Fugitive* Huggins again turned him down. Finally Huggins offered a solution of his own. "Look, it's very simple. I will draw up a list of names of people that you will accept and I will choose the one that I like, and if you like him, we have a deal. I will make a deal with the producer to produce the show for me. I will give him television rights only and I will closely supervise the pilot, but I won't make the pilot."

So, in September 1962 Huggins reached an agreement with producer Quinn Martin, granting him television rights only. Huggins retained all other rights and contracted for a royalty and a

Mel Proctor, left, with Roy Huggins, 1993.

percentage of the show's profits. It was a shrewd move that would provide Huggins with a windfall for the next 30 years.

Although Huggins had great difficulty convincing others of *The Fugitive*'s worth, the show's successful network run and current cult popularity have vindicated its creator. "When I first thought of the *Fugitive* idea, I said to myself, 'This is going to be a classic.' And it turned out that everything that I thought when I first conceived it was right. And yet, this is a very interesting thing. I learned a lesson from that experience. This shows you how easy it is for wrong opinions to influence correct opinions. I knew that it was a good idea, yet other people convinced me I had made a mistake, that this was a bad idea. But the original thinking that I had proved to be true."

While Huggins agreed to monitor the pilot episode, Quinn Martin became *The Fugitive*'s executive producer. Martin had just completed a successful run as producer of *The Untouchables*, which aired on ABC from 1959 to 1963. *The Fugitive* would be the first series made by Martin's newly formed production company, QM Productions.

Remarkably, the pilot is the only *Fugitive* episode Roy Huggins has ever seen." I'm too busy doing other things and I knew that I would see things in it that I wouldn't have done. It sounds like an attitude, but it wasn't an attitude. It was 'this is Quinn Martin's baby' and I don't want to watch it and be tempted to pick up the phone and say, 'Quinn, what the hell do you think you're doing?' The fact is, I don't watch much television. To me, watching television is work."

WANTED

INTERSTATE FLIGHT - MURDER

RICHARD KIMBLE

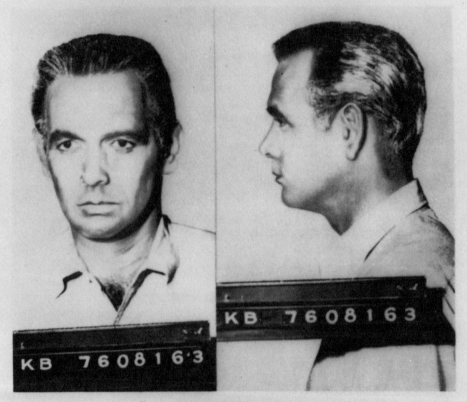

KB 7608163

KB 7608163

DESCRIPTION

Age:	35, born March 27, 1927, Stafford, Indiana	**Complexion:**	Medium
Height:	6 ft.	**Race:**	White
Weight:	175 pounds	**Nationality:**	American
Build:	Medium	**Occupations:**	Doctor
Hair:	Salt and Pepper	**Scars and Marks:**	None
Eyes:	Brown		

Fingerprint Classification: 19 M 9 U 000 13
L 2 U 001

CRIMINAL RECORD

Kimble has been convicted of murder.

A Federal warrant was issued charging Kimble with unlawful flight to avoid confinement for murder (Title 18, U. S. Code, Section 1073).

IF YOU HAVE INFORMATION CONCERNING THIS PERSON, PLEASE NOTIFY POLICE OR CONTACT YOUR LOCAL FBI OFFICE. TELEPHONE NUMBER IS LISTED BELOW.

IDENTIFICATION

ORDER NO. 2771

UNITED STATES DEPARTMENT OF JUSTICE
WASHINGTON 25, D. C.
TELEPHONE, NATIONAL 8-7117

Chapter 2

The Pilot — "Fear in a Desert City"

Roy Huggins was right. He thought *The Fugitive* would strike a nerve and it just happened to come along at the right time where it did.

—*Writer Stanford Whitmore*

The Fugitive was now indeed Quinn Martin's baby. Martin invited Alan Armer, who would later become the show's producer, and director Walter Grauman to his house on Sunset Boulevard to discuss the idea Martin had inherited from Roy Huggins.

"We were chatting after dinner and Quinn mentioned the concept that ABC had given him," said Alan Armer. "He was just curious to see what we thought of it. He mentioned the idea and both Walter and I were very positive. We felt that it was not more of the same thing television was wallowing in. It had a strong element of suspense."

After getting a positive reaction to the *Fugitive* concept, Martin made several changes. "Roy Huggins wanted his wrongly convicted murderer to behave like a jerk, since society was treating him like one anyway," Martin told *TV Guide*. "I

conceived Kimble as something less bizarre, a put-upon but decent person." But that wasn't the way Roy Huggins saw it.

"Quinn Martin became very sensitive to the fact that he had not created the show and began giving

Stanford Whitmore, writer of "Fear in a Desert City," 1993.

out interviews at the drop of a hat, even if he had to supply the hat," said Huggins. "He took credit for creating it and put me down, saying I had in mind a guy who was cynical and all kinds of shit. I called him up and said, 'Look, if you keep this up, I'm going to sue you. Stop doing it.' He stopped it all when I said, 'Don't do this anymore, because this is libelous.' I also had my lawyer write him a letter."

The most important change Martin made was to replace Kimble's pursuer, Roy Huggins's "one man in the state's attorney's office," with Police Lieutenant Philip Gerard. "I had the idea that naturally, for purposes of suspense, Kimble was being searched for," said Huggins, "but I didn't dramatize the search in the character of one obsessed man."

The idea of the obsessed police lieutenant actually came as the result of several long conversations Quinn Martin had with ABC's Dan Melnick, who convinced him that dramatizing the pursuit would be a very important way of getting more excitement into the script.

The name "Gerard" was chosen by writer Stanford Whitmore, whom Quinn Martin selected to write the pilot episode. Whitmore felt the

Quinn Martin, Executive Producer of The Fugitive.

original *Fugitive* treatment was so similar to *Les Misérables* that he based the detective's name on that of Detective Javert in the Victor Hugo classic. "That was my joke, because the detective didn't have a name. I gave him the name Gerard because I didn't want to name him Javert, and that was as close as I could get. I thought I'd have a little fun, a little joke in there for people who saw the resemblance between *The Fugitive* and *Les Misérables*."

Having decided on the personality traits of *The Fugitive*'s main characters, Quinn Martin began to search for the actor to play Dr. Richard Kimble. After considering a field of fifty-odd candidates including Gene Barry, Robert Lansing, Robert Culp, Tony Franciosa, Robert Stack, and James Franciscus, Martin selected thirty-two-year-old David Janssen, who had starred in *Richard Diamond, Private Detective*. Martin had been a film cutter at Universal Studios when Janssen was there and remembered the actor as "a person who would never fade into the woodwork." Janssen also got an endorsement from his poker-playing pal, Roy Huggins.

Although Janssen was Martin's first choice to play Dr. Kimble, the producer did have some reservations. In *Richard Diamond, Private Detective*, Janssen played a glib, self-assured character and Martin feared that style might not be appropriate for *The Fugitive*. Alan Armer eased Martin's trepidations. "I had seen David originally in the Richard Diamond series in which he played a slick, glossy, paper-thin character," said Armer, "and I think everybody's impression of David was that he was 'Mr. Slick,' and not really a very dimensional actor. I told Quinn that I had seen David do a *Naked City* and that I had been very much impressed with his ability as an actor and I suggested to Quinn that he get ahold of that episode and run it."

Martin watched the *Naked City* episode and was convinced Janssen was the right choice to play Kimble. Since Janssen was already committed to another project, Martin had to buy him out of the contract to land him as the lead in *The Fugitive*.

For the role of Richard Kimble's pursuer, Lieutenant Gerard, Martin chose veteran British-Canadian actor Barry Morse. Martin had been impressed by Morse's work in both *The Untouchables* and a failed series called *The New Breed*, and knew Morse could assume any U.S. accent required to portray the obsessed midwestern policeman.

Another small but important role was that of Fred Johnson, the one-armed man who actually killed Helen Kimble. That role went to Bill Raisch, a stuntman and stand-in for actor Burt Lancaster.

With the lead roles cast, Martin chose Stanford Whitmore, a former novelist and short-story writer, to write the pilot episode. Whitmore had worked for Martin on *The New Breed*. Martin called Whitmore and asked, "Would you like to come in to look at an idea here that I'd like you to think about?"

Whitmore went to Martin's office on the Goldwyn lot and was handed Roy Huggins's treatment for *The Fugitive*. "Sit down on the couch over there and read this," Martin told him, "and tell me what you think. I think it's kind of silly; but it might just work. It's a bunch of crap, really . . . but sit down and read it anyhow."

Whitmore read the treatment and found it interesting. He also needed a job and liked the challenge of writing a pilot. "Let's make a deal and do a pilot," Martin suggested.

Whitmore decided to set the pilot in Tucson, Arizona, because he knew the area from having visited friends who were professors at the University of Arizona. Whitmore also liked the idea of leaving Southern California and its palm trees for the desert. He named the show's pilot episode "Fear in a Desert City."

Since Richard Kimble, in the eyes of the law, was a convicted murderer, Whitmore had to provide the doctor with a new identity. Whitmore gave Kimble the alias "Jim Lincoln," and handed him a bartender's apron. "I figured, here's a guy on the run," said Whitmore. "What kind of job would he take where he wouldn't have to answer

Brian Keith and Vera Miles in "Fear in a Desert City,"
1963.

too many questions? I thought, 'Well, a bar-tender.' The idea kind of grew from there, but that was the initial impulse."

"Fear in a Desert City," was also the first episode in which Kimble used a bottle of black hair dye to further hide his real identity. Quinn Martin and David Janssen had done months of research in small towns and police stations, discovering that real fugitives used hair dye to disguise themselves. Janssen told *Newsweek*,: "The police told us that fully ninety-nine percent of all men on the run rarely do more to delude their pursuers. They don't have the money to afford plastic surgery."

After establishing Richard Kimble's dual identity, Whitmore expanded his initial idea and

David Janssen as Richard Kimble in "Fear in a Desert City," 1963.

handed Martin a twelve-page story. He and Martin ironed out the rough spots and Whitmore wrote several revised drafts before completing "Fear in a Desert City."

Later, as Whitmore was working on the final script for the pilot, ABC's programming department raised questions concerning sponsor identification, wondering whether advertisers would want to identify with a fugitive from justice. Whitmore and Martin looked at each other incredulously and told ABC, "Look, Richard Kimble is innocent."

After convincing the network that Kimble had redeeming qualities and assuring ABC that *The Fugitive* could help sell soap and cigarettes, Whitmore knew he had to soften the protagonist's image.

"So, I was really calculated," said Whitmore. "In addition to giving Kimble the alias, I then shaded to get sympathy. I had a little more poignancy with Vera Miles, who played the love interest in the pilot. Kimble had to keep moving on and she was the damsel in distress. She had a son Kimble took to a batting cage and he was the surrogate dad and all that kind of stuff. Then, the most shameless piece of manipulation was at the end of the first episode. That was in the railroad yards. There was a stray kitten, and Kimble just holds it awhile and then puts it down and goes ahead on his own. Well, that was really calculated to tug the heartstrings of America, to make everyone like Richard Kimble. Evidently it worked, because it quieted the folks down at ABC."

Eventually, all of the barriers were cleared and "Fear in a Desert City" was turned over to director Walter Grauman, who read the script and liked it. Then, Quinn Martin called, asking Grauman to join him and David Janssen for lunch at one of Martin's favorite Hollywood restaurants. "I'll never forget," said Grauman, "we left Goldwyn Studios and drove to Musso and Frank's. Quinn loved Musso and Frank's, he ate there practically every day. David was in the front seat, Quinn was driving, and I was sitting in the backseat. David suddenly turned around and said, 'Wally, you're really going to have to help me.' And I said, 'What do you mean, help you?' David said, 'Well, I've been used to doing *Richard Diamond,* all this shallow shit. There's a lot of character here, with Richard Kimble. I don't know whether I can act it.' I said, 'You're a good actor, David, you'll be very good.' I'll never forget him saying, 'You're going to have to help me.' "

Despite Janssen's concerns, he and Grauman and the rest of the cast and crew headed for Tucson to film "Fear in a Desert City."

David Janssen and Brian Keith in "Fear in a Desert City," 1963.

"I remember the first shot of the pilot," Grauman recalled. "We had a crane. I loved Quinn because if I wanted something, Quinn would say, 'Okay, you've got it.' And I wanted a crane for the opening shot. So, they had to drive a huge Titan crane from Los Angeles to Tucson. Nowadays it's nothing, but in the 1960s it was quite a task. Using the crane, the opening shot was of a Greyhound bus coming into town. I loved the crane for that because you could see it from a long distance away. The bus went past the bandstands, apartments, and the center of town to the bus station. Then, there was a young lady, who was built like a brick house . . . a pretty girl. And I decided to shoot her. The crane saw the bus come in, and then a low angle as the bus came right up in the foreground and the doors opened. Then this beautiful pair of female legs came into the camera, and then the camera followed and you saw her behind as she walked away. Then . . . Janssen came into the shot. That was the shot that opened "Fear in a Desert City."

Grauman ran into a few problems in filming the first show. One of his cameramen had worked in motion pictures at MGM, having won Oscars and other awards, but he wasn't used to the faster pace of television work. "It would take him an hour to light a single closeup," said Grauman. "I

remember calling Quinn and saying, 'Quinn, you've got to do something. You've got to either change me or the cameraman.' So, we got another cameraman and we started to make time."

In the opening episode, Kimble, alias "Jim Lincoln," worked as a bartender in a Tucson club. He got involved with the piano player, Monica Welles, played by Vera Miles, who is pursued by her psychotic husband Ed Welles, played by Brian Keith. After being threatened by Welles, Kimble decided to leave town, but Monica and her son decided to go with him. As they attempted to board a bus, Welles and Kimble fought, with Welles pulling a gun. Two military policeman who were in the depot shot and killed Welles. Kimble said good-bye to Monica and left town.

Grauman recalled what happened when David Janssen and Brian Keith filmed the fight scene at the bus depot: "Brian Keith was out on the town, it was like two o'clock in the morning when we filmed the scene, and Brian was feeling no pain. Finally, we found him. He and David were supposed to have a fight. I'd staged it so that David

Barry Morse as Lt. Gerard in "Fear in a Desert City," 1963.

grabbed him and Brian hit him with his elbow and knocked David back against the front of this big Greyhound bus. Brian was a marvelous actor but he was vicious in this part . . . and when he hit David, he hit him so hard he broke two of his ribs. What I loved about David was that even though he was hit that hard, he went right on through the scene, he didn't stop. He hurt terribly. I didn't know his ribs were broken until later."

Aside from Janssen's broken ribs, the exterior shooting in Tucson went relatively smoothly. Then the crew returned to Goldwyn Studios to film the interiors. The climactic scene was to be in a motel room, with David Janssen and Vera Miles.

Before shooting the scene, Walter Grauman said to Vera Miles, "Okay, now let's rehearse."

Walter Grauman, director of "Fear in a Desert City."

According to Grauman, the actress answered, "No, I don't want to rehearse." "What do you mean, you don't want to rehearse?" asked the angry director. "She didn't want to rehearse and I became really upset. I went off the stage and I got Quinn and I said, 'This broad doesn't want to rehearse the scene.' And Quinn said, 'Walter, why don't you try it without her once.' I said, 'No, fuck it . . . I want her to rehearse.' By this time, I'm so angry. Quinn said, 'Oh, what the hell difference does it make?' So, I went back down and said, 'Okay, let's shoot her.' She was marvelous, just marvelous. Why she wouldn't rehearse I don't know."

After all the footage was shot, Quinn Martin, Walter Grauman, and Stanford Whitmore retired to a projection room at Goldwyn Studios to watch "Fear in a Desert City." They were generally pleased with the show except for a scene in which Lieutenant Gerard, played by Barry Morse, looked at a glass map, attempting to locate Richard Kimble's whereabouts. "Barry Morse went absolutely bananas," recalled Whitmore. "He was standing in front of that map, yelling, 'You're out there, Kimble, I know you are.' He really played it so heavily that Quinn said, 'Hold it, hold it. My God, Wally, this guy is nuts. He ought to be in a hospital. He's a lunatic.' And Quinn said to me, 'Stan, you've got to write that scene down again and we've got to reshoot it, because Barry Morse is going to come across as a cop who really needs to be in the booby hatch.' "

In addition to that scene, Roy Huggins, who monitored the pilot, found other faults with "Fear in a Desert City." "They were making some dreadful mistakes," said Huggins. "The lead character, Dr. Richard Kimble, was going to have just one alias, 'Jim Lincoln.' I said, 'Quinn, the first time they get on his trail and they find out his name . . . he's going to call himself the same name in the next town?' And he said, 'Ah . . . I guess you're right.' And I said, 'And the other thing is, you've got Kimble keeping a diary. He carries a diary around in his hip pocket. You can't do that.' And Quinn said, 'Well, he hasn't got anyone to talk to.' And I said, 'He doesn't need anyone to talk to, he doesn't need a diary . . . that's a writer's job . . . that's B-movie stuff, where the hero has to have a sidekick.' "

So, the diary scene was eliminated, Richard Kimble assumed a new alias in every episode, and the scene with Barry Morse was reshot. Slight changes were also made in the graphics used in the show's titles and the music was changed from the temporary music used in the first version to the music of composer-writer Peter Rugolo, which became the show's distinctive theme music.

Also, William Conrad, the former radio star of *Gunsmoke,* was hired to do the show's narration. "I found out Bill Conrad was hired as the narrator," said Stanford Whitmore, "and I liked that because Conrad's got such a terrific voice and I wrote the narration for that deep, resonant voice

Richard Kimble (David Janssen) and Lt. Gerard (Barry Morse) in "Fear in a Desert City," 1963.

he has." Finally, "Fear in a Desert City" was completed.

"I liked some of it," said Whitmore. "I liked the photography and I liked David's performance very much. I liked the mood and the black and white photography. I didn't think it was anything tremendous, I just thought it was sort of a good show."

Walter Grauman had stronger feelings about *The Fugitive*'s first episode. "I sensed it was something special, mainly because of David. I thought the character was a marvelous character, the fugitive man that you know is innocent, who puts himself in jeopardy time after time to help people even though he's being hunted like a dog. David was so good, I thought it was really marvelous."

Grauman recalled leaving the studio after a screening of "Fear in a Desert City." "I was with my late wife Sue, and Quinn, and Arthur Fellows, who was in charge of production, and his wife. We were walking through the lot at Goldwyn Studios and Sue said, 'It was marvelous, but how is it ever going to make a series? A man running away, week after week?' And I said, 'It will make one helluva series.' "

Alan Armer, who was hired as *The Fugitive*'s line producer shortly after completion of the pilot, also sensed the show would be a winner. "A hero is a lonely man. And boy, this was the loneliest of

Barry Morse and David Janssen in The Fugitive.

all heroes. I was very involved with the character and I think that's fifty percent of the success of any series, if you care about the people."

Although David Janssen and Barry Morse went on to major television stardom as a result of *The*

Fugitive, their reaction to "Fear in a Desert City" was lukewarm. "When David and I met, I remember it very well . . . walking down the main street in Tucson," recalled Morse. "David said to me, 'What do you think of this thing?' I said, 'I've been around in a lot of circumstances in this crazy trade of ours and everybody tells me it can't possibly succeed, but then, what do I know? What does anybody know? It's a lot like going to the races and trying to pick the horses . . . trying to conclude which particular kind of format is going to succeed in a series.' At the time, David and I both had other projects. He had become quite well known in *Richard Diamond* and I had made a pilot called *All My Clients Are Innocent,* a courtroom, legal series that everybody assured me was going to sweep the world and make us all rich and famous. So, David and I said to each other, 'Well, we'll make *The Fugitive* and if it doesn't succeed, we've got other pilots.' Needless to say, *All My Clients Are Innocent* was never heard of again, but this little old number called *The Fugitive* started to grow in popularity, became the most popular show in the world, and the most popular show in history until that time."

On September 17, 1963, "Fear in a Desert City" aired at ten P.M. Eastern time on ABC. Narrator William Conrad introduced *The Fugitive* with the now famous words: "The name: Dr. Richard Kimble. The destination: Death Row, State Prison. The irony: Richard Kimble is innocent." With those words, *The Fugitive* was on the air.

The critics' response to the first episode of *The Fugitive* was generally positive although not overwhelming. On September 19, 1963, *Variety* said, " 'The Fugitive' has values — production and histrionic — that could make it a reasonably habit-forming entry with the prime time Charlies." *Variety* also praised the performance of David Janssen, saying, "In Janssen, the show has an appealing masculine figure in the all-important central role," but questioned the show's long-term appeal. " 'The Fugitive' has an outside chance, but for a fellow with one foot in the grave, he's gotta lotta livin' to do. Viewers may get tired of running."

The same day, *The Hollywood Reporter* said, "A season-long chase on TV, meaning a chain of events calculated to hold viewers week after week, might seem a dubious production risk. Nothing but airtight story line and dynamic main character could sustain audience interest over and beyond time gaps. Opening chapter of 'Fugitive' revealed these attributes."

So, with mixed reviews and an uncertain future, *The Fugitive* began to run.

Chapter 3

Off and Running

When you have a hit show, everybody is nice to you, everybody thinks you have the magic answer, and nobody gives you a bad time. It's beautiful.

—*Producer Alan Armer*

The Fugitive wasn't an immediate hit. As the show went into production in 1963, producer Alan Armer and his writers searched for the meaning and direction of the show. Lacking a staff of regular writers, the show used freelancers, who submitted "a crazy spectrum of ideas," according to Armer. "When you start a new series, you really don't know what you're doing. You fall on your butt a couple of times and you find out what you're doing wrong and then eventually you find out what you're doing right, and you throw away the bad things and keep using the good things, and you keep making new, happy discoveries along the way."

Alan Armer, producer of The Fugitive, *1993.*

John Conwell, who was hired as assistant to the producer and was in charge of casting *The Fugitive,* recalled the problems in getting the show under way. "The first few months were a struggle," said Conwell. "The scripts weren't ready and we just had all kinds of production problems." But based on his previous experience, Conwell sensed the early difficulties were good omens. "When things go well, you usually turn out a boring product. When you have all that chaos and all those problems, the product is usually quite rewarding. Give me a happy set and I'll give you a boring show."

One of the early obstacles was an industry belief that the concept upon which *The Fugitive* was

based, just wasn't believable. "When the series was picked up by ABC," said Alan Armer, "all of the smart money in Hollywood said it would never go thirteen shows. They felt you can't have a man escaping from the police week after week. That's ludicrous and the audience would laugh at it." So, part of the challenge was how to make *The Fugitive* believable.

To establish credibility, Armer and Quinn Martin agreed they couldn't do stories that were too far out or too fanciful. They felt the show had to deal with characters who had a realistic base and were believable. "We couldn't do stories that were too bizarre," said Armer, "because we were taking a bizarre concept, a 'way out' concept, and we needed to play against that in order to make it believable."

So, in early shows like Number 2, "The Witch," Richard Kimble became involved with a little girl who lived in a dream world and told tall stories. In Number 3, "The Other Side of the Mountain," Sandy Dennis played a girl longing to leave a small town to fulfill her dreams. In the two-parter "Never Wave Good-bye," Numbers 4 and 5, Kimble fell in love with a sailmaker's beautiful daughter, played by Susan Oliver. These episodes

Susan Oliver as Karen in "Never Wave Good-bye," 1963.

all dealt with Kimble's involvement with relatively average people in realistic environments. The show's gradual development of believable plots and characters allowed the viewing public to accept *The Fugitive.*

ABC thought highly enough of the early episodes to ask Quinn Martin to develop story ideas for ten additional shows. "Quinn called me up and said ABC wants to know what we're going to be doing in the future," said Stanford Whitmore. "I went in and we had a wonderful time. Quinn would say, 'Look at us, we make more money than bank presidents and we look like a couple of bums.' We'd be wearing sneakers or khakis and not dressed up. We'd sit around and look out the window and come up with some kind of ideas. It took us about fifteen minutes and we came up with ten ideas. It was a lot of fun. I remember Quinn and I were fond of the fights at that time, and I said, 'Look, Kimble's a doctor, he gets to be a cut man for a boxer, he works in a boxer's corner.' That became an episode (Number 6, "Decision in the Ring"). It was that kind of relationship I had with Quinn. It was all very relaxed."

David Janssen in "Decision in the Ring," 1963.

It was "Decision in the Ring" that convinced Alan Armer of David Janssen's understanding of the Richard Kimble character. In one scene, Kimble hid in the boxer's dressing room, as the police arrived. "I was just amazed," said Armer. "Boy, just looking at the dailies, you just felt the fear in this man and David was a good enough actor to externalize that so you became aware of what was going on inside of him. From that point on, I was impressed and I became a fan."

The Fugitive was indeed developing a legion of fans. "What I was impressed with were the letters and phone calls we got revealing how deeply people were involved with the character of Richard Kimble," said Armer. "We got letters asking us to give him a second chance, to let him find the one-armed man and return to his medical practice. And I've never worked on a show that brought in so many unsolicited scripts. Everyone seemed to have escape ideas, especially little old ladies. If only some of the stories were any good. After the first half-dozen shows we knew the series was a hit."

"Bill Dozier, who used to be head of Columbia Television and vice president of CBS, was married to Ann Rutherford, who had been a movie star at MGM," continued Armer. "These were people who had been in the business for two dozen years. Ann Rutherford's mother called me one night and pleaded with me to give this poor fellow, Richard Kimble, another trial. The story becomes significant only if you understand that this was the mother of a relatively famous Hollywood actress, married to a studio executive, and the idea of giving Kimble another trial was patently absurd because that would mean the end of the series. The fact that this sophisticated woman would call after one of the episodes and ask me to let this poor fellow have another trial is so revealing because she was totally forgetting the reality of the television world. And I said to her, 'If we give Richard Kimble another trial, and he's convicted, he'll go to the death house. If he's freed, we don't have a series. In either event, we don't have a series.' It was just indicative to me of the incredible degree of emotional involvement."

The show's viewers loved Richard Kimble and loathed Lieutenant Gerard, which was just what the producers intended. David Janssen's fan mail climbed to more than eight thousand letters a month and Barry Morse, who played Lieutenant Gerard, claimed he received "more hate mail than Adolf Hitler."

Although the public embraced *The Fugitive* and the ratings began to rise, network executives were not completely sold on the show. "I remem-

Barry Morse as Lieutenant Gerard.

ber being in a meeting with some ABC guys and Quinn Martin," said Stanford Whitmore. "These guys said they liked the show and they liked the ratings but they were worried that the series didn't have a positive enough tone. They said that Kimble was negative in that he was running from something. They said he should have been running to something. I said, 'That's crazy. He's not just running away, he's looking for the one-armed man.' But they said, 'We want a positive thrust to the show. The guy should give himself up and trust in justice.' And then Quinn and I looked at each other and said, 'Look, the guy is innocent. You're missing the whole point.'"

Midway through *The Fugitive*'s first season, Quinn Martin realized the show had never properly explained Helen Kimble's murder, the appearance of the one-armed man, and the trial and escape of Dr. Richard Kimble. Martin phoned Stanford Whitmore, asking him to find a solution.

"I decided to use a flashback to explain the missing background information," said Whitmore. "But how do you get to the flashback? It's not a shatteringly new idea, but there has to be some kind of mental condition that gets Kimble going into this flashback and I thought, 'The guy is on the road, he doesn't eat well, he doesn't sleep well, and he's probably without shelter.' And I said, 'Look, the guy gets something very ordinary, like a cold. And the cold develops into pneumonia and he becomes delirious and in his delirium he remembers the trial.' So, that was how I was going to do it. So I wrote the treatment of the story. And what I had was that Kimble was in Chicago and was found stumbling around at night. He had pneumonia and was found by a Puerto Rican hooker. And she took him in and he went through the delirium in her apartment. So, I handed it in. And I got home and the phone rang and it was Quinn and he said, 'Puerto Rican hooker!!' And I said, 'Quinn, look . . .' And he said, 'No, you look. If you want to do your little offbeat stuff, that's fine, but wait until we get established to do that.'"

Because Martin's wife Muffet had been a flight attendant, he and Whitmore decided to substitute a stewardess, played by Pamela Tiffin, for the hooker, in "The Girl from Little Egypt," Number 14. Instead of contracting pneumonia, Kimble was accidentally hit by a car driven by the stewardess. As the story unfolded, Kimble flashed back to his wife's murder, the one-armed man, and the trial, allowing the show to fill in the necessary background information.

Midway through the first season, *The Fugitive*'s creative staff realized a mistake had been made. Richard Kimble and Lieutenant Gerard were both from mythical Stafford, Wisconsin. There was just one problem: Wisconsin didn't have a death penalty. So, the writers changed the show's setting to Stafford, Indiana, since that state did have capital punishment. The mistake accounts for the fact that in one early show, a sign on a bus indicated it was headed for "Madison," a city in Wisconsin, and why Dr. John Kimble, Richard Kimble's father, talked of giving his collection of medical books to the University of Wisconsin library.

Another mistake was picked up by Barry Morse's seven-year old daughter Melanie. The opening sequence of *The Fugitive* showed a stock footage shot of a train hurtling down the tracks just prior to the crash that freed Richard Kimble. "Melanie came to me," recalled Morse, "and she said, 'Daddy, I thought you said this was in the States, but that's a French train.' So the producers checked it out and it was indeed a clip of a French train with French lettering on the side. Feeling that most viewers wouldn't know the difference, they left the shot in and nobody else even noticed."

Among the most unique of the first-year shows was a two-parter, Numbers 22 and 23, "Angels Travel on Lonely Roads." Because the character of Richard Kimble was so serious, David Janssen rarely had an opportunity to show his sense of humor. But in these episodes Janssen's humor and comedic timing were allowed to surface. Richard Kimble joined a nun, Sister Veronica, played by Eileen Heckart, on her way to Sacramento. During their journey, the unlikely pair encountered one obstacle after another, but each time a minor miracle bailed them out. After Kimble, alias "Nick Walker," repaired the nun's broken-down car, the two drove away, with the following conversation taking place:

David Janssen with Eileen Heckart in "Angels Travel on Lonely Roads," 1964.

SISTER VERONICA: Nick . . .Walker . . . you said?

KIMBLE: That's right, Sister.

SISTER VERONICA: Well, Mr. Walker, you are a splendid mechanic. This car has not run so well since I left the convent.

KIMBLE: This car isn't running, Sister. It's looking for a quiet place to die.

(Later)

KIMBLE: I don't suppose you made financial provision for the trip?"

SISTER VERONICA: Of course . . . *(looking into her purse)* . . . twenty dollars and thirty five cents.

KIMBLE: Good.

SISTER VERONICA: That's what I had when I started out. *(balance)* a dollar . . . forty five.

KIMBLE: A dah . . . that isn't even going to get us to the top of the next hill.

David Janssen's portrayal of Dr. Richard Kimble, and the quality of the production, allowed *The Fugitive* to overcome the early problems and the network opposition to certain aspects of the series. By the end of the first season *The Fugitive* was a certified hit. *TV Guide* selected *The Fugitive* as the best new show on network television. In 1964 David Janssen was voted the favorite male performer on television in *TV Guide*'s annual poll of its readers. Janssen was also nominated for an Emmy for Outstanding Continued Performance by an Actor in a Series, losing out to Dick Van Dyke of *The Dick Van Dyke Show*.

The second season began with episode Number 31, "Man in a Chariot." While watching television, Richard Kimble saw former trial attorney G. Stanley Lazer (Ed Begley) say that if he had handled the Kimble case, he could have won an acquittal. Injured in an auto accident and confined to a wheelchair, Lazer was teaching at a law school. Although Lazer's students hated him, he believed he could use them in a mock trial to destroy the circumstantial evidence that convicted Richard Kimble, and win a new trial.

The episode was written by George Eckstein, who had earned a law degree from USC, and based this show on his experiences as a law student. "Man in a Chariot," was another example of the exceptional writing that characterized *The Fugitive*.

In the episode's climactic scene, Lazer delivered his summation to a jury composed of law students. In reading the script from "Man in the Chariot," it's apparent that Lazer was on trial as much as Dr. Richard Kimble.

LAZER: But I should like you to consider, if you

will, the defendant himself. What manner of human being are we judging here today?

A member of one of the great professions, he now stands before this court even as the most humble supplicant. And what he asks from you is only this . . . compassion.

(Kimble, watching the proceedings on the university's closed-circuit telecast, begins to understand what Lazer is doing.)

Lazer: He is a man whose very vocation demanded a dedication beyond that required of the ordinary man. And, perhaps, he gave too much . . . shutting out that which should have been most important to him — family, friends . . . and even humanity.

(The twelve law students listen to Lazer's words, moved by them.)

LAZER: Then, suddenly, he was thrust out of the only life he knew — unable to do the very work that, for him, made any life meaningful. He

Ed Begley as G. Stanley Lazer in "Man in a Chariot," 1964.

was exiled to a world he hated — hated only because it was strange to him, and because . . . because memories of mountaintops had blinded him to the beauties of the valley.

LAZER: *(continuing)* He had such an abundance of hate that he built a wall of it, a wall so high that no man could extend a hand over it in friendship.

(The district attorney's assistant leans across the table to him.)

ASSISTANT: (IN A LOW VOICE) He's not talking about

Kimble.

D.A.: "He never was."

LAZER: (addressing the jury) "He is alone now, his wife – a lonely woman – taken from this earth in a pointless and insane moment of violence. And though the woman was dead, the man still selfishly scratched at his *own* wounds, until he was marked by scars that cut deep into his very soul. *(a pause)* This, then, is the man you are asked to judge. I commend him to your mercy.

(The room is hushed as Lazer turns from the jury and wheels himself back to the defense table.)

Ed Begley was so moved by the writing in that final speech by G. Stanley Lazer that he kept a copy in his wallet and carried it with him until his death in 1970.

"Man in a Chariot" was later submitted to a blue ribbon panel at the Academy of Television Arts and Sciences, which determines the Emmy Award winners. During its third year, 1965 to 1966, *The Fugitive* won an Emmy for Outstanding Dramatic Series, beating out *Bonanza, I Spy, The Man from Uncle,* and *Slattery's People.*

The Emmy Awards were presented at the Hollywood Palladium, May 22, 1966. When producer Alan Armer heard the announcement that *The Fugitive* had won, his initial feeling was panic. "I wanted to run," said Armer. "Seriously, and then I said to myself, 'This is ridiculous, you've got to go up there.' " As Armer mounted the stage, presenter Jack Benny congratulated him and extended the prized Emmy. "I remember saying, 'Thank you, Jack,' as if I knew him," said Armer, "which is the kind of thing show business people do, whether they know the person or not. But it was one of the great moments of my life. It was damned exciting."

Because the Emmy Awards weren't broadcast on the West Coast until three hours later, Armer was able to surprise his children, who were watching the show at home. "We kept it a secret," said Armer, "and allowed the kids to see it on their own. They never knew I won until they saw it on television. They were really surprised. They were knocked out."

Although Armer was elated *The Fugitive* won, he was disappointed David Janssen didn't. "I felt bad for David," said Armer, "because David Janssen *was* the fugitive. He was so much a part of the show." Janssen lost again, with *I Spy*'s Bill Cosby winning an Emmy as Outstanding Actor In Dramatic Series.

By the end of its second season, *The Fugitive*

had soared to number five in the Nielsen ratings, with a 27.9 rating, trailing only *Bonanza, Bewitched, Gomer Pyle, U.S.M.C.,* and *The Andy Griffith Show*. It marked the only time during *The Fugitive*'s four-year network run that it reached the top five in the ratings. During its third year, *The Fugitive* dropped out of the Nielsen top twenty, but continued to dominate its time slot, and because it aired in seventy countries, the show was becoming increasingly popular worldwide.

A top German magazine suggested to David Janssen's agent a contest, in which Janssen, wearing a disguise, would walk the streets of Berlin. The magazine's readers would be asked to track down *"Der Fluchtling"* to win prizes. Janssen vetoed the idea.

When Janssen visited the San Isidro bull festival in Spain, fans began to chant *"El Fugitivo! El Fugitivo!"* ignoring the bull and the matador.

In addition to David Janssen's appeal, another reason *The Fugitive* succeeded was that it was based on a proven formula. *"The Fugitive* was based on *Les Misérables,"* said Barry Morse, "a classical novel of a hundred years before, so it was bound to have some good things going for it. In this business, we are all shoplifters. Once you've accepted the fact that you're a shoplifter, you must always be sure you go first to Cartier's and not to Woolworth's, because that's where the best goods are. Roy Huggins would probably be the first to say, 'I'm a discerning shoplifter . . . I go to Cartier's.' "

As Alan Armer and his writers worked on the show's scripts, they knew they couldn't rely solely on Richard Kimble's attempts to elude capture. "If you just have Kimble escape at the end," said Armer, "you're right back to where you were when the episode began."

So, the writers filled the show with an anthology story involving Kimble. Each week the writers allowed Kimble to enter into different situations. One week he was David Benton, working on a Georgia plantation; the next, Pete Glenn, a handyman in an Ohio nightclub; and then, Nick Peters, working in an animal show in Nebraska. *The Fugitive* was a perfect vehicle that allowed Richard Kimble to go anywhere and involve himself in almost every conceivable situation.

Creating aliases, occupations, and destinations for Richard Kimble was almost a job in itself. Kimble used 108 different aliases, held down 42 different jobs, and traveled to thirty-five states, the District of Columbia, and Mexico.

The aliases used by Kimble were mostly products of the writers' imaginations. Occasionally, though, when stumped for a name, the writers would go into Alan Armer's office for inspiration. "I had some old posters, reproductions of authentic posters of the middle 1800s," said Armer. "One was about Abraham Lincoln, one was about Teddy Roosevelt, another about boats sailing up and down the Mississippi River. They were filled with wonderful names, like the names of the captains of the various steamers. And sometimes when we would need a name, I would look at the posters and use one of the names off the posters. 'Taft,' the name of Kimble's in-laws, came off one of those old posters. We'd be sitting there and someone would say, 'Well, what shall we call Kimble's sister?' . . . and I'd look at the poster and say, 'Well, how about Taft.' "

Whether he used the names Jim Lincoln, Nick Phillips, Tom Marlowe, or Jerry Sinclair, to viewers he was still Richard Kimble, and the character's loneliness and fear struck a nerve in the American public. "We are in a world where there is an increasing sense of alienation, frustration, and helplessness on the part of the individual," said *Fugitive* writer and co-producer George Eckstein. "This was such a strong dramatization of that syndrome, with this man, alone, trying to put his life together and not being able to. I think people really identified with that."

Viewers also identified with Richard Kimble's travels and experiences. "The whole tradition of road life in America is one that is very basic to

people and they identified with it," said writer Stanford Whitmore. "If you think back to the times, in the 1960s, you couldn't get on a freeway or an expressway without encountering maybe fifty yards of hitchhikers with dogs, guitars, and so forth. That kind of free-spirited existence, never mind that Kimble was being pursued by a maniac cop, but here he was, he was on the road, that's essentially what it was. I was just surprised

that people took the show so seriously."

Occasionally, *The Fugitive* dealt with serious themes including racism, mental retardation, religious freedom, and rape. "We didn't consciously try to do messages," said Alan Armer. "But if a writer brought us an idea that was entertaining, that was believable, and there was also a social message attached, then fine."

Such an episode was "In a Plain Paper Wrapper," Number 89, written by John Kneubuhl, Jackson Gillis, and Glen Larson. The show dealt with gun control. A group of kids ordered a gun through the mail and decided to arrest Richard Kimble and collect a reward. During a struggle, one of the kids was shot. ABC received thousands of angry letters from viewers, complaining about the show, saying it was impossible for kids to get hold of guns that easily. ABC then reprimanded Quinn Martin.

Martin called Alan Armer into his office and asked, "Alan, is there any validity to the show? Can people buy guns like the kids in that show did?"

"So, I went out on my lunch hour," said Armer.

Kurt Russell as Eddie in "In a Plain Paper Wrapper," 1966.

"There was a newsstand nearby and I bought a bunch of magazines. I came back from lunch and I put twelve magazines on Quinn's desk, each of them opened to a full-page ad saying, 'All you've got to do is send in the coupon and say that you are at least twenty-one years of age and not a convicted felon,' and they will send you a gun. Quinn took the magazines over to ABC and we never heard any more about it."

The Fugitive's writers were some of the most creative minds in television. George Eckstein wrote ten episodes and also served as the show's co-producer. Dan Ullman and Harry Kronman wrote nine episodes. Other key writers included Philip Saltzman, Don Brinkley, Jack Turley, William D. Gordon, John Kneubuhl, Barry Oringer, and Stanford Whitmore. The prolific writing team of Richard Levinson and William Link, who later created *Mannix, Columbo,* and *Murder, She Wrote,* authored two *Fugitive* episodes. And Glen A. Larson, who created and produced shows like *The Six Million Dollar Man, The Bionic Woman, Magnum P.I.,* and *Knight Rider,* co-wrote an episode.

"We had some good writers," said producer Alan Armer, "but the hard work was developing the scripts with the writers and that took about seventy percent of my time. I would come home from a day's sitting in the office, talking to writers, and I would be totally exhausted . . . it's hard work. I was tough to work with and some of the writers complained that I made them work too hard and do too many drafts and was too hard to please. But television is a very tough medium and *The Fugitive* was a tough series to write."

The Fugitive's directors were an equally talented group. Jerry Hopper directed fourteen episodes, while the prolific Walter Grauman directed eleven, including some of the show's most memorable episodes: the pilot, "Fear in a Desert City"; the two-parter "Angels Travel on Lonely Roads"; and another classic two-parter, Numbers 69 and 70, "Landscape with Running Figures."

The Fugitive's list of directors include many who became major motion picture producer-directors. Sydney Pollack went on to direct such films as *They Shoot Horses, Don't They?, The Way We Were, Three Days of the Condor, The Electric Horseman, Tootsie, Out of Africa,* and *The Firm.* Mark Rydell cut his teeth on *The Fugitive* and would eventually direct *The Fox, The Reivers, Cinderella Liberty, The Rose,* and *On Golden Pond.* Richard Donner moved on to direct *The Omen, Superman, The Goonies,* and *Lethal Weapon, 1, 2,* and *3.* Joseph Sargent lists *The Taking of Pelham 1-2-3, MacArthur, Golden Girl,* and *Jaws — the Revenge,* among his credits. One of the early women directors, Ida Lupino, directed three episodes, and *Fugitive* co-star Barry Morse directed one.

Most of the time, *The Fugitive's* creative staff remained true to the serious character of Richard Kimble. But in the series second year, Alan Armer decided Kimble was "a little too good and too pure of heart," and he and writer Jack Turley decided to have some fun in episode Number 54,

"Everybody Gets Hit in the Mouth Sometime." "There was a woman who turned out to be a creep," said Armer, "and she had a kid who was *really* a creep. I was getting the feeling that Kimble was such a goody-goody that we decided to have Kimble whap the kid at the end of the show." Sure enough, in the episode's last act, as Kimble walked down the sidewalk, the kid began to act up. Kimble picked up the boy and spanked him. "It was such a delightful moment," said Armer, "because the kid was such a pain, such a creep, and when Kimble whapped him at the end of the show, it made me feel good. That was fun for me, and sometimes you do things just to make yourself feel good."

In addition to the writing and direction, *The Fugitive's* emphasis on realistic production values also contributed to the show's success. *The Fugitive's* crews spent an average of five out of seven days on location. Richard Kimble's flight supposedly took him across the country, but in reality only the pilot, "Fear in a Desert City," filmed in Tucson, Arizona, was shot outside of California. "We had a remarkable production manager, Fred Ahern," said Alan Armer. "I used the word 'remarkable' because most production managers are so conscious of the budget that they feel their sole function is to put pressure on the producer to keep the show under budget. Fred was one of those rare individuals who really enjoyed seeing production values on the screen. By production values, I mean rich locations and exciting, colorful production elements on the show. He encouraged us to find offbeat and interesting and colorful locations. If we said we were shooting an episode in New Mexico, we would find locations around Los Angeles that would really duplicate the look of New Mexico.

"We had a location manager, Bud Brill, who had books of pictures of various locations around the city and he would suggest locations. He and

David Janssen in The Fugitive, *1963.*

23

Fred would find locations that would make you believe that Kimble was actually in that state. The only problem we had was that every once in a while, a palm tree would show up and we always had to put up a signboard or something to conceal the palm trees, because they gave away the fact that we were shooting in California. But they really made you believe. Sometimes during the course of one show, Kimble would travel through two or three different states and they would make us believe it. They did a remarkable job."

Because *The Fugitive* was a quality production and paid between $3,000-$5,000 for guest stars, the show had no difficulty attracting talent like Jack Klugman, Telly Savalas, Charles Bronson, Carroll O'Connor, Herschel Bernardi, Jack Lord, Melvyn Douglas, and Robert Duvall. David Janssen's rapport with actresses like Angie Dickinson, Suzanne Pleshette, Diana Hyland, Carol Rossen, Brenda Vaccaro, Susan Oliver, and Diane Baker also added quality to the show.

Although *The Fugitive* dropped out of the Nielsen Top Twenty during its third year, 1965 to 1966, the show continued to dominate its time period. But as *The Fugitive* began its final season, 1966 to 1967, the show began to develop cracks.

Alan Armer, who had guided the show through three successful seasons, stepped down as *The Fugitive*'s producer. A science fiction fan, Armer left to produce a sci-fi show, *The Invaders,* another QM production. As Wilton Schiller succeeded Armer, *The Fugitive* began to lose direction. "It was a very peculiar series and you really had to understand how the episodes worked," said Armer. "Every series has its own structure, its own philosophy, its own theme, its own way of putting shows together. For somebody to come in after a series has been on the air

for three years and try to catch that same feeling, it's hard. They were in deep trouble and then Quinn brought in George Eckstein as co-producer. George knew what worked and what didn't work and kind of pulled the potatoes out of the fire."

"We had big problems in the last year," said George Eckstein. A major problem was ABC's directive that the show be shot in color instead of black and white. All of the stock footage shots, like Richard Kimble running along side a train or hitchhiking by the side of a road could no longer be used and had to be reshot in color.

Because the show was now filmed in color, it also limited the locations *The Fugitive* could use. In 1966 David Janssen told *The Chicago Tribune,* "We've always tried to be meticulously accurate about our locales. Color is making the task even more complex. For one thing, Southern California is a dried-up region. We can't use its arid brown hills if we are trying to duplicate the green mountain areas of an eastern state. Sometimes we wrack our collective brains over locations and their color peculiarities."

The change from black and white to color also robbed *The Fugitive* of its "film noir" qualities. "People always say they find something very satisfying and convincing and persuasive about the earlier shows, those shot in black and white," said Barry Morse. "I think that's partly because we've come to believe so much of the black and white archival footage we see on newsreel and documentary shows, so we've somehow come to think that anything that's in black and white must be true."

During its fourth season, *The Fugitive*'s scripts began to weaken. The show even attempted to repeat the success of one of the best episodes from the first year, "Angels Travel on Lonely Roads," bringing back Eileen Heckart as Sister Veronica in Number 109, "The Breaking of the Habit," in 1967. "I walked in and looked at the script and I was very disappointed," said Heckart, "because I thought it would be as good as the first one."

Weaker scripts and difficulties with color filming were only part of *The Fugitive*'s problems during its final year. The fourteen-hour work days and the numbing monotony of playing the same character had taken their toll on David Janssen. "I can play this part falling down or asleep," Janssen told TV Guide. Although Janssen was again nominated for an Emmy, losing out to *I Spy*'s Bill Cosby, his work lacked the clarity and realism he had shown in the previous three seasons. Finally, the biggest blow came when Janssen announced he wanted out of *The Fugitive*.

Telly Savalas and David Janssen in "Stroke of Genius."

Chapter 4

"The Judgment"

This week Dr. Richard Kimble stops running. The threadbare suitcase goes back to the property shop, and the sleazy motels and bleak rooming houses will henceforth have to do without his patronage.

—*Dwight Whitney in* TV Guide, *August 1967*

The fugitive was tired of running. In 1967 David Janssen told Quinn Martin he was thinking of leaving the show after four successful years, but Martin and ABC weren't about to let Janssen go easily. *The Fugitive* was a big money maker for ABC, which grossed an estimated $30,000,000 on the series. While the network and QM Productions pulled Janssen one way, offering him a reported $500,000 for another year on *The Fugitive*, his wife Ellie and his doctor tugged in the other direction, telling him his health was more important than his bank account. Janssen changed his mind almost daily. "First David said 'No,' recalled John Conwell, "and then he said 'Yes,' and then he said 'No.' "

While Janssen wavered, Quinn Martin decided to go ahead with plans to shoot the final episode. If Janssen quit, Martin reasoned, the final episode would bring the show to a conclusive end. If the actor decided to return for another year, the final show could be shelved and new episodes could be shot.

After wrestling with his decision, Janssen finally decided to quit, telling *TV Guide* "They made me an offer. It would have been worth maybe half a million dollars to me. Then I decided against the fifth year. I think I would have fallen apart if I hadn't."

Quinn Martin decided to end *The Fugitive* in an unprecedented manner. Rather than letting the show quietly slip away as most television series did, Martin decided to tie up all the loose ends in one dramatic two-part conclusion, "The Judgment."

The idea to end the show in this fashion had actually originated with Roy Huggins's treatment which stated: "This will be a series which will be brought to a planned conclusion, that conclusion being of course Richard Kimble's release from his predicament and the ultimate salvation of justice."

Actually, over the years, David Janssen had jokingly thought up his own ending for *The Fugitive*. "I said I was going to unscrew my arm and walk off into the sunset, having killed my wife," Janssen remarked on the *Portrait* television show. "That was really sort of an irresponsible statement that I made, just to have a laugh, and then I found it cropping up in a magazine here and a newspaper there."

Over dinner one night, Janssen and Barry Morse dreamed up another imaginary ending. "We said,

how would it be if there was a sequence where we open up on a suburban house in Stafford, Indiana," recalled Morse, "and we now come on a high crane shot down through an upper window of this house, and we see a light turned on suddenly. We push on through this window and we see that in the bedroom, on the upper floor, is a double bed. We see Kimble, our hero, waking up and he's just turned on the light, and he turns over to his partner in the bed, whom we see is Helen, and he says, 'Oh, gee! . . . oh, thank God! I've just had a terrible nightmare.' And that was the end of the whole thing. That was the kind of joke we had between us."

Of course, Quinn Martin had a more serious ending in mind. Martin chose George Eckstein to help write the show's finale. Eckstein, the series' co-producer, had spent four years on *The Fugitive* and understood the show's concept as well as anyone. Eckstein wrote ten episodes and contributed to countless others. "I worked with a writer I knew named Michael Zagor to develop the ending," said Eckstein. "All we knew about it was the one-armed man had to be guilty. I mean everybody was supposing all sorts of alternatives to that, but any other ending would have been a slap in the face to the audience. We felt that after four years of chasing the one-armed man, to finally find out that he didn't do it would have made a mockery of the four years."

George Eckstein, co-writer and co-producer of the final episodes, "The Judgment."

"We wanted to play straight with people on the outside," continued Eckstein. "Everybody was looking for some sort of surprise, but we couldn't

The one-armed man (Bill Raisch) killing Helen Kimble (Diane Brewster) in the final episode of "The Judgment."

give them a surprise because the one-armed man killed Helen Kimble, and Richard Kimble was looking for him and Gerard was looking for Kimble. So it was: Kimble would find the one-armed man, and the fact that Gerard would actually, finally, kill the one-armed man was as much of a surprise as we could deliver."

With suspense building as to how *The Fugitive* would actually conclude, Quinn Martin held a meeting explaining the show's ending and swearing his troops to secrecy. John Conwell carefully numbered each script and included strict

instructions from Martin, warning the cast and crew not to divulge the show's ending. The memo asked the show's participants to "please honor the industry code of not giving the ending away, except to say Richard Kimble will be proved innocent."

As "The Judgment" went into production, tension mounted. "It was exciting," said Conwell. "We had gamblers and oddsmakers calling from Las Vegas . . . they would offer us money to tell how the show ended."

Co-star Barry Morse was also offered bribes to

reveal the show's outcome. "There were all sorts of people," said Morse, "the usual kind of people who think that anything can be bought with money. They're ignorant, stupid people. They offered money. The world is full of people who think the purpose of life on this planet is the accumulation of green pieces of paper called 'bucks.' They're just misled, you just have to try and help them as best you can."

Lieutenant Gerard (Barry Morse) hands a gun to Kimble (Richard Janssen) in "The Judgment."

In "The Judgment" Part One, Richard Kimble discovered that the one-armed man, Fred Johnson, had been arrested in Los Angeles. When asked by Lieutenant Gerard if he killed Helen Kimble, Johnson answered, "No, but I was there and saw the man who did," suggesting that someone else did the actual killing.

Kimble journeyed to Los Angeles, only to discover Lieutenant Gerard had set a trap for him. There, Kimble met Jean Carlisle (Diane Baker), whose father had been a friend of the Kimbles in Stafford, Indiana. Jean quickly became involved in Kimble's life, hiding him at her home and falling in love with him.

Johnson was bailed out of jail by someone giving his name as "Leonard Taft," the name of Kimble's brother-in-law. Johnson murdered the bail bondsman and left for Stafford. Lieutenant Gerard tracked Kimble to Jean Carlisle's apartment and arrested him, taking him, by train, back to Stafford.

In Part Two, as the train neared Stafford, Lieutenant Gerard agreed to give Kimble twenty-four hours to look for the one-armed man.

Johnson lured the man he thought was Leonard

Dr. Kimble fighting with the one-armed man in "The Judgment."

Taft to a deserted stable. Johnson knew that this man, who was really a neighbor, Lloyd Chandler, (J. D. Cannon) was in the Kimble house and saw him murder Helen Kimble. Johnson tried to black

Barry Morse as Lieutenant Gerard shooting the one-armed man, in "The Judgment."

mail Chandler, asking for $50,000. Feeling guilty about having withheld information that would have cleared Kimble, Chandler decided to kill Johnson. Chandler agreed to later meet the one-armed man at a deserted amusement park.

Kimble and Gerard learned of the planned meeting and followed Chandler to the park. Chandler arrived with a rifle, planning to kill

Johnson. As Gerard and Kimble ran toward Chandler, Johnson fired, wounding Gerard in the leg. After falling to the ground, Gerard handed his gun to Kimble, telling him to go after Johnson. Kimble chased Johnson to the top of a tower. There, Kimble and Johnson fought, with Johnson admitting he murdered Kimble's wife. Johnson wrestled the gun away from Kimble, and as he prepared to kill him, Gerard grabbed Chandler's rifle and shot Johnson, who fell from the tower to his death.

The climactic scenes were filmed at Pacific Ocean Park, a deserted amusement park in Venice, California. Despite the complexity of the action, the scenes were shot in only a few takes. Director Don Medford, a meticulous preparer, had choreographed the fight scene in great detail.

In the tower scene, Kimble knocked Johnson down and repeatedly hit him in the face as the actors exchanged the following lines:

KIMBLE: You killed her . . . you killed my wife, didn't you? . . . didn't you . . . didn't you? . . . you killed . . .
JOHNSON: Yeah! . . . yeah . . . I killed her.
KIMBLE: Why?
JOHNSON: 'Cause she wouldn't let me go . . . liked to have clawed my eyes out. I didn't mean to hit her so hard.

As an exhausted Kimble stood up, Johnson managed to pick up the gun which had been knocked to the floor. He pointed the gun at Kimble . . . shouting:

Richard Kimble (David Janssen) shaking hands with Lieutenant Gerard (Barry Morse) in "The Judgment."

Although stuntmen were used, particularly where Kimble and Johnson climbed the ladder to the forty-foot tower, David Janssen and Bill Raisch, who played the one-armed man, did most of the actual fighting.

A problem arose the morning the fight scene was to be shot, when the show's writers changed Raisch's lines. Raisch, who was really more of a stuntman than an actor, panicked and ran to David Janssen and Barry Morse for help. The two professional actors helped Raisch learn his new lines, and with their encouragement, the scene came off without a hitch.

JOHNSON: Yeah . . . I killed her. Now I'm going to kill you . . . won't have to worry about you again . . . no more.

Although Bill Raisch certainly wouldn't win an Emmy for his performance, he did manage to get his lines right. Then Gerard pulled the trigger, killing the one-armed man.

With Johnson dead and unable to confess publicly, Lloyd Chandler agreed to testify and revealed what really happened the night of Helen Kimble's murder.

In the concluding scene, after Kimble was

freed, Kimble and Jean Carlisle walked from the courthouse, approaching Lieutenant Gerard.

Originally, the script called for Kimble and Gerard to exchange some inane lines that both actors felt were inappropriate for the final scene. "We decided the lines were rather mawkish," said Barry Morse, "something like Gerard saying, 'Well, listen, no hard feelings, huh, and Kimble answering, 'Oh, sure.' We decided the most eloquent thing we could do was absolutely nothing, that no dialogue would adequately convey what was going on in either of the character's minds. To make our point, we played the lines as originally written and at the end of the scene, David and I fell into each other's arms and I kissed him heartily on both cheeks. That, of course, raised a laugh from the crew and they realized 'less was more.' "

Finally, the writers agreed to go along with the actors' approach to the scene. In the version that was aired, no words were spoken. As Kimble approached, Gerard nodded and extended his hand. Kimble hesitated, stared at Gerard's hand, and then, finally, the pursuer and the pursued shook hands.

David Janssen with Diane Baker in "The Judgment."

"The Judgment" Part One aired on ABC August 22, 1967. The suggestion that someone other than the one-armed man killed Helen Kimble only whetted the audience's curiosity. For one week the world waited and speculated as the drama built toward the final episode.

Because the writers knew *The Fugitive* would definitely end, they could coordinate the final episode's air date with the script, allowing "The Judgment" Part Two to end with the now

famous line uttered by narrator William Conrad: "Tuesday, August 29. The day the running stopped."

Despite the fact *The Fugitive* was ending, there was surprisingly little emotion following the final day's shooting on "The Judgment" Part Two.

"It wasn't as if there were great emotional feelings about the show ending," said George Eckstein, "because you didn't have an ensemble company. You had only one person really, Richard Kimble, with Lieutenant Gerard appearing only occasionally and the one-armed man very seldom. And the directors changed almost every week, so it wasn't like it was a tight little family. There is always a certain sadness when you've committed yourself to four years on a project. There is always a sadness when it's coming to an end, but there was the other side of it . . . that you want to go out a winner and we knew we were doing that."

Actress Jacqueline Scott, who played Richard Kimble's sister, Donna Taft, remembered the final episode for other reasons. "I remember that I had my son, who was three weeks old, with me in a suite on the Goldwyn lot, so I was running back and forth to feed him. I played Jimmy Stewart's pregnant wife in a movie a week before I had the baby, and I did the last *Fugitive* when he was three and a half weeks old. The final episode was exciting, but I don't think they realized how much people would react to it."

Although Don Medford had directed what proved to be a history-making show, he remembered little about the last episode, saying, "In that kind of situation, the director is so busy getting the film done because there are just so many hours and so much money, that you don't really get involved in little side stories. You almost don't have a chance to stand back and look at what's going on."

The final installment of "The Judgment" aired on ABC on Tuesday, August 29, 1967. More viewers watched the final episode of *The Fugitive* than any television show in history. Seventy-two percent of the American television audience or 25,700,000 households saw *The Fugitive* that night. Stores and restaurants shut down for an hour to allow customers to watch the final episode. In New Zealand, the International Rugby Championship was delayed. The starting times of several major league baseball games were changed to accommodate fans. And during the Minnesota Twins–Baltimore Orioles' game at Metropolitan Stadium in Minneapolis, the scoreboard flashed the message: THE ONE-ARMED MAN DID IT.

Barry Morse recalled a curious thing happening

in England. "In the north of England and Scotland, people saw the final episode a day or so before it was shown in the south of England. Public gambling had just become legal and so there were immense bets placed on who was going to turn out to have been the murderer of Richard Kimble's wife. So people in the south of England spent thousands of pounds telephoning their friends or relatives in the north of England to find out, a day or so before, who it was . . . so that they could place bets. According to the bookmakers, the odds favored Lieutenant Gerard as the culprit."

Diane Baker, who played Jean Carlisle in the final episode, recalled the repercussions of her only *Fugitive* appearance. "In the late sixties, I was in Spain doing a movie with Maximilian Schell," said Baker, "and the last episode of *The Fugitive* was just coming on the air there in Spanish. My God! You would have imagined I was the biggest star in Hollywood. They brought out the press and had me in full-page magazine articles, doing photographs and interviews as a result of it showing over there. It has definitely turned into a cult, historical piece for television. It was a great deal of fun."

In the United States, *The Fugitive*'s forty-six rating and seventy-two percent share were Nielsen ratings' records which stood until 1980, when a *Dallas* episode revealed J.R. Ewing's attacker. In 1994, twenty-six years after it originally aired, "The Judgment" Part Two is still sixteenth on the ratings list for all television shows, and ten of the programs rated ahead of it are Super Bowls. Among weekly television series, the final episode of *The Fugitive* still ranks third after the M*A*S*H Special in 1983, and the aforementioned *Dallas* episode in 1980.

Despite the success of the final episode, Quinn Martin later regretted having ended *The Fugitive* as he did, because it hurt the show in its initial syndication run. Because the outcome was known, the syndicated version was unable to sustain the suspense of the original show. "At the time Quinn ended *The Fugitive*," said George Eckstein, "he was going through some personal problems. His sister was dying of cancer, and he later told me that if he hadn't been so distracted by those problems, he might have changed his mind and not ended the show. He would have ended with a normal episode, to keep the syndication prospects alive."

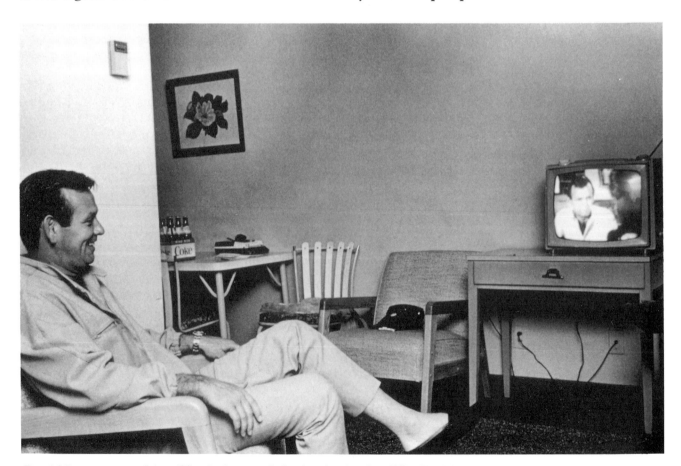

David Janssen watching "The Judgment," the final episode of The Fugitive.

Chapter 5

Paging Dr. Kimble – David Janssen

It was the magic of that son of a bitch, David, and his charm that made the show. He was the most charming bastard that ever lived. I loved him.

—*Actor William Conrad,* Fugitive *narrator*

David Janssen's portrayal of Dr. Richard Kimble was the major reason for *The Fugitive*'s success and enduring popularity. "It was a wonderful marriage of an actor and a part," said John Conwell, who began as the show's casting director and eventually rose to vice president of casting for QM Productions. "It happens once in a while but it doesn't happen too often."

"David fit beautifully," said George Eckstein, *Fugitive* writer and co-producer. "We are in a world where there is an increasing sense of alienation, frustration, and helplessness on the part of the individual, and this was such a strong dramatization of that syndrome. I think people really identified with that."

To television viewers, David Janssen was Dr. Richard Kimble. They experienced Kimble's grief following his wife's murder, his fear during his flight from police Lieutenant Philip Gerard, and his anger and frustration as he chased the one-armed man who murdered his wife.

"Sure I understood Richard Kimble," Janssen told *TV Guide*'s Dwight Whitney. "He is not too far removed from what I am in general. It is the sort of part you can't reach too far outside yourself and successfully play. I relate physically and emotionally. How else could I have done it?"

In expressing the isolation of Richard Kimble, David Janssen reached deep into his own pool of emotion. "David was a loner," said his mother, Berniece Janssen. "As a child he listened to classical music, Beethoven and Chopin, or read for hours. He kept to himself very much."

"David had his own peculiar brand of tension," said Diane Baker, who played Kimble's love interest, Jean Carlisle, in *The Fugitive*'s final episode. "There was something withdrawn and odd and kind of a seriousness about him, and then sometimes a smile would cross his face. I can just see him now. It was surprising how unassuming and quiet he was. There were times when I couldn't even hear him when he was speaking because he was so low-keyed and he spoke kind of swallowing his words. I assumed it was from a shyness. He was so gentle and so sweet and shy. He was adorable."

Adorable. Vulnerable. Sensitive. Those were all words used to describe David Janssen. Certainly his magnetism was universal. "He appealed to both men and women the way Clark Gable did," said John Conwell. "He was a woman's man and a man's man. He had tremendous sex appeal. You just liked him and you wanted him to win all the time."

"People just liked David, everybody liked him," said Jacqueline Scott, who played Richard Kimble's sister, Donna Taft. "Whenever I'd go to my hometown in Missouri or around Los Angeles, people would recognize me and they all would want to know about David. Mechanics would crawl out from under cars and ask about David. There was a quality about him that people liked."

Women loved not only Janssen's sensitivity, but also his physical charm. Six feet tall, 180 pounds, with an athletic build, large ears, dark brown hair, and brown eyes, Janssen was irresistible. "We were shooting in Nevada or Utah or somewhere like that . . . in the parking lot of a bank," said *The Fugitive*'s producer Alan Armer, who also worked with Janssen on a television movie, *The Birds of Prey*. "And there were women at every window of this business building, just trying to catch sight of David Janssen. It was incredible."

David Janssen greets youthful admirers, 1959.

The Fugitive was the perfect vehicle for Janssen to develop his acting talent. After playing a shallow character in *Richard Diamond, Private Eye* and acting in forgettable movies which he characterized as playing "the leading man's best friend's best friend," Janssen finally landed a role that allowed him to use his full range of dramatic skills. "I put myself completely into the character to make him believable," Janssen said. "I close out whatever is beyond the stage light. Once I'm convinced the man is real, he can do anything the story indicates. In front of the camera I forget the ball scores, the family, and what's for dinner."

Director Walter Grauman recalled Janssen's intensity and dedication as being key elements in *The Fugitive*'s success. "Remember the show's opening titles, after the train wreck, where Kimble falls into a little stream and the handcuffs come up and there's a flash of light that comes off the cuffs? I shot all that in Griffith Park, here in Los Angeles. I remember that night, it was very late, and I made David run, over and over again because it was so hard for him to fall and then raise the cuffs exactly to the right spot to get that flash of light. And he was really just so dedicated to doing it right."

David Janssen from the opening titles of "Fear in a Desert City."

"Another night we were shooting in Oxnard at two o'clock in the morning," recalled Grauman. "It was an incredibly cold night on the beach. I wanted David to come up out of the surf and there was this huge pier with the big pilings and I made him come out of the water over and over and over again. Finally David said, 'You son of a bitch, if you don't stop it, you're going to kill me.' I said, 'Not until I get this shot.' "

Another of Janssen's strengths as an actor was his memory. "David was incredibly concentrated," said Grauman. "He had a facility for remembering dialogue. He would glance at a page and inside of a couple of minutes, he'd know the dialogue, it was like he had a photographic mind."

Janssen's dramatic instincts also contributed to

the success of *The Fugitive*. When Alan Armer received a call from Janssen saying he had a problem with a script, the producer would rush to the soundstage and sit down with Janssen and the director. "We would sit there for half an hour, I would change a couple of lines, and we would fix it," said Armer. "I trusted David's instincts. A lot of leading guys in series don't know their ass about how a script is structured, and they bitch and moan because they're not getting enough lines . . . they are prima donnas. But David was really wise enough, that when he had a problem, it was based on something pretty damned legitimate."

During *The Fugitive*'s first season, Janssen wasn't always so cooperative. "David would argue with everybody about faults he'd found in the scripts," Quinn Martin told *TV Guide*. "He baited directors. It wasn't nasty, but he wanted to make sure people paid attention to him. He bugged me."

As *The Fugitive* became successful and Janssen more confident, he mellowed. "Success moves people lots of ways," continued Martin. "Some actors get paranoid. They turn on people. They become selfish. David has become more secure, easier to work with. He's the first guy in town who got nicer as the result of big success."

David Janssen's most endearing quality was his sense of humor. Unfortunately, that side was rarely seen by *The Fugitive*'s viewers. "David had an incredible sense of humor," said Alan Armer. "He had a kind of David Niven–Cary Grant reactive type of humor, that in a series like *The Fugitive*, he never got a chance to show because he was always running, always afraid, and always working under pressure."

If there was criticism of Janssen's performance, it was usually aimed at his limited repertoire of mannerisms. Reviewer Dennis Braithwaite in the *Toronto Globe* wrote: "David Janssen commands the narrowest gamut of facial expressions of any actor since the late Alan Ladd."

"I really found it painful to watch David Janssen grimacing every time a cop came around," said Ed Asner, who guest-starred in *The Fugitive* and later became a major series star himself in *The Mary Tyler Moore Show* and *Lou Grant*. "He looked like the dopiest person in the world, giving himself away to the cops every time rather than playing it cool and smooth. Why he wasn't arrested the second week of the show and sent back to Indiana, I'll never know. I thought David was a good actor, but a lot of the time David didn't give a shit. David had great talent but was lazy and coasted."

Janssen's co-star Barry Morse regarded the

actor's limited facial expressions as virtues. "In today's cliché, 'less is more,' " said Morse. "David was the supreme under-actor. You could have cut almost any single shot of David into almost any situation, whether of elation or despair. You can take that little twitch, that little blink, and cut it into anything. If somebody has just said, 'You've won the lottery,' or somebody has just said, 'Your wife's dead,' you could use the same footage because David's responses would have been more or less the same."

David Janssen with Ed Asner in the Episode 105, "Run the Man Down."

Quinn Martin felt that Janssen's bag of expressions resulted from his lack of self-confidence. "David had never believed he was a really good actor," Martin told *TV Guide*. "He'd blink his eyes or tug at his ears or stroke his chin. He was a glib, good-looking, well-dressed guy who refused to probe his own talent."

Gradually, as Janssen's talent surfaced, his stock mannerisms disappeared. "He used them only when he was tired," said Martin. "I'd watch the dailies – the unedited film of each day's shooting – and I'd say to David: 'I counted two bug eyes, one ear tug, and one chin pull. Tired?' And he'd say, 'You rat, you caught me.' The next day there'd be no gimmicks. Just talent."

In playing a character, an actor strives to become the character. In his portrayal of Richard Kimble, David Janssen was so believable that the television audience couldn't separate Kimble from Janssen, the role from the actor. "There were all kinds of things implied in David's performance

which he didn't even have to state," said Barry Morse. "Viewers could fill all that in with their own reactions like 'Oh, that poor man, he hasn't had a good night's sleep or a decent meal,' and people would say, 'let me hide him under my bed, or better yet, let me hide him in my bed.' There is a particular skill in being a series actor and David was dynamite."

To *The Fugitive*'s fans, David Janssen was Dr. Richard Kimble. Without Janssen, it's doubtful the show would have connected with viewers as it did. "It was the ideal chemical combination of this sad man, David, with the character of Richard Kimble," said Walter Grauman. "David was exactly right and I can't imagine anyone else in the part," echoed Quinn Martin.

Long before he played Richard Kimble, David Janssen was born David Harold Meyer in tiny Naponee, Nebraska, March 27, 1931. David's father was Harold Meyer, a banker whom his mother Berniece divorced shortly after David's birth. Berniece had been Miss Nebraska of 1928 and a runner-up in the Miss America contest the same year.

Using her maiden name, Berniece Dalton, David's mom toured as a dancer with Ziegfeld's Rio Rita road show, and at the age of one, David got his first taste of show business, sometimes traveling with his mother.

When he was three, David won a Sears & Roebuck beautiful-baby contest and claimed a silver loving cup. Shortly after that he made his first theater appearance in Alma, Nebraska, singing and dancing in a talent contest. David took second place in a field of four, finishing behind Berniece's brother Merlin.

When David was eight, he and his mother moved to Los Angeles. The first place Berniece took David was Grauman's Chinese Theater. "We walked down Hollywood Boulevard," said Berniece, "and we tried our feet in the different stars' footprints. I told David that someday he would have his footprints there. He just smiled and said, 'Yeah, I will, Mother, I'll have mine there.' "

When David was ten, Berniece placed her son in the McKinley Home for Boys, sponsored by the Kiwanis Club of America. Janssen's second wife Dani maintained this was an orphanage, a charge Berniece vehemently denied. "It's not an orphanage," said Berniece. "I had an appendectomy and I didn't want David to stay alone in the apartment. They took David, he survived, he loved it. He stayed for a year because where I was living, you could not have children at the time, and he came home every weekend."

Eventually Berniece married trucking executive Eugene Janssen, who adopted David, giving him his name and a home.

Berniece enrolled David in acting lessons and had him performing in little plays all over Hollywood. Although Berniece Janssen bristled at the term "stage mother," it's obvious she was determined to see her son become a star. "I enjoyed the Ziegfeld Follies so much, and I saw the money there, for doing what you liked. So, I thought, why not?"

David with his mother Berniece Janssen.

David Janssen at age eight.

"My mother's career in movies didn't amount to much," Janssen told *Globe* writer David Ragan. "So, from the time I was eight years old, she turned all her attention on me."

In 1945, at the age of fourteen, David Janssen made his screen debut in *It's a Pleasure,* starring Sonja Henie, and a year later he played Johnny Weissmuller's younger brother in *Swamp Fire.*

Then Janssen discovered an alternative to the road to movie stardom his mother had mapped out for him. At John Burroughs Junior High School, he began to display athletic talent, and by the time he reached Fairfax High, the once-aspiring thespian had become a basketball and track star. As a pole vaulter, Janssen cleared a then-respectable 12 feet 2 inches, and was recruited by several colleges including UCLA. Then his athletic career took a strange twist.

Pole vaulting for publicity photos for *The Hollywood Citizen News,* Janssen suffered a serious knee injury, dashing his dreams of someday competing in the Olympics and playing pro basketball. Years later, in 1968, Janssen wrote a letter to Abe Grunberg's Voice of Hollywood column, in which he said:

David Janssen, 1949.

Dear Abe:
    You know how to hurt a guy, as our friend Don Rickles would say. Yesterday, when we chatted at Fairfax, you had to mention the most painful moment of my life. Seriously, if I had not sustained that accident on the Fairfax athletic field in my junior year, life for me probably would have been markedly different.

    In those days, my only dream – day and night

— revolved around a flaming desire to set the sports world on fire. So how can one be modest? They say I was a pretty fine basketball player — for a six footer — obviously before the Alcindor days. Some believe my track prospects were even brighter. I was a pole vaulter, a high school occupation that, if accomplished, always was good for at least three athletic scholarship offers.

And that's where the *Citizen-News* entered my life.

One afternoon, I was in great form — I thought — after completing the best vault of my young career. Jerry Weiner, one of your sportswriters, sidled up innocently and asked if I would pose for a photograph. "Of course we could lower the bar a few feet for the picture," Jerry suggested. "No one would notice

the difference from the angle at which it was to be taken."

"Should I tempt the fates and lend my support to this little deception? My friends always joshed me about being as honest as the day is long. I did, and excuse the pun, the days got awfully darn short in a hurry.

"I sailed over the bar with all the agility of a gazelle — feet to spare. But somehow — other than superstition, I don't know why — I twisted my knee on the grand descent.

Crack!

No, I didn't want any support. I could walk it off in a few minutes. That night the knee looked like a big black and blue balloon, two colors that never have suited my complexion.

The leg was in a cast for six months. Later, after hours of treatments, the best I could do was hobble around gamely in a heavy bandage from calf to thigh, always, naturally, with that sickly brave expression on my face.

Expressions don't elicit athletic scholarships and neither did this one. Luckily I had some drama training — really good at Fairfax — and I had my first movie behind me. So I veered from sports to stage and film work — and here I am!

Everyone who knows about the vaulting accident laughs at the irony of the biggest factor in my career — playing Dr. Richard Kimble, the man wrongfully convicted of murder, who spends life running, yes, running, from the law.

With his athletic career over, Janssen spent a semester at UCLA, a couple of months at a community college, and then turned to acting full-time. Janssen worked in a Los Angeles amateur stock company, where its director, Jack Holland, remembered him as "the stiffest actor I've ever worked with."

At age eighteen Janssen landed Sue Carol, a former movie star and Alan Ladd's wife, as his agent. She took him to Twentieth Century-Fox studios, where the producers took one look at Janssen's oversized ears and had them glued back. "They did it with white rubber cement," Janssen told *TV Guide*. "The cement was applied to the side of the head and the back of the ear. But this didn't work, because the ears lay too flat. So they wanted me to have them fixed surgically. I was against that. Incredible? Yes, but it was the kind of thing Fox was doing in those days."

Fox also tried changing Janssen's hairline and dying his hair blond. "In those days," Janssen said, "the studios weren't satisfied until they had you looking like some star. When they got me to look like Clark Gable they dropped me cold."

David Janssen injured his knee pole vaulting for the Hollywood Citizen News *in 1948.*

39

After Fox dumped him, Janssen appeared in summer stock productions in Maine, and then rehearsed for two Broadway plays which closed before they opened. In New York, Janssen worked as an elevator operator and drugstore counterman while waiting for his big break.

Returning to Hollywood in 1951, Janssen signed a five-year contract with Universal Inter-

David Janssen in his first movie at Universal Pictures, Yankee Buccaneer, *1952.*

national Pictures. His classmates at Universal included Clint Eastwood, Rock Hudson, Richard Long, Martin Milner, and Angie Dickinson. Janssen's first movie at Universal was *Yankee Buccaneer* but then he entered the army, spending his two-year hitch in Special Services at Fort Ord, California.

In 1955 Janssen returned to Universal, appearing in *Chief Crazy Horse*. While at Universal, Janssen had small roles in thirty-two mostly forgettable pictures, playing what he called "agreers." "The star would approach me and ask, 'Don't you think so, Harry?'" Janssen said. "I'd agree and disappear."

Janssen also described his typical scene in a Universal movie, saying, "There would be a scene in which the two leading characters would be standing in the foreground and they'd be saying, 'Hey, listen, why don't we go into town tonight and see if we can find some broads.' Then they would turn back to a figure dimly in the background who was sitting on his bed in the barracks and they'd say, 'Do you want to come, Joe?' And

this out-of-focus figure would say, 'Yeah, sure.' That out-of-focus figure was me."

When his Universal contract expired, Janssen

David Janssen co-starred with Tab Hunter (left) in Lafayette Escadrille, *1958.*

went freelance and worked sporadically. "I was part playboy and part bum," Janssen told *TV Guide*'s Dwight Whitney. "My life consisted mainly of cashing my paycheck and paying off my tailor and my bar tabs. I had a bad case of that Hollywood psychology which says, 'Here's the face and body, so love me, world.'"

During this period, Janssen did two Warner

David Janssen as Richard Diamond, Private Eye, *1957 to 1960.*

Bros. movies starring Tab Hunter: *The Girl He Left Behind* in 1956 and *Lafayette Escadrille* in 1958, a film which would lead to his first big break in television.

In *Lafayette Escadrille*, Janssen worked with famed director William Wellman. Intrigued by Janssen's unusual gravelly voice and motion picture personality, Wellman touted Janssen to Dick Powell, a partner in Four Star Films, who was looking for someone to play the part of private detective Richard Diamond, a part Powell himself had played on radio. After auditioning twenty-four other actors, Powell interviewed Janssen and without even a screen test, hired him to play Richard Diamond.

At the age of twenty-six, David Janssen finally had his first major role on television. In 1957 *Richard Diamond, Private Eye* began its run on CBS as a summer replacement series. It remained on the air on both CBS and NBC until September 1960. For playing Richard Diamond, Janssen was reportedly paid the trifling sum of $750 a week.

During a three-month period when Richard Diamond was off the air, Janssen also played a killer on *Zane Grey Theater,* an oil engineer in *The Millionaire,* and a detective on *Alcoa-Goodyear Theater.*

When *Richard Diamond* ended, Janssen returned to Hollywood movies. He had a featured role as a tough marine in *Hell to Eternity* in 1960, a movie that was both a box office and critical

Hell to Eternity, 1960: David Janssen (right), Vic Damone (center), Jeffrey Hunter (left), and Guy Gabaldon, seated.

success. In 1961 Janssen appeared in a series of pictures including *Dondi,* based on a comic strip, which Janssen told UPI's Vernon Scott was "one of the great bombs of our time"; *King of the Roaring Twenties,* in which Janssen played gangster Arnold Rothstein; and *Twenty Plus Two* in which he portrayed a tracer of lost persons. The same year Janssen also played a deputy sheriff in a low-budget film, *Ring of Fire.* A *Variety* reviewer thought that Janssen gave evidence "that he may become one of Hollywood's top stars. He has the looks, the masculinity, the personality, and he can act. His reactions and his timing are keen."

Janssen's film career continued in *Man Trap* in 1961, in which he played a young man planning a big robbery. In 1963 he acted opposite Debbie Reynolds in *My Six Lovers,* a film that was so bad that Janssen's press agent Frank Lieberman "winces at the memory."

In 1962 Janssen's luck changed as television producer Quinn Martin selected him for the role of Dr. Richard Kimble in the new series Martin was producing called *The Fugitive.* Martin agreed to buy Janssen out of a preexisting contract to do another show, and glad to take a break from his lukewarm film career, Janssen accepted Martin's offer. It was the best decision Janssen ever made.

Although *The Fugitive* made Janssen a wealthy man, in the beginning the financial prospects weren't bright. During the filming of the pilot episode, "Fear in a Desert City," Janssen and Barry Morse walked the streets of Tucson, Arizona, discussing their remuneration for the new show.

"Are they paying you decently for this?" asked Janssen.

"Well, no, I'm nobody in Hollywood," answered Morse. "I'm just an ordinary working actor. They're paying me fairly enough, but nothing too extravagant."

"You know what? They can't even meet my ordinary going price, but they've offered me a piece of the show."

"Well, that may not be too bad."

"Well, you know what five percent of nothing is?"

Actually, Janssen's "five percent of nothing" became twenty percent of *The Fugitive*'s earnings, and twenty percent of the hit show, plus a reported salary of ten thousand dollars per week, made Janssen a millionaire many times over.

Janssen and his first wife Ellie used his television and movie earnings to enjoy the good life. The couple lived in the fashionable Trousdale Estates section of Beverly Hills. Barry Morse remembered being invited to Janssen's house:

"David said, 'Come out and have a meal . . . I'll have a couple of people there.' He didn't tell me it was indeed his birthday party. When I got close to the house I realized this must be an enormous 'do' because I couldn't park within a couple of

David with first wife Ellie, 1965.

blocks of his place. I went up to the house and rang the bell and the door was opened by Jack Benny and he said, 'Oh, come in . . . come in.' Then I saw Lucille Ball. The place was swarming with everybody in our trade . . . the most unbelievable people, and there was David basking in the middle of all this."

In addition to their Beverly Hills home, the Janssens also owned a posh weekend retreat in Palm Springs and drove his-and-her Lincoln Continentals.

Although *The Fugitive* made Janssen rich and famous, the show took its toll. "At that time, David Janssen did a harder day's work than probably any actor in the whole history of the world," said Barry Morse. Janssen rose each day between four and five and was on *The Fugitive* set by 6 A.M. A typical shooting day lasted twelve to fourteen hours. By his own estimate, Janssen was on camera for 85 per cent of every show and he appeared in all 120 episodes.

Not only was Janssen in *The Fugitive* most of the time, his role was also grueling. Although Janssen had a stuntman and a stand-in, he did much of his own stunt work as Dr. Richard Kimble was blinded by an explosion, run over by a car, knocked unconscious, stabbed, survived fights, concussions, gunshot wounds, cases of

amnesia and pneumonia, and was arrested countless times.

The most taxing part of Janssen's work was the constant running the show required. Richard Kimble was always running – up a hill, through a stream, over the mountains, or through a desert – running to catch a bus, a car, or a train – and always running from the relentless pursuit of Lieutenant Gerard. And all this on a bad left knee. Janssen's old high school pole-vaulting injury flared up. His knee ached and swelled, and by the end of the show's run, Janssen could be seen limping perceptibly. His ailing knee eventually required surgery.

The Fugitive also frequently employed "night-for-night shooting," in which night scenes were actually photographed at night. This meant Janssen often worked late into the evening. He once complained to writer Stanford Whitmore, "Can you write me a show with no night shooting?"

"Sure, David," Whitmore answered. "What's the big deal?"

"Ellie and I have box seats for the Dodgers' games. We were at the game and Ellie poked me in the ribs and she said, 'Wake up David, Sandy Koufax is pitching to Willie Mays and fifty-two thousand people are watching you sleep.' "

In 1965 Ellie Janssen told *TV Guide:* "He is physically tired. He pushes himself beyond his endurance. In a way he has to. He doesn't want to lead an existence that is solely eat-work-sleep. He must have a social life. He is smoking more these days – two to three packs a day – and he is drinking more. He feels it gives him zing, it peps him up."

David Janssen's drinking has become legendary. One rumor had it that when Janssen died in 1980, his favorite Hollywood haunts all went dark for an hour in his memory.

"David began drinking at parties," said Ellie Janssen, "when he had to be 'David Janssen,' in the public eye. He would drink to bolster his courage." The physical and mental strain of doing *The Fugitive* caused him to drink even more. "He was not a mean drunk or anything like that, he just enjoyed it," recalled John Conwell. "I think a lot of it came from the pressure of performing all the time. When he went home, he wanted to relax and would take a drink or two. It never interfered with his acting."

Although Janssen's drinking sometimes created problems later in his career, it rarely affected his performance on *The Fugitive*. "All these years, people have said David was a bit of a boozer," said Barry Morse. "Anybody who did the day's work that he did could not possibly have survived on alcohol. He was absolutely impeccable in his discipline on the set. He never put a foot wrong

The Formosa Cafe, located near Goldwyn Studios.

in hitting the marks and working with the cameras. He never failed in absolute courtesy towards the crew. He was the absolute, ultimate pro."

It was well known that Janssen drank heavily away from the set, but had amazing recuperative powers. "If I saw him drunk a few times, it wasn't when he was shooting," remembered Walter Grauman. "It would be late at night. I could never figure out how he could drink and live like that and come in the next day and work. He was never drunk on *The Fugitive*, where it interfered with his work."

One of Janssen's favorite retreats was the Formosa Cafe, across from Goldwyn Studios where *The Fugitive* was filmed. Still in existence, the Formosa is a converted railroad car with

autographed stars' pictures on the wall, and a menu of Chinese food. In the 1960s, the Formosa was a haven for television and movie stars like Janssen. While working on *The Fugitive*, actress Eileen Heckart frequently joined Janssen for cocktails at the Formosa. "David was heaven," said Heckart. "When he had a few drinks, he just got like more of a pussycat and he was more and more charming. You just wanted to take care of him. Oh, he was dear. Drunk or sober, he was wonderful."

Heckart recalled one time, though, when over a long lunch at the Formosa, Janssen had one drink too many. "David had come back from lunch," said Heckart. "Normally he was a page reader, he'd look at the script once and would know it. I don't know what he had to drink, but he couldn't do a thing, and I finally sat down after eleven takes, I was so tired. And I said, 'David, if you don't get it on this next take, I'm sitting down and we're going to cancel this whole thing.' " Then Executive Producer Quinn Martin called and told David he looked terrible in one shot. The filming stalled as an angry Martin and Janssen's manager arrived on the set to deal with the problem. "And David said to me, 'Cancel Easter because you won't get home for Easter,' recalled Heckart. "And I said, 'I intend to go home for Easter, David, you're going to have to work out your own problems.' But he was darling and fun."

Financially secure but physically and emotionally drained, David Janssen left *The Fugitive* after four enormously successful years. When *The Fugitive* ended in 1967, Janssen had few regrets. "I didn't weep," he told *TV Guide*. "I was not being shipped off to the elephant's graveyard to have my bones bleached in the sun. I was gaining time to flush out the brain." The respite from series TV gave Janssen an opportunity to again pursue an unfulfilled dream: to become a movie star.

Janssen had often done quickie movies during his hiatus between seasons of *The Fugitive*, but now he could devote his full energy to motion pictures. His first effort was *Warning Shot* in 1967, an action-filled drama, ironically about a cop's attempt to clear his name after killing a supposedly innocent doctor. *Warning Shot* got good reviews and Janssen followed that with a co-starring role opposite John Wayne in *The Green Berets*, a critically acclaimed performance in *The Shoes of the Fisherman*, and other movies including *Generations, Marooned,* and *Where It's At.*

While working on *Where It's At,* in 1968, Janssen became involved in an affair with actress

Rosemary Forsyth. Janssen's wife of eleven years, Ellie, answered by filing for divorce. She hired famed divorce attorney Marvin Mitchelson and the case turned into one of the longest and nastiest divorce trials in California history.

The affair with Rosemary Forsyth was really just the culmination of Janssen's Hollywood dalliances. As an attractive and popular television and film star, Janssen had his pick of the most desirable women in the entertainment world and made the most of his opportunities. "David was a playboy," said his friend director Walter Grauman. "He was really an attractive, charming guy that women flipped for and he lived it up all the time."

For Ellie Janssen, the affair with Forsyth was the last straw. "We had a wonderful marriage for as long as it lasted," said Ellie. "But the women in Hollywood throw themselves at the feet of celebrities, a celebrity as attractive as David was. When the women in the industry started trying to take over, my own ego and self-respect were what was being attacked." According to Los Angeles newspaper reports, Ellie Janssen was awarded an estimated ten million dollars in the divorce settlement. Although the court later reduced that amount, Ellie continued to receive half of Janssen's twenty percent share of *The Fugitive*'s profits.

David with second wife Dani, 1976.

"There is only one thing I do regret," said Ellie Janssen. "When I divorced David, I still loved him but I couldn't live with him under the circumstances. Had I stayed with him, I think he might still be alive today. After the divorce he was under a terrible strain and I think he drank himself to death."

Devastated by the financial and psychological effects of the divorce, Janssen began a three-year plunge into debauchery. "After eleven years of marriage," Janssen told the *Chicago Sun-Times*, "I dived into what I considered a newfound freedom. I was working hard and playing hard. Flying my own plane to parties all over the country and down to Mexico, having what I thought was a great time.

"I participated in life on what might be considered the grand scale, before I decided I had had one hangover too many; one party too many; one chartered plane and fourteen servants too many; too many cars that I never got around to drive."

In 1971 Janssen moved in with a curvaceous blonde, Dani Greco, who had recently divorced jazz great Buddy Greco. Four years later the couple was married. Janssen had been friends with the Grecos for years, and had originally met Dani in 1954, when she and David were both under contract to Universal Studios. Dani provided Janssen with stability, handled his investments, and even helped him stop drinking for a while. She also tolerated his lifestyle. When a national television interviewer asked Dani, "Do you think your husband cheats?" she answered, "Is the Pope Catholic? Look, David gives me everything I need emotionally, physically, financially, everything that I need. Now, if he has anything left over, he can give it to whoever he wants. I don't really care and I don't want to know about it."

Fourteen months after they were married, the couple separated, as Janssen became involved with songwriter Carol Connors, an Oscar-nominated lyricist who co-authored the theme song for the movie *Rocky*. During their five-month relationship, Janssen and Connors wrote music for a PBS kids' show and for *A Sensitive, Passionate Man*, a television movie starring Janssen.

Eventually, the Janssens reconciled and David returned home. Actually "home" consisted of two residences: a million-dollar Century City town house, complete with movable interior walls, and a $1.5-million beach house in Malibu.

In 1971, Janssen also decided it was time to go back to work. He returned to television, starring as treasury agent Jim O'Hara in *O'Hara, U.S. Treasury* on CBS. O'Hara reportedly paid Janssen

$30,000 per episode, but the show was dropped after only twenty-two segments. O'Hara was produced with the approval and cooperation of the Department of the Treasury, but Janssen maintained the U.S. government interfered with the show's scope, resulting in its failure.

Janssen came back to television again in 1974, starring as private detective Harry Orwell in *Harry O* on ABC. "Working in television is like making love to a gorilla," Janssen said of his return. "You don't stop when you want to stop; you stop when the gorilla wants to stop."

With *Harry O,* David Janssen again struck gold. The show was hailed as a small television masterpiece, and many who knew Janssen felt the character of Harry Orwell was a lot like Janssen himself. Orwell was a laid-back bohemian who lived on the beach and often used the city bus for transportation. Orwell would rather use his wit and sense of humor than gunfire to solve a case. "David was like Harry O," said Dani Janssen.

David Janssen with Robert Vaughn in the 1980 ABC TV movie, City in Fear.

"His sense of humor was the best. David originated a lot of sayings like: 'This is the only business in which you fail upwards,' and 'In my house, when the going gets tough, the tough go shopping.' He had a punch line for everything." When *Harry O* went off the air in 1976, David

Janssen's career as a star in episodic TV ended.

David Janssen was a superb television actor who understood how to use the medium. As one critic put it, Janssen was "an actor able to create a sense of character through the rhythms of his speech, the way he cocked his head or shrugged his shoulders, an actor alert to all the minute physical and vocal maneuvers that define our ordinary individuality."

As his career in series TV wound down, Janssen moved into motion pictures, television movies, and miniseries and from 1975 to 1980 did some of his best work, including Jacqueline Susann's *Once Is Not Enough, Two-Minute Warning, The Swiss Conspiracy, Centennial, The Word, S.O.S. Titanic, City in Fear, The Golden Gate Murders,* and *High Ice.* Janssen's favorite was *A Sensitive, Passionate Man,* a 1977 NBC movie in which he co-starred and reportedly cavorted with Angie Dickinson. Janssen played a self-destructive alcoholic, a role that may have been at least partly autobiographical.

Although he was one of television's brightest stars, Janssen never attained the same stature in motion pictures. His failure to achieve movie stardom was undoubtedly due in part to unwise selections he made in roles. "Some of his choices were not the smartest choices," said Janssen's close friend actress Suzanne Pleshette. "He sabotaged himself in some ways. David was a wonderful actor who never got his due. I don't think people really acknowledged how good David Janssen was. He really should have been our generation's Cary Grant."

Rather than being selective in accepting movie roles, Janssen seemed to grab almost everything that was offered. "I have always considered myself basically unemployed," said Janssen. "I'm from Nebraska and I feel guilty when I'm not working."

"There are a lot of television actors who don't make the transition to movies," said John Conwell. "You're going from that little box, television, to suddenly being sixty feet tall on the motion picture screen. I would have thought that David would do well in the movies, but he didn't."

"David possessed a particular skill in being a series actor," said Barry Morse. "He could develop his character cumulatively, week by week. But the skills required for a movie are higher profile, you have to state more, you have to commit more, because you're not going to be back next week. You have to summon up the character's response to a given situation in one take. In series television you don't have to do that."

Although Janssen never attained super stardom in movies, he was always in demand and enjoyed making films. "You know what I feel like? I feel like a little boy playing hooky from school," Janssen said. "I keep expecting my mother to come down on the set and come over to me and say, 'All right, come home!' They'll come and get me. They'll send the truant officer."

In all, Janssen acted in over one hundred movies. He had just finished a major film *Inchon* with Sir Laurence Olivier and had begun work on a TV movie, *Father Damien,* when he died.

Ironically, a few days before his death, Janssen had visited his doctor and had passed a physical. Although the tabloids speculated wildly about his death, the truth seemed to be that Janssen died February 13, 1980, after suffering a heart attack at about four A.M. in his Malibu beachfront home. His wife Dani phoned Los Angeles County paramedics. Two paramedics and four fireman arrived at the Janssen residence and administered CPR. Janssen's longtime friend, actor Stuart Whitman, drove by about four-thirty A.M. Seeing an ambulance and fire trucks, Whitman rushed inside and saw the paramedics working on Janssen. "They

Berniece Janssen, David's mother, 1993.

David Janssen with Suzanne Pleshette in Episode 67, "All the Scared Rabbits," 1965.

had taken him out of bed and they were working on him," Whitman told the *Los Angeles Times.* "It must have been half an hour altogether. Then one of the paramedics said, 'I think I've got a heartbeat,' and they took him to the hospital."

Whitman and Dani followed the ambulance to Santa Monica Hospital, but a short while later Janssen was pronounced dead in the emergency room. He was forty-eight. The fugitive had finally stopped running.

David Janssen's farewell was pure Hollywood. Close to a thousand people attended his funeral at Hillside Memorial Park and seven hundred the wake that followed. Mourners included execu-

tives from all three television networks and four major movie studios as well as celebrities like Gregory Peck, Rod Stewart, Richard Harris, Gene Kelly, Milton Berle, Johnny Carson, Angie Dickin-

son, and Linda Evans. Also paying their respects were the behind-the-scenes people: grips, guys on the crew, stunt men, and minor actors who had worked with Janssen. Among those who delivered eulogies were producer Quinn Martin, Janssen's longtime friend Richard Lang, and Suzanne Pleshette. "Dani Janssen asked me to speak for the girls," said Pleshette, "because David had so many women friends." "So, I spoke for the girls. We all loved him so much."

According to Dani Janssen, following the actor's death, a family dispute broke out when Janssen's will was released. Although the actor was worth a reported nine million dollars, he left his entire estate to his wife Dani, and left his mother Berniece exactly one dollar.

"That's exactly what he left her," said Dani Janssen, "because he had to legally or she could have contested the will. She made his life as miserable as she could." Dani Janssen wouldn't specify exactly what Berniece Janssen did to provoke her son's action, saying only, "David put up with such embarrassing situations that my heart went out to him. You can't even imagine your worst enemy would pull this stuff."

"I never had any trouble with David over the years," said Berniece Janssen. "We got along fine. She [Dani] manipulated the will and I know it. David didn't know he was going to die. I don't think he even made the will. I didn't even get the dollar. Where is the dollar? I'll take it. She's a manipulative, lying woman."

Years later a friend of Berniece Janssen's, Ken Custer, suggested that her son should have a star on the Hollywood Walk of Fame. Berniece, Custer, and Janssen fan Dave Brown began a campaign to raise the necessary $3500 needed to pay for the star. During a three-year fund-raising drive, Janssen's family members, fans from fifteen different states, and Janssen's Hollywood friends including James Garner, Lee Meriwether, Linda Evans, and silent star Buddy Rogers all contributed the necessary funds for the plaque. The movement gained momentum when the Motion Picture Mothers Club (Berniece Janssen is a member) joined the cause. Finally, the Hollywood Chamber of Commerce Committee approved David Janssen's star. In 1989, fifty-one years after he first

set foot on Hollywood Boulevard, David Janssen joined other entertainment legends on the Hollywood Walk of Fame.

Ken Custer, Berniece Janssen and Dave Brown at the Walk of Fame ceremony honoring David Janssen, 1989.

Ken Custer, Ellie Janssen and Dave Brown at David Janssen's star on the Hollywood Walk of Fame, 1989.

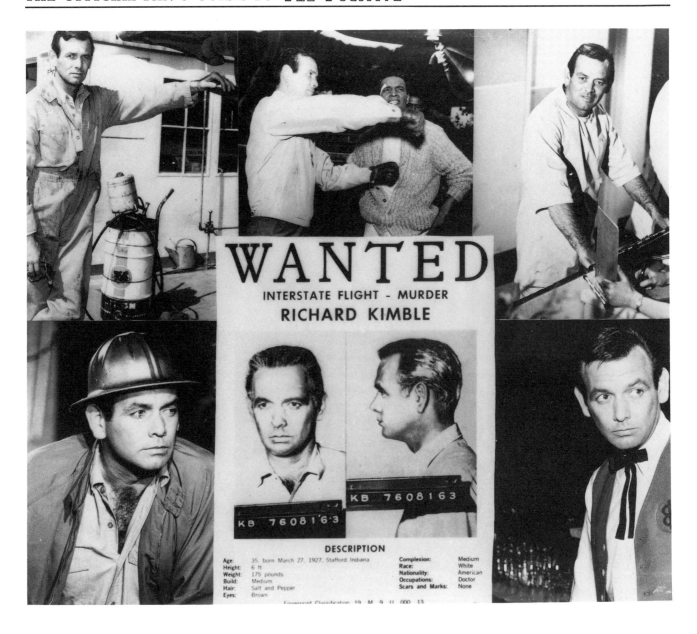

Chapter 6

Lieutenant Gerard –
Barry Morse

I learned that I had to protect myself when people took Lieutenant Gerard so seriously. Little old ladies would hit me with their purses and say, "You rotten, mean man, why don't you leave that nice doctor alone."

—Barry Morse

Talking with Barry Morse is like speaking with William Shakespeare himself. Could this classically trained actor with the rich British accent be the same man who played Lieutenant Philip Gerard, the obsessive Stafford, Indiana, cop who spoke in a flat, midwestern tone and chased Dr. Richard Kimble across our television screens?

"It's an ancient craft known as acting," said Morse. "Not many people do it anymore, but in the days when I was trained for this trade, you were expected to be able to make any kind of noises you were asked to. So, if somebody wants me to be not just an American, but any specific kind of American from Maryland to Missouri to California, I'll give them that kind of accent. I'll play in Sanskrit or Chinese if required, because that's what I take to be part of our trade. It's one of my private pleasures . . . that all over the U.S.A. people regard me as being from America although I'm not an American at all."

Born in 1918, the son of a poor London shopkeeper, Morse was educated, he says, "during truancies from a London Council elementary school." Naturally left-handed, Morse was beaten by teachers intent on making him write with his right hand. Tired of the beatings, he took to the streets and educated himself in public libraries, art galleries, and museums. At the age of fourteen Morse took a job as an errand boy, delivering parcels on a bicycle.

When he was fifteen Morse won the principal scholarship at the Royal Academy of Dramatic Art, becoming the youngest student ever to be admitted. At the end of two years of study, Morse played the title role in *Henry V* which was presented in honor of the Royal Academy's patron, King George VI.

Morse then began what he refers to as his "jail term," spending four years in repertory companies, where he had "the opportunity to fail in three hundred parts," more than many actors play in a lifetime.

When World War II broke out, Morse attempted to enlist in the navy, but a physical revealed he had tuberculosis. Instead of spending his time on the battlefront, Morse was sent to a sanitarium, where his TB was caught in the early stages and cured. Medically unfit for duty, Morse went back to acting, entertaining throughout the region during the war.

Morse acted for the BBC on radio and in 1937 made his television debut on the BBC when the industry was still in the experimental stages. "A famous stage actor in England told me I was foolish to waste my time on television," he recalls. "He said it was just a passing fad."

In addition to television, Morse performed on stage, on radio, and in movies in Europe, Canada, and the United States. "I hold over a dozen union cards from actors' guilds all over the world," he said. "In this day and age an actor has to be prepared to travel anywhere."

In the late 1950s Morse began to commute to New York and Los Angeles to act in various U.S. television shows including *Alfred Hitchcock Presents, Wagon Train, Twilight Zone, The Defenders, The Nurses,* and *Playhouse 90.* Among the shows Morse guest-starred in were *The New Breed* and *The Untouchables,* produced by Quinn Martin. "I played a number of roles in those series," Morse remembers. "All the way from a French champagne smuggler to a Romanian drug peddler to an East Side thug; I played everything, but never, as far as I recall, an English character."

When Quinn Martin began to cast *The Fugitive,* he remembered Morse's work and called him. "I'm working on a pilot for a proposed new series in which there is a recurring role I'd like you to play," Martin told Morse. "I won't tell you anything more about it, I'll send you a script, and then let's have lunch and talk about it."

"This script arrived," recalled Morse, "and I read this story vaguely reminiscent of Victor Hugo's *Les Misérables.* I saw that the two principal characters were this middle America doctor, who was obviously meant to be the hero of the piece, and the obsessive, dedicated police officer who was bent on capturing him, based on the char-

Barry Morse as Lieutenant Gerard.

acter of Inspector Javert from *Les Misérables*. I thought, 'How stupid, somebody in Quinn's office has sent the wrong script. He can't mean that I play either of these characters.' "

"Quinn, both of these characters are quintessentially middle American," Morse told Martin over lunch at Musso and Frank's restaurant.

"Yes, I know . . . that's the challenge," answered Martin. "There's something about this detective which is a bit too conventional. I know how much you enjoy tilting and shading different characters, so perhaps you can come up with something that's a bit off-center."

"Quinn, you know if that's what you want, I think it would have to be something beyond the normal Hollywood concept of a police officer," replied Morse. "You know what you want, but there are a whole lot of guys in Hollywood who could do this much better than me. I'm not even an American to start with."

At Martin's urging, Morse arrived in Tucson, Arizona, to film *The Fugitive*'s pilot episode, determined to get away from "the conventional cop figure in movies . . . with the raincoat and fedora." But on the set, the wardrobe department immediately handed him a raincoat and a fedora. "You will see that only in the pilot did I wear that dreadful raincoat and that cliched fedora," Morse laughingly recalled. "After the pilot was completed, I threw them behind some bushes and they were never seen again. You may have noticed that I never wore any kind of hat or coat ever afterwards."

In creating Lieutenant Gerard, Morse drew upon his interpretation of Inspector Javert in *Les Misérables,* his observations of American police officers, and the experiences of his older brother Leonard, a bobby in the Metropolitan Police Force in London.

"My brother and Lieutenant Gerard had some general moral qualities in common," said Morse. "What I had learned from Leonard was that he regarded himself merely as an instrument of the law and I made use of that thinking in the character."

One of the joys in watching *The Fugitive* is seeing Morse's gradual development of Lieutenant Gerard. "This is one of the great advantages of series television," said Morse. "That you start to tell more as the weeks and months and years go by than you can ever hope to tell once around. You can start to let people gradually understand what sort of guy this is and there are all kinds of characterization features."

Initially, Lieutenant Gerard's professional pride was wounded by Richard Kimble's escape, and recapturing the fugitive became an obsession. Gerard didn't seem to care whether Kimble was innocent or guilty. "I enforce the law," Gerard often said. "The law pronounced him guilty. Whether the law is right or wrong is not my concern."

Barbara Rush and Barry Morse in "Landscape With Running Figures," Episode 69, 1965.

As the series continued, Gerard's obsession grew and Morse added flesh to the character's skeleton. "I know everything about Kimble — what kind of books he likes, what kind of toothpaste he uses," said Gerard. In the episode "The 2130," when Gerard was told that a computer found Kimble 98 percent incapable of committing murder, Gerard responded, "The remaining 2 per cent is good enough for me."

Gerard's behavior even began to affect his family. In the classic two-parter "Landscape with Running Figures," Gerard's wife, played by

Barbara Rush, became so disgusted with her husband's obsession with Kimble that she left him. Later, when she had been blinded and was in the hospital, Gerard told her, "He's [Kimble] stuck in my throat and I can't swallow him."

Although Barry Morse appeared in only 37 of the 120 Fugitive episodes, the specter of Lieutenant Gerard was a constant presence. The viewer always knew that Gerard was on the trail of Richard Kimble and was a threat to show up at any time.

One of Morse's biggest challenges in playing Lieutenant Gerard was to lose his natural English accent and sound like an Indiana cop. He prepared by going to a local library and listening to tapes of midwesterners talking. "The greatest compliment," said Morse, "was when I started to get mail from people in Indiana saying, 'Gee, you talk just like my uncle Fred. You must have been born in our state.'"

"It wasn't that easy," continued Morse. "Because quite often I would have been in New York or Toronto playing a character with a quite different accent, totally unlike my own, and I would have to be a bit careful the first day back on the *Fugitive* set." To insure that Morse sounded the same in every episode, the show's soundman kept footage of Morse's last performance. Before Morse resumed shooting, he would listen to his previous work, making sure there was consistency in the accents.

Morse's ability to emulate almost any speech pattern dated back to his childhood. "I was lucky enough to be born in a slum in the East End of London," he said, "where people spoke in an impenetrable cockney accent like Liza Doolittle in *My Fair Lady,* and I grew up thinking that everybody spoke like that. Then, when I got my first job as an errand boy and began riding around other parts of London, I learned that not everybody did talk like that. A couple of years later, when I went to the Royal Academy of Dramatic Art, I discovered there were such things as beautiful girls, who besides speaking differently, smelled quite differently than any girls I'd ever known. So, I began to be introduced to a world of sights and smells and sounds, all totally different. Then I started watching movies and I heard these strange noises, where a cowboy would say, 'Gee, pardner, I left my horse down in the gulch,' or a gangster would snarl, 'You dirty rat.' I became aware that in different parts of this planet, they made different noises, and if you had your ears washed out, you could understand the different noises they made. The whole business of having an ear for sounds, for accents, for the way other people speak, is really a knack, a God-given instinct to remember what sounds are like."

Away from *The Fugitive* and Lieutenant Gerard, Morse lapsed back into his natural British accent. One day he drove to Beverly Hills to see film producer David O. Selznick and his wife Jennifer Jones. Unable to find the Selznicks' house, Morse spotted a woman washing her car and pulled up to ask for directions. "I said, 'Hello, could you tell me where the Selznicks live . . .'" Morse recalled. "And this woman lifted her head up, and it was Katharine Hepburn and she said, 'Oh, it's you . . . from that television series. You don't talk like that, do you? Oh, you're not an American.' And I said, 'Well, you can't believe everything you see on television.' And she directed me to the Selznicks."

Because elementary-school teachers had forced Morse to use his right hand, he became ambidextrous and used that trait to enhance Lieutenant Gerard. "I'm by nature left-handed," said Morse, "but I thought it would be fun to introduce a kind of divided personality in Lieutenant Gerard. So one week I would write with my left hand and then a couple of weeks later I would use my right hand. It's astonishing what viewers notice. People would stop me on the street and ask what it all meant, and I would say, 'it means Gerard has a divided personality.'"

Television had never seen a character quite like Lieutenant Gerard. "At the time, continuing characters in television always had to be adorable because the sponsors, all of these people who want to sell deodorant or automobiles or whatever, didn't want to have anybody involved in their series who was less than adorable," said Morse. "There had never been a running character who was deliberately intended to be disliked.

Richard Kimble (David Janssen) and Lieutenant Gerard (Barry Morse) in Episode 1, "Fear in a Desert City," 1963.

Being brought up in a theatrical tradition, I knew very well that if you wanted to play the most rewarding parts, they were often characters like Richard III, carefully designed to be disliked."

After the pilot was made, ABC tested the audience reaction to *The Fugitive*'s main characters. "The network people, the ad agencies, and sponsors," said Morse, "all those people who know the price of everything but the value of nothing, said, 'The viewers just love David Janssen, but you've got to get rid of that guy Morse. They all hate him.' And Quinn Martin, of course, very wisely nodded and said, 'Yeah, yeah . . . that's what we want.' "

The public not only disliked Lieutenant Gerard, they loathed him. During Morse's travels, little old ladies bashed him with their umbrellas and, said Morse, "Guys would loom over me in cafés and bars saying, 'You dumb copper, don't you understand Kimble is innocent.' I took it as a compliment because they didn't for a moment grasp that this was fiction and had nothing to do with real life."

Occasionally, when Morse felt particularly threatened, he would affect an even stronger British accent and tell his accusers, "I'm not that actor, whatever his name is. In fact, I'm a professor of English at Yale University."

Even real policemen critiqued Lieutenant Gerard. "I went to Chicago to be inducted as an honorary chief constable," remembered Morse, "and these cops were all very satirical, saying, 'Listen, that's not the way it happens.' And I said, 'Don't talk to me about it, talk to the writers.' "

Although Morse enjoyed the public's response, part of their reaction bothered him. "The sad thing was, so many people assumed the legal system of the United States was flawed, because they would say, 'Can't you see Kimble is innocent?' And I would say, 'This police lieutenant whom you feel so strongly about is simply a functionary, an instrument of your law. Under the system of legal process, this guy Kimble has been tried and found guilty. Now, if there's some flaw in the legal system and some mistake has been made, there are ways to correct this. It is not down to the law officer, the police lieutenant; his only function is to carry out the law in the same way that a waiter's function is to deliver the meal. Don't blame him if its badly cooked. It's not his responsibility. The responsibility is with the legal system as a whole.' "

As a result of *The Fugitive*'s worldwide exposure, Barry Morse was known from the United States to Europe. Several years after *The Fugitive* left network air, it was still being shown abroad. The Morses purchased a villa in Spain, and upon arriving stopped at a local bar to ask for directions to their new home. When Morse walked in, the surprised proprietor was watching *The Fugitive*. He looked from Morse to his television and back to Morse again and began shouting excitedly, "El fugitivo! El fugitivo! El teniente! El teniente!" During the years in which he vacationed in Spain, Morse became known as "El Teniente." I think the children in the streets knew Lieutenant Gerard's lines better than I did," Morse recalled.

While Lieutenant Gerard and Richard Kimble were adversaries, Barry Morse and David Janssen became close away from the show. "David was always glad to see me turn up in town," said Morse, "because that meant he was going to have a few days off. We all became immensely excited by the success of the series and David and I became very good friends."

The Morses and Janssens sometimes got together for dinner, much to the dismay of ABC, which didn't like the idea of the public seeing the fugitive and his pursuer dining together. So, most of the dinners were in seclusion at either the Janssens' Beverly Hills mansion or Morses' apartment.

When he began *The Fugitive,* Morse was forty-five, thirteen years older than Janssen. "I like to think David regarded me as a kind of proxy parent, since I was virtually old enough to be his father," said Morse. As their relationship developed, the younger Janssen frequently relied on Morse for fatherly advice. "David had a succession of ever more youthful wives, which is a very expensive habit in California," said Morse. "I used to say to him, 'David, son, if you are going to go on collecting, do, please, if you can, collect something which is relatively inexpensive, like stamps or coins. Don't go on collecting wives. It's a very expensive habit.' "

Despite their success, Morse and Janssen both maintained a sense of humor about their profession. During one hiatus between seasons of *The Fugitive,* ABC would often ask the actors to make promotional tours with network executives. One night in Chicago, the two staged a prank, at the expense of the one-armed man. "We arranged for David to have a prosthetic device built into his suit with a false and removable arm," recalled Morse with a twinkle in his eye. "We wrapped up our pitches, saying, 'We'll see you next season on ABC,' and I turned and shook hands with David and we walked off in opposite directions, with me carrying his arm, and he proceeding in the other direction with only one arm. ABC was not pleased because none of those fellows with the tight silk suits and the frightened faces had much of a sense of humor."

The Fugitive was a perfect vehicle for Barry Morse. He would show up on the set a dozen times a year to play Lieutenant Gerard, but avoided typecasting. "I had a recurring part in this immensely popular series," said Morse, "and at the same time I was able to play all sorts of other characters for NBC or CBS in New York, go back to Canada for the CBC for television or radio, or back to England for the BBC."

After *The Fugitive* ended, Morse and Janssen maintained their friendship, and would get together whenever Morse showed up in Hollywood. In 1980 Morse phoned Janssen to tell him he was coming to town and the two arranged to meet for dinner. A couple of days later, a journalist awakened Morse early in the morning, asking, "Mr. Morse, have you heard the news?"

"Well, no, I haven't gotten up yet," answered Morse, thinking the writer was seeking his opinion on "World War Three or whatever was in the news."

"Then perhaps you haven't heard," said the man. "David Janssen has died."

"I was really quite horrified," recalled Morse. "Because David was only forty-eight and that seemed to me to be a ludicrously, tragically young age. It was a great waste, because, in my view, David was never properly or fully extended as an actor. I was able to get a hint of what he was capable of and I don't think his full capabilities were ever properly made use of."

In addition to playing Lieutenant Gerard, Barry Morse also directed one episode of *The Fugitive*, "The Shattered Silence" in 1967.

After *The Fugitive* ended, Morse continued his television career, appearing in numerous movies and miniseries including *A Tale of Two Cities*, *Innocents Abroad*, *Sadat*, *Master of the Game*, and *A Woman of Substance*. Among his motion picture credits are *Daughter of Darkness*, *Kings of the Sun*, *Justine*, *Running Scared*, *Asylum*, *The Shape of Things to Come*, *Love at First Sight*, and *The Changeling*. Morse also starred on Broadway in *Hadrian VII* and directed productions of *Staircase* and *Who Goes Bare?*

At the age of seventy-five, Morse is still active as both a director and actor in theater and film. He has been married for almost fifty-five years to actress Sydney Sturgess and the Morses divide their time between residences in Toronto and London. The Morses have two children, a son Hayward and daughter Melanie, both actors, and two grandchildren, Vanessa and Hegan Louise.

Barry Morse's major project today is raising money for P.A.L., Performing Arts Lodges, a retirement home for actors in Toronto. In the summer of 1993 Morse staged a one-man show, "Merely Players" to raise funds for P.A.L.

Morse rarely watches reruns of *The Fugitive* and regrets only faintly that he hasn't profited from the show's continuing success. He recalled that he was paid "about $1,500 or $2,000 an episode" for playing Lieutenant Gerard, but gets nothing in the way of residuals today. "In those days nobody ever thought anybody would dream of wanting to watch 30-year-old shows. We all had similar contracts, with residuals which vanished down to nothing after five years. So, for the last twenty-five years, we've not been paid one nickel."

Paul Birch (left) as Captain Carpenter and Barry Morse as Lieutenant Gerard.

Although Barry Morse has lost count of the number of shows he's appeared in, he is perhaps best known on television for his role as Lieutenant Gerard.

"Still, to this day," said Morse, "I always know when a new country is getting *The Fugitive*, maybe Tanzania or Zimbabwe, because I get this mail written in pidgin English, finding its way around the earth, saying, 'What you think, you rotten mean detective person? You do not pursue that nice doctor no more.'"

Chapter 7

The One-Armed Man —
Bill Raisch

Yeah, I killed her! Now I'm gonna kill you! Won't have to
worry about you again no more!

—Fred Johnson, the one-armed man to Richard Kimble

The one-armed man, Fred Johnson, was an integral part of *The Fugitive*, but it's hard to believe the character appeared in only nine of the show's 120 episodes. Johnson appeared in one episode in each of the series' first three years and in six shows during *The Fugitive*'s final season, but viewers will always remember the sinister-looking character who haunted Dr. Richard Kimble until the show's final episode.

Roy Huggins's original treatment mentioned "a gaunt and red-haired man" seen running from the Kimble house, but did not go into great detail.

Stanford Whitmore had Huggins's idea in mind when he wrote a first draft of the show's pilot, "Fear in a Desert City." As Whitmore was writing a more detailed second draft, Quinn Martin called him in great alarm, saying a researcher had looked at the script and felt the idea was stolen from the Sam Sheppard murder case.

Dr. Sam Sheppard, an Ohio osteopath, was convicted of the 1954 murder of his wife. After serving ten years behind bars, Sheppard won a second trial and an acquittal. "Sheppard had seen either a bushy-haired stranger or a red-haired stranger, " Stanford Whitmore said. "We couldn't do that because Sam Sheppard was still facing trial."

Whitmore went into Quinn Martin's office and the writer and producer tried to dream up some sort of distinguishing physical characteristic for Helen Kimble's murderer. "I remember being a kid," Whitmore told Martin. "And when I went to these horror movies they would always have somebody with a club foot and the foot was dragging, and they showed a close-up of it coming up the stairs and it scared all the kids to death." Then the two men realized a villain with a club foot wouldn't work. "It would be an unequal situation," said Whitmore. "We can't have Richard Kimble running after a guy who can't really run. So we had to think of something else, and I said, 'What about a man with one arm?' "

Quinn Martin told his assistant John Conwell, "Find me a one-armed man and I want a real one. I don't want to tie the arm back and all that."

Conwell remembered seeing a movie called *Lonely Are the Brave* starring Burt Lancaster and Kirk Douglas. In one scene, Douglas got into a knock-down drag-out saloon fight with a one-armed man. Conwell and Producer Alan Armer screened the film. "We got hold of the picture and ran it," said Armer. "The one-armed man was actor Bill Raisch, and he was so wonderful, he was scary."

The husky (5'9 1/2", 170 pounds) Raisch was actually a stand-in for Burt Lancaster and occasionally played one-armed roles in movies. Raisch had also appeared in *Spartacus,* another Lancaster-Douglas movie. In that film, Douglas chopped Raisch's arm off — an artificial one attached to his real arm — but the scene was edited out because it was too gory.

John Conwell brought Raisch in for an interview. "He was very sinister," said Conwell. "But he wasn't a very good actor. As the show went on, he became good. But we didn't need the lines, we just needed the look. He was also the only one-armed man I could find," laughed Conwell, "the only one listed with Screen Actors Guild. He didn't have an agent, so I had to make a deal with him personally."

At age 59, Bill Raisch was cast as the one-armed man.

At the age of fifty-nine, Raisch was overjoyed to land the part. "Usually, amputees are used as newsboys or down-and-outers," Raisch told the New York *Sunday News.* "Up to now, no one has shown the slightest interest in me. They just wouldn't consider me for an acting job because I have one arm."

Raisch lost his right arm, two inches above the elbow, after he was severely burned fighting a shipboard fire during World War II. "The doctors removed it in 1945," explained Raisch, "in order to save my life. Since then I've worn an artificial arm, but it's an awful nuisance. It's wonderful to be working in this series during which I can throw this thing into a corner and forget about it."

Raisch was born of German immigrant parents on April 5, 1905, in North Bergen, New Jersey. After leaving grade school, he took a job in construction, hauling cement. When he wasn't working, he lifted weights at Sig Klein's gym in New York.

Later, Raisch was seen by a society girl who was looking for a dancing partner. He was seen dancing with her at parties around New York and eventually came to the attention of Marilyn Miller, star of the Ziegfeld Follies. She eventually introduced Raisch to Florenz Ziegfeld, who signed him up.

In the late 1920s Raisch danced for Ziegfeld at the New Amsterdam Roof, where Maurice Chevalier was making his first American appearance and also appeared in *Whoopee,* starring Eddie Cantor.

"Boy, that was show business in those days," Raisch told *TV Guide.* "I played the Capitol and Radio City Music Hall so many times, I can't recall the actual number."

While he was dancing in New York, Raisch was attacked by five muggers on the street. Although he was worked over, Raisch got his licks in, and the next day a New York newspaper ran a picture of Raisch with the headline, "Don't Say Dancers Are Sissies."

Raisch fondly remembered the old days on Broadway. In 1965 he told *TV Guide* "One month, you'd walk up the street with fifteen cents in your

Dr. Richard Kimble in pursuit of the one-armed man.

pocket to eat at the Automat. Six months later, you'd walk down the other side of the street with your pocket full of money, but you didn't feel hungry."

While in New York, Raisch got to know many show-business types like Walter Winchell, Mark Hellinger, and Ben Hecht. Years later, after Raisch had lost his arm, Hecht brought him to Hollywood, promising to get him a part in a movie. Hecht wrote the part in *Spectre of the Rose* in 1946, and Raisch played it with an artificial arm.

In 1952 Raisch became Burt Lancaster's stand-in. "Burt's a good guy," Raisch told the New York *Sunday News*. "He's sincere and has helped me on every picture he's made except those in Europe. I'd even travel with him abroad, but the foreign countries do not permit outside stand-ins." It was Lancaster who helped Raisch land the part in *Lonely Are the Brave*. "Kirk Douglas was seeking a one-armed man for his picture," said Raisch. "Burt, who is one of Kirk's best friends, called him up and asked him to put me in the movie. I had one scene in which I fought with Kirk. Kirk said, 'Let's make it look real.' We really went at it. When it was over, we were both black and blue. Many critics wrote that it was one of the best movie fights of all time."

After Raisch's appearance in *Lonely Are the Brave,* he received another call from a studio looking for a one-armed man.

"Everything was all set," Raisch said. "The next day, the casting director phoned. 'Which arm of yours is missing?' he asked. I told him the right one. 'Sorry,' he said, 'we need a man with his left arm off.' The story circulated throughout Hollywood. It became a running gag."

After Raisch became known as the one-armed man on *The Fugitive,* there were other jokes at his expense. "Bill's busier than a one-armed paper hanger," said one wag. "Bill won the role all by himself, he did it single-handedly," cracked another.

Roles for one-armed actors don't surface very often, and during lean times, Raisch had even signed up for unemployment. He hoped *The Fugitive* would provide him with steady employment. When Raisch's wife, former Ziegfeld star Adele Smith, asked him, "Is Kimble ever going to catch you?" Raisch answered, "I really don't know. I don't even think the producers know. If he does manage to grab me, I hope it doesn't happen for some time."

Although Raisch's appearances on *The Fugitive* were limited, his impact on the public was not. Producer Alan Armer remembered the time Los Angeles police spotted Raisch, and believing that he was wanted, arrested him. "Bill was minding his own business, walking down the street or coming out of a restaurant, when a police car pulled up at the curb. The cops asked him to get into the car, and Bill said, 'What for?' The police recognized him and were convinced he was wanted for something. He said, 'Look, I'm a guy in a television series.' But unconvinced, they put him in the police car and took him downtown." Finally, someone from *The Fugitive* had to go to police headquarters and convince them that Bill Raisch was just an actor.

"I am amazed at the number of persons who now recognize me on the street," said Raisch. And he proudly received fan mail. "Some of the letters," he said, "even declare the writers think I'm innocent. They want this Kimble to give himself up and take the heat off me."

Raisch was hired for his looks, not his acting ability. He was limited mainly to short speeches like, "I'm sick of running!" "Kimble, that guy's been bugging me for years. Says I killed his wife," or "No skin off my nose if the doctor burns."

"As we began to give Bill more and more," recalled John Conwell, "we began to get nervous as to whether he could deliver the lines or not. I always thought he was very effective."

The Fugitive's stars, David Janssen and Barry Morse helped Raisch develop as an actor. "We were very supportive," said Morse. "David and I would give Bill encouragement because we knew he had almost no experience speaking lines and he was considerably nervous. As so often happens in our profession, people who've had no training and not very much experience turn out to be as effective as people who've been working at it for years. He turned out to be very, very good."

Except for the opening sequence of *The Fugitive*, the one-armed man was rarely seen. "We tried to make him an ethereal image, to create a mystique about him," said Quinn Martin. " I don't think he ever said more than ten words a year, but he had a wild-eyed look that worked out perfectly."

Raisch worked a total of only four days in the first two years of the show, appearing in Number 19, "Search in Windy City," and Number 39, "Escape into Black." In the third year, Raisch worked in only Number 77, "Wife Killer." During the show's final year, he appeared in Number 93, "A Clean and Quiet Town," Number 97, "Second Sight," Number 100, "Nobody Loses All the Time," Number 111, "The Ivy Maze," and in the two-part finale, Numbers 119 and 120, "The Judgment."

Because Raisch was so recognizable as *The*

Fugitive's one-armed man, it was almost impossible for him to get work on other shows. So Quinn Martin put Raisch on a retainer, giving him a degree of security.

Although David Janssen and Barry Morse were able to avoid typecasting when *The Fugitive* ended, Bill Raisch was not. After the show wrapped, Raisch rarely worked. He died in 1984 of lung cancer at Santa Monica Hospital. He was seventy-nine.

Bill Raisch, David Janssen and Barry Morse on the set.

Chapter 8

The Voice of God – William Conrad

You haven't got a chance in hell of it going more than thirteen weeks. It's a good show, but it's a one-timer and that's it.

—William Conrad to Quinn Martin
after watching The Fugitive *pilot.*

When Roy Huggins pitched his original *Fugitive* concept to ABC, he suggested that the show use a narrator, "the all-knowing voice of God."

Quinn Martin had the same idea in mind when he called veteran radio actor and narrator William Conrad in 1963. "Bill, I'm doing a show and I've made the pilot and I want to have narration in it. I don't want to tell you any more than that. I want you to do the narration if you're interested."

The next day, Martin arranged for Conrad to watch *The Fugitive*'s pilot in a screening room at Goldwyn Studios. Conrad sat by himself in the darkened room and watched "Fear in a Desert City." When the show was over, Martin walked in and asked, "Well, Bill, what did you think . . . did you like the show?"

"Well, it's an interesting show," Conrad answered, "but as I understand it, you're doing the same show every week. Not even theme and variations, you're doing the same show every fucking week."

"I never thought of it that way. I see your point, yes."

"You have the same plot, all you do is change the locale and change the supporting characters," continued Conrad. "One week it's a man, and the next week it's a woman. You have the same guy going through the same bullshit every week and you expect this to become a hit series? You haven't got a chance in hell of it going more than thirteen weeks. It's a good show but it's a one-timer and that's it."

"That was my worst 'famous' opinion," laughed Conrad thirty years later.

Despite his doubts, Conrad agreed to narrate *The Fugitive*, and his intonation of the show's prologue and epilogue has become one of the show's most memorable elements. All *Fugitive* fans know the distinctive voice which spoke words like, "The name: Dr. Richard Kimble. The destination: Death Row, State Prison. The irony: Richard Kimble is innocent."

William Conrad was exactly what Quinn Martin was looking for in a narrator, although Conrad discounts his "voice of God" quality. "What I had was a ridiculous pomposity that I could put on," said Conrad with a laugh, "that made it sound like it was very important."

The Fugitive narration was just a secondary job for the busy Conrad. He had starred for eleven years as Matt Dillon in the radio version of *Gunsmoke*, voiced *The Lone Ranger* and *Bullwinkle* cartoon shows, and narrated thousands of radio and television shows. Conrad also produced and directed movies and television, including shows for ZIV Television, located next door to *The Fugitive*'s soundstage at Goldwyn Studios. "It was hardly a job," recalled Conrad. "I'd drive in the gate to do my producing and directing at ZIV and somebody from *The Fugitive* would say, 'We've got three or four scripts ready.' And I'd pick them up and read them cold and leave. Except for the pilot, I don't think I ever saw more than two episodes of *The Fugitive*."

Although Conrad narrated all of the 120 shows and later became a major television star himself, he never acted in a *Fugitive* episode. "I was busy doing other things," said Conrad, "and I don't think it paid enough money. I think I was making more money as a narrator than most of the actors were making."

Speaking of money, Conrad's association with *The Fugitive*'s executive producer Quinn Martin would pay enormous dividends later. Conrad was on his boat one day in 1971 when Martin called to tell him that Fred Silverman (CBS's vice president, programs) had seen him in a movie, loved his work, and wanted him to play the lead in a television series. "What . . . you mean somebody wants me to do a lead in television, I think you have the wrong man," Conrad told Martin.

"No, no . . . I think you'd be great."

"Well, is there good money in it?"

"More money than you've ever thought of making in radio," said Martin.

"God . . . yes, I'll do it."

The next day Martin called back to discuss story ideas with Conrad. "What do you want to do?" asked Martin.

"As long as I get my paycheck, I don't give a shit what it is."

"How about a detective, a private eye."

"Okay . . . how about a fat private eye." countered the portly Conrad.

"That's even better."

And thus was born Frank Cannon, private eye.

By putting William Conrad in front of the camera, Quinn Martin shattered the traditional concept of the private detective. Overweight, balding, and middle-aged, Cannon drove around in an enormous Lincoln Continental, chasing bad guys and enjoying high ratings.

While starring in *Cannon,* which aired on CBS from 1971 to 1976, Conrad strengthened his friendship with David Janssen. "I had met David at parties and I always liked him," said Conrad.

"When we started doing *Cannon,* we started using him on the show. I think we did four shows with him. He was a joy, we had so much fun."

While working together, the two actors became friends and would sometimes meet at the Formosa Cafe. "That's where we really got to know each other," said Conrad, "in the Formosa, drinking. In those days, he could really drink and so could I."

Conrad used his heft to advantage again in 1987, playing district attorney J. L. "Fatman"

McCabe in CBS's *Jake and the Fatman.* "There's no better-paying game in the world than being a successful actor in a successful TV series," said Conrad. "You get a job and it runs eight years and it keeps escalating all those years. You become a millionaire very easily. It's beautiful."

On February 11, 1994, William Conrad died of a heart attack, in North Hollywood, California. He was 73. Conrad is survived by his wife Tippy and son Christopher.

William Conrad and David Janssen on the set of Cannon, *1973.*

Chapter 9

Wasn't That So-and-So . . . ? The Guest Stars

Quinn left the casting to me. A lot of those people were friends of mine from New York.

—*John Conwell, vice president of casting, QM Productions*

John Conwell was sitting in his office at the *Twilight Zone set*, when his secretary buzzed him. "John," she said, "

"Quinn Martin is calling."

"Who's Quinn Martin?" asked Conwell.

After admonishing her boss for not knowing that Quinn Martin was one of the hottest young producers in television, Conwell's secretary transferred the call. "Hi, John, this is Quinn Martin. I've just done a pilot for a show called *The Fugitive*, and I wonder if you'd do me a favor and take a look at it."

The next morning Conwell joined Martin in a screening room at Goldwyn Studios. After watching the pilot, the two adjourned to Martin's favorite restaurant, Musso and Frank's. When Martin asked him what he thought of *The Fugitive*, Conwell answered, "It's a terrific pilot, but it will never sell."

"I had no idea that Quinn was actually interviewing me for a job," Conwell recalled, "and that's why I was so candid. But that challenged him and Quinn loved challenges."

Within an hour Martin hired Conwell as his assistant and put him in charge of casting *The Fugitive* beginning an eighteen-year working relationship between the men. Later, Conwell was promoted to vice president in charge of talent. Eventually, QM Productions had six shows on

John Conwell (1993) was Casting Director and Vice President of Quinn Martin Productions.

network television, and each show had a casting director, with Conwell overseeing them all. His ability to match actors and roles was an important

factor in the success of QM Productions.

Typically, Conwell would read the script for each *Fugitive* episode, and then meet with Martin, producer Alan Armer, and the director to determine the types of actors needed for each week's show. A former New York actor himself, Conwell relied heavily on his friendships and knowledge of actors from his days in theater. Auditions were rare and as Conwell discovered, auditions could be dangerous.

Bruce Dern as Mitch in "The Devil's Disciple," Episode 102, 1966.

"The first time Bruce Dern came in," said Conwell, "he got carried away and almost beat the shit out of me. He was supposed to be in a fight and he grabbed me and threw me across the room. Having been an actor myself, I thought he was terrific and he got the part. And after that, he didn't have to read again." Dern appeared in five episodes of *The Fugitive,* at the start of a long career in television and movies.

Ed Asner, Jack Lord, Kevin McCarthy, Fritz Weaver, Pat Hingle, and Nancy Wickwire were just some of Conwell's New York friends who guest-starred on *The Fugitive* without benefit of an audition.

"Quinn was great about that, particularly in the early days," said Conwell. "He didn't know who Robert Duvall was and I said, 'Quinn, he'll be perfect for this and Quinn said, 'Fine, fine.' "

"Robert Drivas was another one. We were looking for someone to play the part of a young law student on "Man in a Chariot" and I told Quinn, 'I saw a kid last night on *Naked City* and he was terrific. Quinn said, 'Fly him in.' "

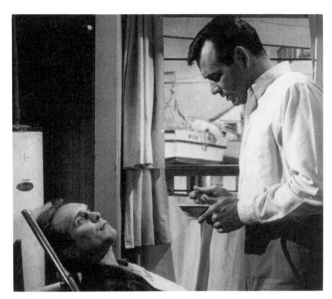

Robert Duvall as Leslie Sessions with Janssen in "Brass Ring," Episode 46, 1965.

Another of Conwell's friends was Jack Klugman, already an established film star. Conwell and Klugman had been struggling actors together in New York and Conwell prevailed upon his friend to appear in Number 13, "Terror at High Point," in 1963. Klugman played a construction boss, and the episode was shot on top of a mountain near Hollywood called Mt. Olympus. "It was the rainy season," Conwell recalled, "and one night it was pouring and Jack finished what he had to do and

Jack Klugman and David Janssen in "Terror at High Point," Episode 13, 1963.

went to his trailer and fell asleep. An hour or so later he realized the rain had stopped and there was no sound. Jack opened the door and everybody had gone. The production company, everybody . . . they had finished shooting and they all got in the trucks and drove back to the studio and left poor Jack on top of this mountain, in his dressing room. Oh, God, he walked down to somebody's house and called a cab. Well, the next day Jack came to the studio but he wouldn't go on the soundstage — he was so angry he wouldn't work. I couldn't blame him."

"So Quinn came to me and said, 'John, we've got to do something. You know Jack and you've got to go to his dressing room and get him onto the soundstage.' And so I did. Because he has a great sense of humor, I said, 'Jack, that is really funny, it's hilarious that we left you up there in the rain and someday we're really going to laugh about this. But I need you back on the stage now.' So he went back."

Mickey Rooney was another major star who appeared on *The Fugitive*, in Number 78, "This'll Kill You," in 1966. Writer–associate producer George Eckstein recalled the casting meeting for

Nita Talbot and Mickey Rooney as Paula and Charlie in "This'll Kill You," Episode 78, 1966.

that episode: "Alex March was directing and Alex was a very extravagant kind of person and somebody brought up Mickey Rooney. And people were saying, 'Mickey's got a reputation, he's very difficult to work with.' And Alex very grandly said, 'Listen, whether I'm a good director or not, that's up for grabs, but as far as being in control on my set, don't worry about it.' And so we cast Mickey Rooney, and by the end of the second day I was on the stage and Alex was off in a corner on the phone, trying to get off the show, because Rooney was driving him berserk. Mickey can be a lot of problems. He can drive a director up a wall, as he drove Alex."

The diminutive Rooney's size also presented a problem. Nita Talbot, a very tall actress, was cast as Rooney's girlfriend in "This'll Kill You." "Somebody said Nita Talbot," recalled John Conwell, "and we said, 'Oh, terrific' completely forgetting that she's twelve feet tall. And oh God, about seven o'clock the night before we were supposed to shoot, Meryl O'Laughlin, who was casting, said to me, 'Oh, I just remembered Nita's so tall' and I said, 'me too.' We called Alex March, who said he knew Nita and not to worry about it. But it was shot, Mickey Rooney was terrific, and nobody knew the difference."

Rooney wasn't the only pint-size actor to appear on *The Fugitive*. Many child stars also made guest appearances. One was Ron Howard, who played Opie on *The Andy Griffith Show* and

David Janssen and Ron Howard.

is now a successful motion picture director. In 1964, Howard was just a precocious nine-year-old with freckles and red hair who came in to audition for a role in Number 41 "Cry Uncle." John Conwell, a talented artist, was sitting at his desk, one of his prized paintings on the wall behind him. "Ronnie looked up at that painting and asked, 'Who did that?' remembered Conwell. "I said, 'I did,' and he said, 'What did you do, just throw cans of paint on the wall?' Fortunately, I thought that was very funny and we hired him."

Another child actor who appeared on the show was Kurt Russell, now a major motion picture star. Russell worked in two episodes, Number 35, "Nemesis," and Number 89, "In a Plain Paper

Wrapper." "Oh, my God, that little kid," said Conwell. "He was so good, but then he went off to play baseball, and I couldn't get him anymore. When I see Ronnie's work or Kurt's today, that's when it comes back to me how long ago it was."

Beau Bridges, Tim Considine (*My Three Sons*), and Tommy Rettig (*Lassie*) were other young actors who appeared on the show.

The Fugitive had no problem attracting the best talent in both New York and Hollywood. It was a hit show and top guest stars were paid as much as $5,000 per episode, big money for the 1960s.

Sandy Dennis had won a Tony Award for Best Supporting Actress in the Broadway production

Sandy Dennis as Carrie in "The Other Side of the Mountain," Episode 3, 1963.

of *A Thousand Clowns* in 1963. John Conwell wanted her for *The Fugitive*'s third show that year, "The Other Side of the Mountain," but had heard Dennis had caused difficulties on an MGM show and had to be replaced. "So I called MGM," said Conwell, and asked, 'What was the problem with Sandy?'"

"She refused to wear a girdle and we just wouldn't have it," answered MGM's casting director. "She has a lousy figure and wouldn't wear a girdle and she looked terrible."

Confident he could handle the problem, Conwell hired Dennis, but warned her, "Now, Sandy, you have to wear a girdle."

"Oh, yeah, sure," she answered, "of course I will, don't worry about it."

"Of course she didn't wear the girdle because she appeared in jeans," laughed Conwell, "but what were you going to do? And she was terrific."

A pre-*Kojak* Telly Savalas made the first of three *Fugitive* appearances on Number 18, "Where the Action Is" in 1964. Savalas's agent called John Conwell, saying, "Telly's house has burned down and he doesn't have any clothes, so you'll have to take him to Carroll's department store and get him some clothes."

So Conwell called Quinn Martin, who said, "What are we going to do? John, take him over to Carroll's and wardrobe him."

"When the show was over, Telly took off with the clothes," said Conwell. "They weren't his and he didn't say, 'May I buy these?' He took them! So I had to call his agent and say, 'We want the clothes back.' 'Oh, you cheap sons of bitches,' said the agent. And I said, 'Telly's welcome to the clothes. We'll sell them to him at half price, but we can use them.' In the end, he kept them and we never saw the clothes again. After that, whenever he worked for us, we were prepared for it, and would say, 'If we use Telly, we'll have to go get some clothes.' "

Long before he ever starred as Archie Bunker on *All in the Family*, Carroll O'Connor appeared on Number 24, "Flight from the Final Demon" in 1964, playing a town sheriff. In an opening scene, the sheriff (O'Connor), wearing only a towel around his waist, is lying on a table, being mas-saged by Richard Kimble. O'Connor was quite heavy at that time, and Qunn Martin found the sight of the actor hanging over the table offensive. Martin reprimanded John Conwell, saying, "You shouldn't have cast him in that part."

"Well, I'm casting Carroll because he was right for the part," answered Conwell, "and if we'd known that you objected to the way he appeared without any clothes, I would have told the director and he would have shot him differently."

Another actor who bared his chest on *The Fugitive* was Charles Bronson, in Number 107, "The One That Got Away" in 1967. John Conwell

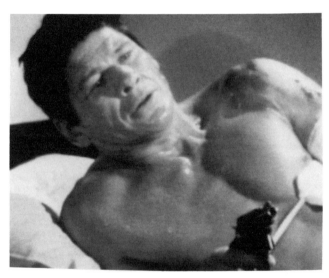

Charles Bronson in "The One That Got Away," 1967.

remembered his old friend being "terrific" in the show, but more vividly recalled the attire of Bronson's co-star. "Anne Francis had to appear in a bathing suit, they wanted to make it as sexy as possible," said Conwell. "But in those days we had a rule against actresses wearing two-piece suits, we couldn't show her navel. So, it seemed sexy at the time, but if you look at it today, it looks like she's practically fully clothed."

Ed Asner eventually became a major television star in *The Mary Tyler Moore Show*; *Rich Man, Poor Man*; and *Lou Grant*, but when he made his first *Fugitive* appearance in Number 56, "Masquerade," in 1965, Asner was struggling through a difficult period as a freelance actor. "I don't have fond memories of *The Fugitive*," recalled Asner, "because most of my roles didn't thrill me. I got the feeling that by the time they called me, they had already called Simon Oakland or Don Gordon, or other character actors of that period. I thank God for the show though. I flew in the face of its popularity because people loved it. It kept my face out there and provided a pay-

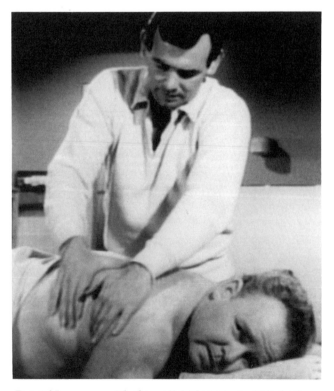

David Janssen with Carroll O'Connor in "Flight from the Final Demon," 1964.

check, and they were lovely people to work for." Asner also appeared in Number 66, "Three Cheers for Little Boy Blue," and Number 105, "Run the Man Down."

Another future star, Dabney Coleman (*Buffalo Bill, The Slap Maxwell Story*), had small parts in three episodes of *The Fugitive* before moving on to bigger roles in other QM shows. "I always loved using him because his performing was really based on truth," said John Conwell. "He was always so believable and real."

Gloria Grahame had won an Oscar as Best Supporting Actress in *The Bad and the Beautiful* in 1952. With her movie career fading, Grahame turned to television in the 1960s. She was picked to play the role of a southern belle in Number 28, "The Homecoming" in 1963. While dressing for the role, Grahame informed John Conwell of a curious habit. "She said, 'I want you to know I put cotton under my upper lip,'" Conwell remembered. "Of course, I already knew this, but played along with her, saying, 'Oh . . . Why?' She said, 'Well, I'm going to show you.' She then proceeded to show me how she put cotton under her lip and turned to me and said, 'You see, it really makes my mouth much more sexy.' I couldn't have cared less if she put cotton up there although it made her talk kind of funny. And I said, 'Oh, okay,' fine . . . that's terrific.' As I recall, she came on our set and her southern accent was just terrible. It was one of the seven hardest days of my life."

Tuesday Weld (*The Many Loves of Dobie*

Carol Rossen as Irene Cheyney in "Tiger Left, Tiger Right," Episode 36, 1964.

Gillis) was already a well-known actress when she was asked to play the role of a blind girl in Number 38, "Dark Corner" in 1964. "In those days, if you got Tuesday Weld to be in your show, it was like bringing Garbo out of retirement," said Conwell. "It was a big deal. Her agent made a big thing out of it, saying we had to treat her in such a way, but she was terrific."

Competitors often accused QM Productions of having a "repertory company," since Quinn Martin often used the same talent many times. Martin had a group of actresses he particularly liked, including Shirley Knight, Diana Hyland, and Carol Rossen.

Carol Rossen, daughter of producer/director/ writer Robert Rossen (*All the King's Men, The Hustler*) appeared in five episodes of *The Fugitive*. Among them was Number 62, "Middle of a Heat Wave," in 1965, in which she played a

Tuesday Weld as Mattie Braydon sculpting Richard Kimble in "Dark Corner," Episode 38, 1964.

young girl who was sexually assaulted. "I think the one thing that was interesting about the show," Rossen recalled, "was that in those days nobody could even say 'rape' on television." Unfortunately for Rossen, life imitated art. In 1964, in a Southern California park, Rossen was attacked and beaten by a man wielding a hammer. She wrote about the incident in her book *Counterpunch*: "I swear to God, I'd played the scene before. There used to be all these melodramas on TV, and I was in all of them, 'Kildare,' 'The Fugitive,' 'Naked City,' 'The Untouchables,' and if you were a young leading lady in those days, your job was to be mugged, or doped, or raped, or roughed up by some guy who really didn't mean it, you know?"

Rossen and Leslie Nielsen played a married couple in Number 36, "Tiger Left, Tiger Right."

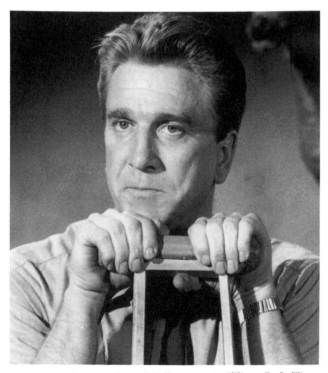

Lelslie Nielsen as Harold Cheyney in "Tiger Left, Tiger Right," Episode 36, 1964.

Today Nielsen is best known as Lieutenant Frank Drebin in the motion picture comedies *Naked Gun* and *Naked Gun 2 1/2*. In 1964 Nielsen was a respected character actor, but according to Rossen, certainly wasn't known for his sense of humor. "Leslie was a very straight-arrow guy, he wasn't particularly funny," said Rossen. "Somebody decided it might be interesting to play a trick on him. In that episode, I think we're all locked in a log cabin and suddenly the cops are going to show up, and finally the knock comes at the door,

and the cameras are rolling, and Leslie opened the door with great intensity, and there was Marty Landau, (*Mission: Impossible*), dressed like an American Indian. He had come over from another set." Nielsen, Rossen, and the rest of the crew cracked up and the scene had to be reshot.

Eileen Heckart played a Catholic nun, Sister Veronica, in the two-parter "Angels Travel on Lonely Roads," (Numbers 22 and 23), in 1964, and returned in Number 109, "The Breaking of the Habit," in 1967. Heckart loved doing *The Fugitive* because it gave her a chance to socialize with David Janssen. One day she and David went to the Formosa Cafe for lunch. They sat down at the bar, with Heckart still dressed as a nun. "I was in full nun's habit because I didn't dare take it off," said Heckart. "I think I wore thirty-six pieces by the time I got through the crucifixes, and it took me forever to put it on. I said to David, 'Oh, I would love to have a cigarette.' And David said, 'Well, go ahead and have it.' And I said, 'Well, I certainly can't have it in a nun's habit.' And he said, 'Don't be silly.' So I lit up my cigarette, and sure enough there was a man looking at me with such a mean expression on his face like, 'What are you doing?' And David turned around and said to the man, 'What's the matter with you? Haven't you ever seen a nun smoke before?' Oh, I wanted to die."

Later that evening, following a long day on the set, Heckart, Janssen, and director Walter Grauman stopped at a bar on Santa Monica Boulevard to have a few drinks. As the well-oiled group was leaving the bar, Heckart missed a turn and mistakenly drove her car onto railroad tracks that ran down the middle of the street. "All of a sudden I look and Eileen has gone off the road and is driving her car down the railroad tracks, bouncing and hitting the ties," laughed Grauman. "I pulled up along side of her and yelled, 'Stop it, stop the goddamned car.' And she stopped and I got in and got the car off the tracks and back onto the road for her. Jesus, she had sure banged the shit out of that car. I'll never forget it as long as I live."

Suzanne Pleshette made her first *Fugitive* appearance in Number 32, "World's End," in 1964. Pleshette had already moved into feature films and her agent told John Conwell, "Suzanne doesn't do television." But Conwell felt Pleshette would enjoy playing the role of Elinor Burnett, a young woman who falls in love with Dr. Kimble, and he urged her agent to ask Pleshette to consider. After looking at the script and liking it, Pleshette said she wanted to check with her then-husband, actor Troy Donahue, before accepting the role. "Troy obviously said okay," said Conwell, "so she did the show. Well, you know what happened. She and David Janssen took one look at each other. I think they fell madly in love really. But David was married and she was married. So she and David had an affair."

The affair created serious problems between Janssen and his first wife Ellie. "Suzanne Pleshette was the basic cause of almost everything that happened to us," said Ellie, blaming Pleshette for the start of the couple's marital problems.

When Suzanne Pleshette was offered a part in another *Fugitive* episode, Number 67, "All the Scared Rabbits," a year later, Ellie Janssen was incensed and called the show's executive producer. "I was really angry at Quinn Martin," said Ellie, "because he knew what we went through the year before because of Suzanne Pleshette, and he hired her back to do another show, which I

thought was very insensitive. I asked him why he was doing it and if there was some way he could undo it, but naturally he paid no attention to me."

The night before the episode was to be shot, John Conwell received a call from Martin. "Listen, John, I just got a call from Ellie Janssen that makes me nervous. She said if Suzanne does the show beginning tomorrow, she's going to arrive on the set with a gun and she's going to shoot her. What shall we do?"

"Well, I think I should call Suzanne and tell her. We can't let her go on the set and be shot."

Before calling Pleshette, Conwell lined up another actress to play the role, assuming Pleshette wouldn't want to take the risk. Then Conwell phoned Pleshette, informing her of Ellie Janssen's threats. "I told Suzanne, 'I'm sure you don't want

David Janssen kissing Suzanne Pleshette in "World's End," Episode 32, 1964.

to show up tomorrow.' She said, 'Are you kidding? I'll be there. Oh, she's not going to kill me.' "

Conwell then called Martin, telling his boss, "Suzanne doesn't want to be replaced, she's going to be there. She's loving it, as a matter of fact."

According to Conwell, when Ellie Janssen arrived on the set the next day, she didn't bring a gun, but did everything she could to disrupt the shooting. "When the red light went on, when they were doing a take," said Conwell, "Ellie would walk through the soundstage. She tried to ruin every take of Suzanne's. We eventually talked her into leaving the studio and letting us proceed."

Janssen with Angie Dickinson as Norma Sessions in "Brass Ring," Episode 46, 1965.

William Shatner as Tony Burrell in "Stranger in the Mirror," Episode 72, 1965.

Of her relationship with David Janssen, Suzanne Pleshette said, "I will not talk about anything personal. I never have and I never will." She described Janssen as "wonderful, bright, talented, funny, loyal, a great friend." Although their affair eventually cooled, the two remained friends until the end of Janssen's life.

Suzanne Pleshette, Angie Dickinson, Lee Grant, Diane Ladd, Lois Nettleton, Fay Spain, Susan Oliver, Lee Meriwether, Claude Akins, Steve Forrest, Greg Morris, Earl Holliman, William Shatner, Melvyn Douglas, Jack Warden, Martin Balsam, William Windom, James Farentino, Joseph Campanella, Tom Skerritt, Herschel Bernardi, Ted Knight, Norman Fell — *The Fugitive*'s guest roles read like a Who's Who of television.

Ted Knight as Lieutenant Mooney in "The White Knight," Episode 86, 1966.

Chapter 10

Family Feud —
the Kimbles, the Gerards,
and Others

People all over town would say, "How's your brother?"
And I'd say, "I don't have a brother."

—Jacqueline Scott, who played Richard Kimble's sister

As all *Fugitive* fans know, Dr. Richard Kimble was married to Helen Kimble before she was murdered by the one-armed man. Helen was played by Diane Brewster and showed up only in flashbacks as in Number 14, "The Girl from Little Egypt," in 1963. Before playing Helen Kimble, Brewster had previously appeared as Miss Canfield in *Leave It to Beaver*, Samantha Crawford in *Maverick*, and Wilhelmina Vandeveer in *The Islanders*.

Helen Kimble's family was introduced in Number 53, "The Survivors" in 1965. Hearing that his wife's father, Ed Waverly, had gone bankrupt, Richard Kimble returned to Indiana to help. Ed Waverly was played by Lloyd Gough, who later appeared as the hard-nosed reporter Mike Axford in *The Green Hornet*. Mrs. Waverly was played by Ruth White.

A central character in "The Survivors" was Helen Kimble's younger sister, Terry, who had fallen in love with her sister's former husband, Richard Kimble. Terry was played by Louise Sorel, who guest-starred on many other series in the mid-1960s, and later played Don Rickles's wife on *The Don Rickles Show*, a vampiress on *Curse of Dracula* and the boss, Elaine Holstein, on *Ladies' Man*. In the mid-1980s Sorel appeared on the daytime soap opera *Santa Barbara*.

In *The Fugitive*, Richard Kimble was the son

Dr. Richard Kimble (David Janssen) with his father, Dr. John Kimble (Robert Keith), in "Home is the Hunted," Episode 15, 1964.

of another M.D., Dr. John Kimble, and his wife Elizabeth. The elder Kimble was played by veteran actor Robert Keith, Brian Keith's father. The elder Keith appeared in only one episode, Number 15, "Home Is the Hunted," in 1964, in which Kimble returned to Stafford, Indiana, to find that his father had suffered a heart attack and had retired to a country house.

Also appearing in "Home Is the Hunted" was Andrew Prine, who played Richard Kimble's embittered brother Ray. Prine also appeared in

Andrew Prine as Ray Kimble in "Home is the Hunted," Episode 15, 1964.

Number 74, "End of the Line," playing a delinquent youth named Neil Hollis. Prine was seen often in westerns of the 1960s and co-starred in two short-lived western series, *Wide Country* and *The Road West*. Prine is still active today and frequently shows up on network television, including a role on *Dr. Quinn Medicine Woman* on CBS in 1993.

The most prominent of the family members was Jacqueline Scott, who played Kimble's sister, Donna Taft. Scott appeared in only five episodes of *The Fugitive* but her character's relationship with Kimble elicited strong reactions. "When people would say, 'How's your brother?'" said Scott, "I didn't know what the hell they were talking about . . . until I put the pieces together. Then, whenever anybody asked about my brother, I knew they were talking about Richard Kimble."

Scott made her first *Fugitive* appearance in "Home Is the Hunted." There was a scene in which Kimble phoned Donna, telling her he is coming home. The scene required Donna to express several different reactions: fear for her brother's safety, the joy of seeing him again, and the concern for maintaining secrecy. Worried about being convincing in the telephone scene without David Janssen's participation, Scott expressed her fears to director Jerry Hopper. "This will not be as good if I have to do the scene without David," Scott told Hopper. "So he agreed to shoot around that scene until David arrived. Finally, he said, 'I have nothing else left to shoot, I'll have to do your scene.' Then David came walking on the set, he came to work early, and I went leaping up to him and said, 'Oh, my God, you're here. I'm so glad.' Well, he thought I was crazy. It was the first show I'd done and he didn't know who I was." Janssen agreed to stand off camera and supply his end of the conversation, and it made for a very realistic scene.

Jacqueline Scott as Donna Taft (Kimble's sister) in "Trial By Fire," Episode 64, 1965.

Jacqueline Scott's role was supposed to be just a one-shot appearance, but Quinn Martin liked her so well, he kept asking his writers to include Donna Taft in the scripts. "Somebody told me I was the only woman Quinn could ever stand to watch cry," said Scott, "which I think is hysterical." Martin also saw a physical resemblance between Scott and David Janssen. He thought their eyes were similar and figured she'd be perfect playing Dr. Kimble's sister.

Scott appeared in four additional episodes:

Number 64, "Trial by Fire" and Number 82, "Running Scared," in the show's third season, 1965–66, and in the two-part finale "The Judgment" in 1967. Today Scott lives in Southern California and is still active in theater and television.

Donna Taft's husband Leonard was played by three different actors. Because the same actor wasn't always available, James Sikking, Lin McCarthy, and Richard Anderson all played Leonard Taft, and the public never knew the difference.

James Sikking had small roles in many television shows and films in the 1960s and was in more than a dozen mostly forgettable TV movies during the '70s and '80s. After working without fanfare for more than twenty years, Sikking found stardom on *Hill Street Blues,* in the role of Lieutenant Howard Hunter, the trigger-happy leader of the precinct's SWAT team.

Lin McCarthy later played Lieutenant Hauser in Joseph Wambaugh's television drama *The Blue Knight* and Blinker Vance in *The Winds of War.*

Richard Anderson was originally discovered by Alan Armer and Walter Grauman on their 1950 television show *Lights, Camera, Action,* a summer talent show originating in Hollywood. Per-

Richard Anderson as Col. Lawrence in "The Iron Maiden," Episode 43, 1964.

forming comedy skits, Anderson won "a trip to La Jolla plus an acting part in a movie which was never made." "But it did launch my career," recalled Anderson, "because I got offers from Paramount, MGM, and Fox."

Anderson appeared as a supporting actor in many 1950s movies, including *Twelve O'Clock High, The Long Hot Summer,* and *Paths of Glory.* In the 1960s Anderson began a long television career that saw him playing mostly authoritative roles like a district attorney on *Bus Stop,* a colonel on *The Lieutenant,* a police officer on *Perry Mason* and *Dan August,* and government agent Oscar Goldman on both *The Six Million Dollar Man* and *The Bionic Woman.* The last role made Anderson the first actor in television history to play the same regular character on two different series simultaneously.

In addition to playing Leonard Taft, Anderson played other roles on *The Fugitive,* including an air force colonel in Number 43 "The Iron Maiden," a sheriff in Number 57 "Runner in the Dark," a prosperous businessman in Number 66, "Three Cheers for Little Boy Blue," and a policeman in Number 94, "The Sharp Edge of Chivalry."

Today Anderson is still working, acting in, and executive-producing *Return of the Six Million Dollar Man,* and *Bionic Woman Three,* for Universal Pictures and CBS.

Leonard and Donna Taft had two sons, David and Billy. Child actor Billy Mumy portrayed David and appeared later in television series including *Sunshine* and *Lost in Space.* Both Johnny Jensen and Clint Howard played Billy. Jensen appeared in the final episode, "The Judgment," while Howard was in Number 15, "Home Is the Hunted." Howard is the younger brother of Ron Howard, who played Opie on *The Andy Griffith Show.* Clint made his television debut in his brother's show and went on to appear in other series including *The Baileys of Balboa, Gentle Ben,* and *The Cowboys.* Ron Howard also appeared in an episode of *The Fugitive* Number 41, "Cry Uncle." In addition to his work on *The Andy Griffith Show,* Ron also played Richie Cunningham on *Happy Days* and has gone on to become a major motion picture director, with credits like *Night Shift, Splash, Cocoon, Gung Ho, Parenthood,* and *Backdraft.*

Jean Carlisle was not a family member, but *The Fugitive's* concluding episode, "The Judgment," left little doubt that Richard Kimble's love interest would eventually become Mrs. Kimble. Jean Carlisle was played by Diane Baker, who had previously appeared in films including *The Diary of Anne Frank, Marnie,* and *The Prize.*

If Jean Carlisle had married Kimble, what would life with the doctor have been like? "I'm sure he would have had obsessive nightmares," said Baker. "He probably would have been difficult to live with for a while, until he calmed down and lived a quiet life. I probably would have ended up as a nagging wife who went berserk every time he had to leave the house." In addition to acting, Diane Baker has been producing and directing both television and movies and heads up her own production company, Artemis Productions.

Barry Morse played Lieutenant Philip Gerard, but three different actresses appeared as the lieutenant's wife: Barbara Rush, Rachel Ames, and an uncredited actress. The best known of the three was Barbara Rush, a former movie starlet

Barbara Rush as Marie Gerard in "Landscape with Running Figures," Episode 69, 1965.

of the 1950s who has had a respectable career in TV and films. Rush has appeared in such series as *Saints and Sinners, Peyton Place, The New Dick Van Dyke Show,* and *Flamingo Road.* Rachel Ames was best known for playing Audrey on the daytime soap opera *General Hospital.* To further confuse the issue, Mrs. Gerard was known as both Ann and Marie during *The Fugitive's* run.

The Gerards had a son, Phil, Jr. In an early episode, that role was played by an uncredited actor, and in Number 35, "Nemesis," child star Kurt Russell played Phil Jr. Russell acted in many series in the 1960s as well as films, many of them Disney productions. In 1979 Russell received an

Emmy nomination for his portrayal of Elvis Presley in the TV biography *Elvis*. Today Russell lives with actress Goldie Hawn and has starred in films including *Silkwood*, *The Mean Season*, *Tequila Sunrise*, *Tango & Cash*, *Backdraft*, and *Unlawful Entry*.

Russell's father Bing also appeared in five episodes of *The Fugitive*, usually playing a policeman. Bing is best remembered as the sheriff on *Bonanza*.

Although not technically a family member, Lieutenant Gerard's boss, Captain Carpenter, must have seemed like family to the lieutenant, appearing in thirteen episodes of *The Fugitive*. Carpenter was played by Paul Birch, a respected New York theater actor whose credits include having played Captain Randolph Sothard in *The Caine Mutiny Court-Martial* with Charles Laughton in 1953. Birch died in 1969.

Paul Birch as Captain Carpenter in "Fear in a Desert City," Episode 1, 1963.

Lieutenant Gerard (Barry Morse) with son Phil Gerard, Jr. (Kurt Russell) in "Nemesis," Episode 35, 1964.

Chapter 11

The Mighty Quinn –
Quinn Martin

I've either met the nicest guy in Hollywood or the greatest con artist. As it turned out, he was both.

—John Conwell's reaction upon meeting Quinn Martin

The words "A QM Production" were a familiar sight on television screens from the late 1960s through the late 1970s. Shows like *The FBI, Cannon, The Streets of San Francisco,* and *Barnaby Jones* all bore the QM stamp, but the first to wear it was *The Fugitive* in 1963.

"QM" stood for Quinn Martin, but that wasn't really his name. He was born Irwin Cohn on May 22, 1922, in New York City, the son of Martin Cohn, a film cutter. While growing up in Los Angeles, young Irwin picked up the nickname "Quinn." According to Martin's wife Muffet, the nickname developed when his friends started calling him "Co-en" which became "Ca-win" and eventually was shortened to "Quinn." When he returned from duty in World War II, Irwin "Quinn" Cohn discovered that his sister Ruth had changed her last name to "Martin." He liked his nickname and her new last name so well that he had his name legally changed to Quinn Martin.

After breezing through Fairfax High school, dreaming of becoming an architect, majoring in English at the University of California at Berkeley, and a stint in the army, Quinn Martin took a job as a film cutter because that was the only job offered. Martin then moved into television, writing teleplays for shows like *Four Star Playhouse, Fireside Theatre,* and *Desilu Playhouse.*

Martin got a major break when he was asked to write and produce an installment for *Desilu Playhouse* in 1959 entitled "The Untouchables." The show eventually became a hit series with Martin promoted to line producer. Starring Robert Stack as Eliot Ness, *The Untouchables* aired on ABC from 1959 to 1963. Then ABC and Roy Huggins asked Martin to produce *The Fugitive,* under the banner of his new company, QM Productions.

Of all the hit television shows that Quinn Martin produced in his career, *The Fugitive* remained his favorite. "When I formed my own company in 1960, one of our first shows was *The Fugitive,*" said Martin. "It became the number-one show and won an Emmy for Best Dramatic Show. Even though *The Untouchables* was the show that gave me a big start, *The Fugitive* is the one I'll always have in my heart because it cemented the company's name as a producer of quality products."

The Fugitive was a quality show because Martin

Quinn Martin, 1965.

demanded high production values and was willing to spend money to insure realism in the show. Martin was one of the first television producers to take shows out of the soundstages and onto locations. QM Productions spent six to seven days on a typical *Fugitive* episode, with three of them on location.

In addition, the show used a lot of "night for night shooting," a very expensive procedure, meaning night scenes were actually filmed at night, rather than on a soundstage.

Martin was also a stickler for accuracy. If a scene wasn't done absolutely right, he would insist that it be reshot, over and over, until it was correct. A typical *Fugitive* episode cost $230,000 to produce, and Martin estimated he spent $10,000 to $12,000 more per show than his competitors.

Martin was also willing to spare no expense when it came to hiring actors for *The Fugitive*. He frequently flew in actors from New York rather than hiring the same old recycled Hollywood talent, and he paid top dollar. Martin had extreme likes and dislikes when it came to actors. He loved actors like Bruce Dern, Joseph Campanella, Ed Asner, and Telly Savalas, and frequently used them on *The Fugitive*. Martin's favorite actresses included Diana Hyland, Shirley Knight, Lois Nettleton, and Carol Rossen, who made five guest-star appearances on the show. "Each time I

on *The Fugitive*, Carol Rossen and David Janssen were leaving Goldwyn Studios to go have a drink. "A guy waved at us and said, 'Hi, David, Hi, Carol,' " remembered Rossen. "I asked David who that was and he said it was Quinn Martin. I never met him other than that one time. I don't think that was a testament to indifference, but to how wonderful he was as a producer, because he didn't need to come on the set and make a big deal about being known. He knew that actors get very frightened when the person who hires them walks on the set. Actors need space to make mistakes, to learn, to find out what the scene is about, and Quinn never imposed his presence.

Telly Savalas and Carol Rossen guest starred as husband and wife in "May God Have Mercy," 1965.

did one of Quinn's shows," said Rossen, "he would raise my salary and he did it on his own. And he was right to do it, because I was worth more to him, but who ever does that for you?"

Martin believed in hiring the best talent and leaving them alone. He rarely made an appearance on the set. One night after a long day's shooting

You never felt that 'Big Daddy' was watching you. That was as structured and professional a relationship as I've ever had, and also the most loving and caring . . . and that was Quinn."

Martin left most of the casting decisions up to John Conwell, his casting director, who later became a QM vice president. Conwell would select the talent for each week's show and then send his list to Martin for approval. "He used to grade my suggestions," said Conwell. "He would put: 'A+. . . A . . . B . . . C . . . D . . . and F' and then those he just hated, he would write, 'Boo . . . Boo . . . Hiss . . . Hiss.' It was hilarious. He loved those grades because they made me laugh. He did it because it was fun."

Although he had a sense of humor, Martin could be very tough in evaluating actors' performances on *The Fugitive*. During a screening of a day's footage, Martin would sit in the first row and would encourage John Conwell to join him. "No . . . no . . . I can't," Conwell would tell Martin. "I don't want to sit next to you."

As the lights were turned off and the dailies began to roll, Conwell would become aware of "an awful silence" as Martin watched an actor bomb. "John," Martin would say loudly.

"Yes."

"Whose relative is that?"

"No one's, Quinn."

"Well, couldn't we have just given them a check?" said Martin.

The Fugitive succeeded because Quinn Martin instinctively understood what kind of characters a TV audience would be attracted to. "One of Quinn's major talents was that he could look at a show and react as pure audience," said *Fugitive* producer Alan Armer. "He was a good audience. And I think when he picked people he looked at them as an audience would. 'Is this someone that I can root for, that I can care about, that I can get emotionally involved with?' I think he saw those qualities in David Janssen."

Another Martin strength was his ability to judge story material. "I look for scripts that deal with human emotions, that don't write down to people," said Martin. "I believe you have to give people credit. If they don't understand it intellectually, they'll understand it emotionally. Whatever success we've had comes from the attitude that people deserve better."

"You can't argue the success of the show," said writer George Eckstein, who later became *The Fugitive*'s associate producer. "Quinn loved what he did, he loved the shows, he liked the way they were done, and you didn't even think of deviating from that. Quinn had 'the public's ass.' He would sit down and what he liked, a thirty-five share would like."

Quinn Martin also used *The Fugitive* to establish what became a standard format for QM shows, dividing each episode into four acts plus an epilogue. "Quinn liked to use 'a drive-up,'" explained Eckstein. "If a policeman was going to

go to somebody's house, you'd see the police car drive down the street and see the policeman get out of the car and go up to the door, instead of cutting directly to the policeman knocking on the door. Quinn loved that because it gave him time to put 'Act III' on top of the film."

Martin hired not only the best on-screen talent, but the most creative production talent in the industry. He lured producer Alan Armer away from *The Untouchables,* snatched his assistant, John Conwell, from *The Twilight Zone,* and hired producer David O. Selznick's former assistant, Arthur Fellows, to work on *The Fugitive.* "I surround myself with good people," Martin said. "You should always try to get the best people. You can't learn anything from someone who is dumber than you are. Then you set a climate that they can work well in."

"Quinn was a hands-on producer," said writer Stanford Whitmore, "but hands-on didn't mean fooling with the product. He got people he knew and trusted and he just left them alone and didn't meddle with them. He was a good guy to work for."

"Quinn was wonderful," recalled George Eckstein. "Quinn was one of the great, classy men I've ever worked with in television. He was intelligent, he had a good sense of humor, and he was wonderful to his people. A lot of people were with him for many years; the tenure of Quinn's unit was extraordinary."

"Quinn's production unit was unique," continued Eckstein. "I've never before or since been in a position like that. The producers dealt only with the writing, ninety-five percent of what we did was to get out the scripts. So we could devote that concentrated effort to the script without having to pick locations or worry about the editing or dubbing or looping. That was all handled by another unit." In Martin's compartmentalized system, the producers dealt with the scripts, while other units handled the show's casting, pre-production, and post-production, with Martin, a self-described "benevolent dictator," overseeing the entire operation.

Although *The Fugitive* was critically acclaimed and was a ratings success, Martin knew that not every episode was perfect. "I figure I make ten good *Fugitive*s a year," Martin told *TV Guide* in 1965. "Ten that are pretty good and ten that are shot just because you have to shoot something."

Built like a middle linebacker, Martin wore dark-rimmed glasses and favored monogrammed shirts and checkered sport coats. He claimed to have an IQ of 148 and carried a briefcase with "QM" stenciled on the side. Martin usually arrived at his office in the Goldwyn Studios around ten A.M., watched dailies of *The Fugitive* at eleven, and then adjourned for lunch at Musso and Frank's, his favorite Hollywood restaurant, around one P.M. He was gregarious at times, shy at others. And sometimes during the week he would try to coax his assistant John Conwell into joining him at the local horse tracks, Hollywood Park and Santa Anita.

Conwell, who was later promoted to vice president in charge of talent for QM Productions, spent eighteen years at Martin's side. "Quinn was honest, as honest as one can be in show business,"

said Conwell. "He was bright, generous, tasteful, kind, humorous, devious, cunning, he was a great belittler, but he was supportive and he was very very loyal."

Conwell recalled Martin imparting some of his philosophy for swimming in the shark-infested waters of Hollywood: "Quinn always said, 'If somebody screws you, don't scream, don't fight, you'll lose the battle. Bide your time and get 'em.' If he was wronged, he would never scream at anyone, he would just say 'all right' and every time he would eventually get the person who betrayed him. And they deserved it."

Martin also had the ability to sense when a member of his television family was unhappy. "I don't know why I was down," remembered Conwell, "but one time, I went into the office one morning and there was Quinn, smiling broadly and holding up the front page of *Variety* with the headline 'Martin Ups Conwell,' and a story telling how I was promoted. And I asked Quinn, 'Did you up my salary too?' And he said, 'No, maybe later, that was just to cheer you up.' And I said, 'I'd be more cheerful if my salary was up too.' "

Director Mark Rydell worked on Number 93, "A Clean and Quiet Town," in 1966. Rydell wanted to make a script change and went to John Conwell, asking him to arrange a meeting with Quinn Martin. Rydell was confident he could get *The Fugitive*'s executive producer to agree to the change. Conwell set up the meeting, but warned Rydell, "I'll tell you what's going to happen. You'll see Quinn and you'll have the greatest meeting and you'll come out of there just feeling great and then you'll be in your car going home, and all of a sudden it will hit you: 'My God, Quinn talked me into doing it his way.' "

Rydell met with Martin and left, feeling confident the suggested script changes would be made. "And later that night," said Conwell, "Mark called me at home and said, 'You were right. I'm doing it Quinn's way.' Quinn was a great manipulator."

Martin was also shrewd when it came to dealing with *Fugitive* star David Janssen. "Quinn was able to diagnose what people really need, what people want," said *The Fugitive*'s producer Alan Armer. "He would give David things before David asked for them. He would give him ego-gratifying things in place of money."

Martin bought his star a lavish aluminum Airstream trailer to use as his on-location dressing room. The trailer was complete with a kitchen, shower, library, and fully stocked bar. Martin had the van delivered to Janssen on location. When Janssen opened the door and entered the van, he found a special surprise. Suzanne Pleshette was lying on the bed. Janssen collapsed with laughter.

Janssen decided to leave the show in 1967. Although the fugitive stopped running, Quinn Martin was merely catching his second wind. From 1964 to 1977 Martin produced his biggest hit, *The FBI*, as well as *Twelve O'Clock High, The Invaders, Dan August, Cannon, The Streets of*

San Francisco, Banyon, Barnaby Jones, The Manhunter, Caribe, Bert D'Angelo/Superstar, and *Most Wanted*. At one time Martin had three shows running on CBS and two on ABC.

Martin jealously guarded his status as an independent producer, but as QM Productions grew in size, the pressures mounted. "There's a game you play," Martin told *TV Guide*, "I have a lot of people to please. The network. The sponsor. The studio that puts up the production facilities. Most of all myself. It gets tougher as you get bigger. QM Productions, wholly financed by ABC, employs four hundred people."

Increasing network involvement and changing viewer tastes led to the decline of QM Productions. By the late 1970s, glitzy shows like *Charlie's Angels* and *Starsky and Hutch* grabbed the audience's attention while Martin's shows began to decline in the ratings. Then Martin produced a number of made-for-television movies, hoping the

networks would spin one of them off as a series, but there were no takers. When *Barnaby Jones* went off the air in 1980, it was the first time since 1959 that not one Quinn Martin show was being aired on prime time in network television.

During his nearly two-decade run as president and chief executive officer of QM Productions, Martin produced sixteen one-hour network series and twenty movies of the week. Embittered by increasing network interference, Martin became tense and lashed out at his friends who had helped him build QM Productions. Sinking into deep depression, Martin reached the breaking point in 1979, and decided to leave the business, selling QM Productions to Taft Broadcasting. As part of the sales agreement, Martin agreed to stay out of television production for at least five years.

The family moved to Rancho Santa Fe, California, where Martin eventually regained his mental health, became involved in community activities, occasionally taught at the University of San Diego at La Jolla, and raised and raced Thoroughbreds. Quinn Martin died of a heart

Roy Thinnes starred in "The Invaders," a Quinn Martin production.

attack in 1987. He was sixty-five. Martin was survived by his wife Muffet, three children, Jill, Cliff, and Michael, and his mother.

At a memorial for his friend of twenty-five years, John Conwell recalled his reaction upon meeting Martin for the first time. "I've either met the nicest guy in Hollywood or the greatest con artist. As it turned out, he was both."

Chapter 12

The Imitators

Roy, everyone else is stealing from *The Fugitive*,
why don't you?

          —ABC president Leonard Goldenson

The basic theme of *The Fugitive* was used in many other television shows. The most obvious imitation was *Run for Your Life,* which was developed by Roy Huggins, the man who conceived the original idea for *The Fugitive*. Several years after *The Fugitive* had begun its run on ABC, Huggins returned to television as a writer, producer, and executive at Universal Studios. One day in the studio's dining room he was joined by ABC president Leonard Goldenson, who told him, "Roy, everyone else is stealing from *The Fugitive,* why don't you, now that you're back in television?" "You know, Leonard, I think I already have," replied Huggins, who had just sold *Run for Your Life* to NBC.

"Jennings Lang, who was a senior vice president at Universal, talked to me and my assistant, Joe Swerling, one day," recalled Huggins. "Jennings said, 'I've got a great idea. A guy finds out he's got only two years to live and his doctor is telling him that. And he leaves the office in a daze and the doctor puts the file away and somehow or other, we find out that it's the wrong file. The guy isn't sick at all, but he thinks he is. And Joe and I left the office laughing, saying, 'Christ, what a bad idea.' I got to my office and sat down and began thinking about it and I said to myself, 'That's not a bad idea except the "mistake" is a bad idea. Because what if it's true? What if the guy really has only two years to live.' And that is how *Run for Your Life* came into being. I took it from there."

Run for Your Life aired on NBC from 1965 to 1968. "There was no imitation of *The Fugitive* that worked except for *Run for Your Life,*" said Huggins. "It was the only one that was successful."

The similarities between the two shows were obvious. *The Fugitive*'s main character was Richard Kimble, a successful doctor in his mid-thirties, played by a dark-haired, sensitive actor, David Janssen. *Run for Your Life*'s chief protagonist was Paul Bryan, a thirty-five-year-old lawyer, played by an intense, dark-haired actor, Ben Gazzara.

Like *The Fugitive*'s Kimble, Bryan was also handed a death sentence when told by doctors that he had an incurable illness and had only a short while to live. Just as Kimble abandoned his successful medical practice, Bryan shut down his law office and began to travel the world, trying to make the most of his remaining time.

Rather than running from Lieutenant Gerard as Richard Kimble did, Bryan ran from an even more terrifying pursuer: death. Much like Kimble, Bryan's travels took him to a variety of places and put him in contact with a diversity of people. "It was another way of doing, in a modern context, a man who moves around like a western hero," said Roy Huggins. "And he did it because he was going to die." Not content to just oversee the production of *Run for Your Life*, Huggins wrote many of the show's episodes using the pseudonym John Thomas James, the first names of his three sons. Even though Paul Bryan supposedly had only two years to live, the show ran for three years, and Bryan was still running when *Run for Your Life* left the air in 1968.

Other shows whose central themes were reminiscent of *The Fugitive* included *Run Buddy Run* (CBS, 1966-67), in which Jack Sheldon played Buddy Overstreet, a man who overheard mobsters planning a murder and is forced to run from them; and *The Loner* (CBS, 1965-66), which saw Lloyd Bridges as William Colton, an ex-Union cavalry officer who wandered the frontier following the conclusion of the Civil War.

Lloyd Bridges as William Colton in "The Loner."

Still another such show was *A Man Called Shenandoah* (ABC, 1965-66). Robert Horton played a wounded stranger who was shot and left to die. Found by two buffalo hunters on the prairie, the man recovered from the wounds but couldn't remember his name. He assumed the name Shenandoah and spent the rest of the season wandering through the West in search of his identity.

Quinn Martin returned with a story line similar to that of his ABC hit on *The Invaders* (ABC, 1967-68). Produced by *The Fugitive*'s Alan Armer and narrated by William Conrad, *The Invaders* told the story of architect David Vincent (Roy Thinnes) who witnessed the landing of a flying saucer. Much like Richard Kimble, Vincent traveled from town to town, trying to convince others that the population had been infiltrated by aliens. Although Alan Armer said there was no conscious effort to emulate *The Fugitive,* he admitted there were similarities between the two shows. "The leading character is a character who is not recognized or applauded by society," said Armer. "One is a refugee from the law. The other is a guy whom nobody will believe. And in a sense, that's what Kimble is, because Kimble says the real killer is the one-armed man, and nobody will believe him. We've all been in the position where nobody will believe us, and there is such audience empathy for the character. It worked for us in *The Fugitive* and I recognized that factor in *The Invaders,* either consciously or subconsciously, and I said, 'Let's go.' "

David Vincent and Carol Lynley in "The Invaders."

Another show which resembled *The Fugitive* was *The Immortal* (ABC, 1970-71). In this show, Christopher George played a handsome race car driver, Ben Richards. Peculiar antibodies in Richards's blood made him immune to disease and aging. Because others sought his gift of immortality, Richards was constantly chased,

mainly by ruthless billionaire Arthur Maitland, played by David Brian, and his henchman Fletcher, played by Don Knight.

Kenneth Johnson wrote and produced *The Incredible Hulk,* which aired on CBS from 1978

Lou Ferrigno as "The Incredible Hulk."

to 1982. Although *The Incredible Hulk* was based on the comic-book character created by Stan Lee in 1962, the show's story line was quite similar to *The Fugitive.* Bill Bixby played Dr. David Banner, another doctor banished to a life on the run after being exposed to radiation during a freak accident in his research laboratory. Every time he became angry, Banner turned into a huge green monster, played by bodybuilder Lou Ferrigno. Banner traveled across the country, searching for a cure for his condition, and trying to elude the investigative reporter bent on catching him.

Johnson returned with *Hot Pursuit,* on NBC in 1984. Instead of one fugitive, this show featured two: Kate and Jim Wyler, a young couple who had the world by the tail. Kate was an auto engineer developing a high-performance car, while Jim was a veterinarian. Much like the fate that befell Richard Kimble, the Wylers' lives became a nightmare when Kate was falsely convicted of murdering her employer. *Hot Pur-*

suit starred Eric Pierpoint as Jim Wyler and Kerrie Keane as both Kate Wyler and her evil twin double, Cathy Ladd, who framed Kate for the murder. The Wylers traveled from city to city, trying to find the double, the one person who could prove Kate's innocence. This show even featured a train-wreck escape and also worked a one-armed man into the story.

During the summer of 1993 *Johnny Bago* appeared on CBS. *Johnny Bago* was a satire of shows like *The Fugitive* as well as a parody of every gangster movie ever made. Peter Dobson played Johnny, a small-time hood released from prison who is promptly framed for the murder of a crime-family heir. Johnny jumped in an RV, a Winnebago (from which he borrows his name), and drove cross-country, on the run from both the mob and his parole officer, who also happened to be his ex-wife.

Roy Huggins, who conceived the original idea for *The Fugitive* and produced *Run for Your Life*, resurfaced in 1989. "A movie producer named Keith Barish came along and wanted the movie rights to *The Fugitive*," said Huggins. "And I said,

'What in the world makes you think anyone is going to watch *The Fugitive* as a movie? I mean the television show is still on the air and any movie that could come from *The Fugitive* has already been done, because in the show's two hour conclusion, they catch the one-armed man. And Barish looked at me and said, 'How long ago did you do *The Fugitive*. . . . twenty-five years ago? That's the answer. The movie audience is people about twenty-five years old or a few years older. They don't know anything about *The Fugitive*. They've just heard about it. And there's tremendous interest in it because it's a classic.' And I said, 'I'll be damned, I think you may be right. Let's talk.' "

So, with Roy Huggins and Keith Barish as executive producers, Arnold Kopelson as producer and Andrew Davis as director, *The Fugitive* became a Warner Brothers feature film. Released in August 1993, the movie starred Harrison Ford as Dr. Richard Kimble and Tommy Lee Jones as Sam Gerard, the U.S. Marshal who pursued the fugitive.

The Fugitive, the movie, was an immediate hit,

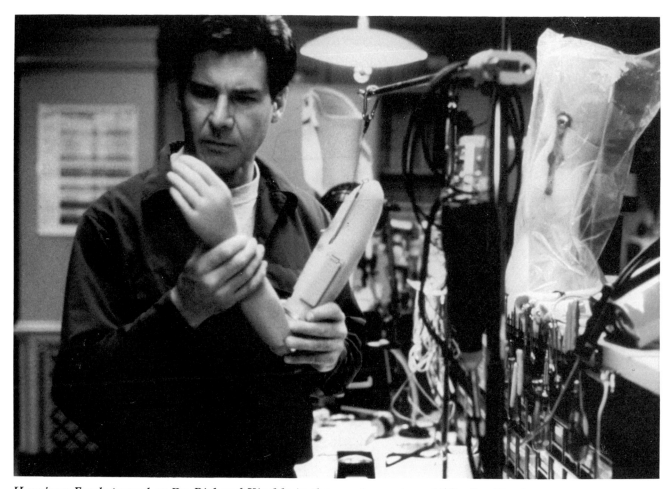

Harrison Ford starred as Dr. Richard Kimble in the movie version of "The Fugitive."

grossing a record $23.8 million during its first week in release and $181.5 million in thirty weeks.

Because of health problems, Roy Huggins was able to make only infrequent contributions to the movie. "I got sick and had to leave it," said Huggins. "When I came back, I made some mildly important contributions, but the credit really goes to Arnold Kopelson, who was like a hen with one chick. He just never allowed anything to happen on that show that he didn't analyze. And I really think the credit for the tremendous quality of the show goes to Andy Davis. Andy Davis has suddenly come out as one of the really fine directors in our industry. He is now set to embark on a tremendously prestigious career."

In addition to becoming the biggest hit of the summer, *The Fugitive* was also a critical success. *CinemaScore*, a ratings service that polls movie audiences, gave *The Fugitive* a rare grade of A+. Roger Ebert of the *Chicago Sun-Times* gave the movie a four star rating, saying, "One of the year's best films. A tense, taut and expert thriller. Pure filmmaking on a master scale. Director Andrew Davis deserves comparison with Hitchcock and also with David Lean and Carol Reed." And critic Janet Maslin of *The New York Times* proclaimed *The Fugitive* "a smashing success, sensationally directed and acted to steely perfection by Harrison Ford, Tommy Lee Jones and a flawless supporting cast." *The Fugitive* received seven Academy Award nominations with Tommy Lee Jones winning an Oscar as Best Supporting Actor.

Thirty-three years after Roy Huggins sat by his pool and created the original idea, *The Fugitive* is still running.

Tommy Lee Jones as Sam Gerard in the movie version of "The Fugitive."

Chapter 13

The Episodes

First Season

Second Season

Third Season

Fourth Season

Production Credits 1963–67

The Fugitive*'s Original Sponsors*

First Season

EPISODE 1:
"FEAR IN A DESERT CITY"
(9-17-63)

Written by: Stanford Whitmore
Directed by: Walter Grauman

Guest Cast:

Lt. Gerard . . . . Barry Morse
Evelyn . . . . Abigail Shelton
Monica Welles . . . . Vera Miles
Mark Welles . . . . Donald Losby
Edward Welles . . . . Brian Keith
Ticket Agent . . . . Bryan O'Byrne
Sgt. Burden . . . . Harry Townes
Sgt. Fairfield . . . . Dabbs Greer
Cleve Brown . . . . Barney Phillips

While working in a Tucson, Arizona, hotel, Richard Kimble becomes involved with Monica Welles, a beautiful piano player who is being pursued by her estranged and jealous husband, Ed Welles. Welles threatens Kimble and tries to force him to leave town. When Monica decides to leave with Kimble, Welles comes after them with a gun. In a shootout at the bus depot, Welles is killed and Kimble resumes his flight.

Notes:
• In addition to enjoying a long movie career, Brian Keith starred in television series including *Family Affair, The Brian Keith Show,* and *Hardcastle & McCormick.*

EPISODE 2:
"THE WITCH"
(9-24-63)

Written by: William D. Gordon
Directed by: Andrew McCullough

Guest Cast:

Mrs. Ammory . . . . Madeleine Sherwood
Jenny Ammory . . . . Gina Gillespie
Emily Norton . . . . Patricia Crowley
H.R. Ammory . . . . Crahan Denton
McNary . . . . Ray Teal
Mrs. Sturgis . . . . Claudia Bryar
Ty Tyson . . . . Arch Johnson
Mr. Sturgis . . . . George Mitchell
Sailor . . . . Elisha Cook

Kimble becomes involved with a little girl, Jenny Ammory, who talks to a doll, lives in a dream world, and tells tall tales. The girl convinces people in a small town that Kimble has attacked her and that he is involved with the local schoolteacher.

The girl's accusations create a scandal, and when the townspeople attempt to fire the schoolteacher, Kimble comes to her defense.

Notes:
• Patricia Crowley played Joan Nash on *Please Don't Eat the Daisies* on NBC from 1965–67 and Georgia Cameron on *Joe Forrester* on NBC from 1975–76.
• Elisha Cook, a legendary movie heavy, played Francis "Ice Pick" Hofstetler on *Magnum P.I.* from 1980–88.

EPISODE 3:
"THE OTHER SIDE OF THE MOUNTAIN"
(10-1-63)

Teleplay by: Alan Caillou and Harry Kronman
Story by: Alan Caillou
Directed by: James Sheldon

Guest Cast:

Lt. Gerard . . . . Barry Morse
Jackson . . . . Frank Sutton
Cassie . . . . Sandy Dennis
Bradley . . . . R.G. Armstrong
Grams . . . . Ruth White
Leo . . . . Hugh Sanders
Quimby . . . . John D. Chandler
Martin . . . . Bruce Dern

Sandy Dennis as Cassie with David Janssen in "The Other Side of the Mountain."

Kimble goes into a depressed West Virginia coal-mining town, and the locals coax him into a fight. As Kimble tries to escape, he meets Cassie Bowlen, a lonely girl who hides him but doesn't want to let him go. As Lieutenant Gerard closes in, Kimble flees, but not before encouraging Cassie to follow her dream of leaving the small town.

Notes:
• Sandy Dennis won a Tony Award for *A Thousand Clowns* and an Academy Award as Best supporting Actress in *Who's Afraid of Virginia Woolf*.
• Frank Sutton is best known as Sgt. Vince Carter on *Gomer Pyle, U.S.M C.* on CBS from 1964–70.

Gerard. Tired of running, Kimble decides to stay in Santa Barbara, hoping that his strategy of staying put will confuse Gerard.

Notes:
• Susan Oliver appeared in hundreds of series episodes from the 1950s to the 1970s. She was also a regular on *Days of Our Lives* in the mid-70s.
• Robert Duvall was seen frequently in television dramas of the 1960s before moving on to a career in films. Duvall won an Oscar for *Tender Mercies* (1983) and has appeared in countless other films including *The Godfather* (1972), *The Godfather Part II* (1974), *The Great Santini* (1979), and the *Lonesome Dove* miniseries.

EPISODE 4:
"NEVER WAVE GOODBYE" PART ONE
(10-8-63)

Written by: Hank Searls
Directed by: William A. Graham

Guest Cast:
Lt. Gerard	Barry Morse
Dr. Brooks	Lee Phillips
Lars	Will Kuluva
Flip Gerard	Roger Parvis
Ann Gerard	Rachael Ames
Eric	Robert Duvall
Karen	Susan Oliver

In Santa Barbara, California, Kimble falls in love with a sailmaker's beautiful daughter. Hearing that a one-armed man has been arrested in Los Angeles, Kimble goes there, only to encounter Lieutenant

Robert Duvall as Eric with Barry Morse as Lieutenant Gerard in "Never Wave Goodbye."

EPISODE 5:
"NEVER WAVE GOODBYE" PART TWO
(10-15-63)

Written by: Hank Searls
Directed by: William A. Graham

Guest Cast:
Lt. Gerard	Barry Morse
Coast Guard Skipper	Bert Remsen
Karen	Susan Oliver
Dr. Ray Brooks	Lee Phillips
Eric	Robert Duvall
Watch Commander	Nick Nicholson

Tired of running and deeply in love, Kimble risks staying in Santa Barbara as Lieutenant Gerard closes in. Trying to deceive Gerard, Kimble fakes his own death at sea. When Gerard's boat crashes and the lieutenant is injured, Kimble returns to help him before resuming his flight.

EPISODE 6:
"DECISION IN THE RING"
(10-22-63)

Written by: Arthur Weiss
Directed by: Robert Ellis Miller

Guest Cast:
Joe Smith	James Edwards
Laura	Ruby Dee
Bragan	James Dunn
Dan Digby	Hari Rhodes

In Los Angeles, Kimble is hired as a cut man by pro boxer Joe Smith, who once wanted to be a doctor. When Kimble discovers Smith has

David Janssen with James Edwards as Joe Smith in "Decision in the Ring."

suffered possible brain damage, he encourages him to retire and pursue his medical studies.

Notes:
• Although it was aired as the series' sixth show, "Decision in the Ring" was actually the first episode filmed after the pilot. It was also the first episode produced by Alan Armer.
• Ruby Dee appeared as a regular on *The Guiding Light* on CBS in 1967 and *Peyton Place* on ABC, from 1968–69.

EPISODE 7:
"SMOKE SCREEN"
(10-29-63)

Written by: John D. F. Black
Directed by: Claudio Guzman

Guest Cast:
Lt. Gerard . . . . Barry Morse
Maria . . . . Pina Pellicer
Paco . . . . Alejandro Rey
Doris . . . . Beverly Garland
Fire Chief . . . . James Seay
Johnny . . . . Peter Helm
Cardinez . . . . Pepe Hern

Employed as a migrant worker in California, Kimble joins a group of men asked to fight a forest fire. When a co-worker's pregnant wife needs a cesarean section, Dr. Kimble overcomes the others' resentment and performs the surgery, as Lieutenant Gerard closes in.

Notes:
• Beverly Garland played Bing Crosby's wife on *The Bing Crosby Show* on ABC from 1964–65, Barbara Harper Douglas on *My Three Sons* on CBS from 1969–72, and Dotty West on *Scarecrow and Mrs. King* on CBS from 1983–87.
• Alejandro Rey was best known as casino owner Carlos Ramirez on *The Flying Nun* on ABC from 1967–70.

EPISODE 8:
"SEE HOLLYWOOD AND DIE"
(11-5-63)

Written by: George Eckstein
Directed by: Andrew McCullough

Guest Cast:
Joanne . . . . Brenda Vaccaro
Vinnie . . . . Lou Antonio
Miles . . . . Chris Robinson
Ray . . . . J. Pat O'Malley
Mr. Burgess . . . . William Fawcett
State Trooper . . . . Lane Bradford
Les . . . . William Challee
Sam . . . . Ken Tilles
Tim Cates . . . . Jason Wingreen

Kimble and a beautiful girl are taken hostage by two hoodlums heading for Hollywood. Kimble tricks them into thinking he's a master thief on his way to a big score. When Kimble enlists their help, they walk right into his trap.

Brenda Vaccaro as Joanne, Lou Antonio (left rear) as Vinnie and Chris Robinson (right rear) as Miles with David Janssen in "See Hollywood and Die."

Notes:
• Lou Antonio has enjoyed a successful career as an actor and director in television and movies. One of his most memorable roles was as Koko in

Cool Hand Luke (1967). He has also directed episodes of *McCloud; Owen Marshall, Counselor at Law*; and *McMillan and Wife*, and was twice nominated for an Emmy for his direction of tearjerkers *Something for Joey* (1977) and *Silent Victory: The Kitty O'Neill Story* (1979).

• Brenda Vaccaro was nominated for Tony Awards for *Cactus Flower*, *How Now Dow Jones*, and *The Goodbye People*. On television she starred on *Sara* on CBS in 1976 and played Julia Blake on *Paper Doll* on ABC in 1984. In addition to guest-starring on numerous series, she also worked in TV movies like *The Star Maker* (1981), *A Long Way Home* (1981) and *The Pride of Jesse Hallam* (1981).

• Jason Wingreen played Harry Snowden on *All in the Family* on CBS from 1977–79 and on *Archie Bunker's Place* on CBS from 1979–83.

EPISODE 9:
"TICKET TO ALASKA"
(11-12-63)

Written by: Oliver Crawford
Directed by: Jerry Hopper

Guest Cast:

Adrienne Banning	Geraldine Brooks
Capt. Carraway	John Larkin
George Banning	David White
Ruth Wyatt	Gail Kobe
Paul Vale	Gene Lyons
Earl Morehead	Murray Matheson
Celia Decker	June Dayton

On a freighter bound for Alaska, Kimble runs into passengers who also have something to hide. When a government agent boards the ship looking for a spy, he is murdered. With Kimble's help the spy is uncovered and arrested.

Notes:

• Geraldine Brooks played Lou Carson on *Faraday and Company* on NBC from 1973–74 and Angela Dumpling on *The Dumplings* on NBC in 1976.

• Tim O'Connor has had a busy career as a character actor on television. He also played Elliott Carson on *Peyton Place* on ABC from 1965–68.

• David White played Larry Tate on *Bewitched* on ABC from 1964–72.

EPISODE 10:
"FATSO"
(11-19-63)

Written by: Robert Pirosh
Directed by: Ida Lupino

Guest Cast:

Lt. Gerard	Barry Morse
Davey	Jack Weston
Mrs. Lambert	Glenda Farrell
Mr. Lambert	King Calder
Frank	Burt Brinckerhoff
Crowley	Vaughn Taylor

Following a traffic accident, Kimble is jailed and befriends Davey Lambert, a young man arrested for drunkenness. After they're released, the two men go to the Lambert's ranch, where Kimble foils a devious family plot to ruin Davey.

Notes:

• This was the first of three episodes directed by Ida Lupino, a successful actress turned producer-director. Lupino also directed segments of other series, including *Four Star Playhouse*, *The Dick Powell Show*, *The Big Valley*, *Alfred Hitchcock* and *Bewitched*.

• Jack Weston played Walter Hathaway on *The Hathaways* on ABC from 1961–62 and Danny Zimmer on *The Four Seasons* on NBC from 1970–71.

• Glenda Farrell often played wisecracking characters on television and in movies. She won an Emmy for her performance as a guest star on *Ben Casey*.

EPISODE 11:
"NIGHTMARE AT NORTHOAK"
(11-26-63)

Written by: Stuart Jerome
Directed by: Chris Nyby

Guest Cast:

Lt. Gerard	Barry Morse
Jen	Sue Randall
Al Springer	Frank Overton
Capt. Carpenter	Paul Birch
Wilma Springer	Nancy Wickwire
Dr. Babcock	Ian Wolfe
Matty	Barbara Pepper

When Kimble rescues children from a school bus accident, he becomes a small town hero, but also attracts the attention of Lieutenant Gerard. With the help of the appreciative townspeople, Kimble escapes.

EPISODE 12:
"GLASS TIGHTROPE"
(12-3-63)

Teleplay by: Robert C. Dennis and Barry Trivers
Directed by: Ida Lupino

Guest Cast:
Martin Rowland . . . . Leslie Nielsen
Lewis . . . . Warren Parker
Angstrom . . . . Edward Binns
Pascoe . . . . Robert Quarry
Ginny Rowland . . . . Diana Van Der Vlis
Floyd . . . . Jud Taylor
Tibbets . . . . Jay Adler

Working for a department store, Kimble witnesses a fight in which his employer, Martin Rowland, knocks a man down in a parking lot. When the man dies, a skid row character is charged with the murder, and Kimble risks his safety and works to clear him.

Leslie Nielsen guest starred as Martin Rowland in "Glass Tightrope."

Notes:
• In addition to appearing in two episodes of *The Fugitive*, Leslie Nielsen helped provide the show with one of its most prolific writers, Stanford Whitmore, who penned four episodes, including

the pilot, "Fear in a Desert City." "My wife worked at MGM with a girl who eventually married Leslie Nielsen," recalled Whitmore. "We were friends with them and my wife and I stood up at their wedding. I was trying to break into television, so Leslie told Quinn Martin that I was a good writer. Leslie was working on one of Quinn's shows called *The New Breed*, and Quinn asked me if I would be interested in writing an episode. I wrote a number of episodes and then when the show was dropped, Quinn called about *The Fugitive*."

EPISODE 13:
"TERROR AT HIGH POINT"
(12-17-63)

Teleplay by: Peter Germano and
Harry Kronman
Story by: Peter Germano
Directed by: Jerry Hopper

Guest Cast:
Buck Harmon . . . . Jack Klugman
Dan . . . . James Best
Ruth Harmon . . . . Elizabeth Allen
Charley . . . . Richard Wessell
Jamie . . . . Buck Taylor
Rufe . . . . Russ Vincent
Mrs. Hendricks . . . . Doreen McLean
Mike . . . . Billy Halop
Krips . . . . Richard Webb

Working on a Utah construction site, Kimble defends a retarded boy accused of attacking the foreman's wife. He uncovers the real culprit and patches up his boss's marriage.

Notes:
• Jack Klugman starred as Oscar Madison in *The Odd Couple* on ABC from 1970–83, Quincy on *Quincy, M.E.* on NBC from 1976–83, and Henry Willows on *You Again?* on NBC from 1986–87. Klugman won Emmy Awards for *The Odd Couple* and for a guest-starring role on *The Defenders* in 1964.

EPISODE 14:
"THE GIRL FROM LITTLE EGYPT"
(12-24-63)

Written by: Stanford Whitmore
Directed by: Vincent McEveety

Guest Cast:

Lt. Gerard . . . . Barry Morse
Ruth Norton . . . . Pamela Tiffin
Helen Kimble . . . . Diane Brewster
Jim Prestwick . . . . Jerry Paris
Judge . . . . William Newell
Doris Clements . . . . June Dayton
Paul Clements . . . . Ed Nelson
Ratliff . . . . John Rodney

After being run down by a young woman, Kimble winds up in the hospital, where he becomes delirious and reveals his past. The woman befriends Kimble and he helps her straighten out her tangled love life.

Notes:
• The title of this episode comes from the Illinois area where writer Stanford Whitmore grew up. "It's got towns named Cairo and New Thibes and Metropolis and the whole area is known as Little Egypt."
• Whitmore also recalled David Janssen's reaction when told the guest star would be Pamela Tiffin: "David said, 'What's a Pamela Tiffin?'" Whitmore didn't think much of Tiffin's performance, nor did he like this episode. "I thanked Quinn Martin for airing it on Christmas Eve," Whitmore said, "because nobody would see it. I thought it came out terribly."

EPISODE 15:
"HOME IS THE HUNTED"
(1-7-64)

Andrew Prine as Ray Kimble with David Janssen in "Home is the Hunted."

Written by: Arthur Weiss
Directed by: Jerry Hopper

Guest Cast:

Lt. Gerard . . . . Barry Morse
Ray Kimble . . . . Andrew Prine
David . . . . Billy Mumy
Dr. John Kimble . . . . . . Robert Keith
Donna . . . . Jacqueline Scott
Billy . . . . Clint Howard

Kimble returns to his hometown to visit his ailing father, his sister, and his angry younger brother. With Lieutenant Gerard hot on his trail, Kimble effects a reconciliation with his brother, who then helps him escape.

Notes:
• Robert Keith enjoyed a stage, screen, and television career that lasted over forty years. He was a regular on *The Great Gildersleeve* on NBC from 1955-56. His son is actor Brian Keith, who appeared in *The Fugitive*'s pilot, "Fear in a Desert City."

EPISODE 16:
"GARDEN HOUSE"
(1-14-64)

Written by: Sheldon Stark
Directed by: Ida Lupino

Guest Cast:

Harlan Guthrie . . . . Robert Webber
Ann Guthrie . . . . Peggy McKay
Carol . . . . Pippa Scott
Hannah . . . . Hanna Landy
Police Lieutenant . . . . . . Jason Johnson

Working for a wealthy Connecticut couple, Kimble's true identity is discovered by his employer, Harlan Guthrie. Guthrie, unhappy with his marriage and in love with his wife's sister, plots to use Kimble to help him out of his fix.

Notes:
• Robert Webber played Alexander Hayes, father of Maddie Hayes, on *Moonlighting* on ABC from 1987-88.
• Pippa Scott played Molly Wood on *The Virginian* on NBC from 1962-63 and Maggie Hearn on *Jigsaw John* on NBC in 1976.

EPISODE 17:
"COME WATCH ME DIE"
(1-21-64)

Teleplay by: Stanford Whitmore
Story by: Perry Bleecker
Directed by: Laslo Benedek

Guest Cast:

Bellows	Robert Doyle
Clement	John Anderson
Benjy	Randy Boone
Charley	Bruce Dern
Shrader	Russell Collins
Bowers	Judson Pratt
Sheriff	David McLean
Stella	Diane Ladd

When a young man is accused of murder, Kimble is deputized and asked to drive a bus to transport him to the county seat. Fearing the man will be killed before he gets a trial, Kimble helps him escape, only to find out he's really a killer. When Kimble helps recapture the murderer, he's offered a permanent job as a deputy.

Bruce Dern guest starred as Charley in "Come Watch Me Die."

Notes:

• We were shooting just before Christmas," recalled Barry Morse, "and everybody was anxious to get home. We had a sequence in a bus with the old rear screen projection, using a mockup of a bus in the studio. We were just about to roll, when our clapper boy said to the assistant director, 'I think that rear screen projection is going the wrong way . . . all the trees and the telegraph poles make it look like the bus is going backwards.' And they said, 'Shut up, son, just clap the boards.' "They shot the master scene," remembered producer Alan Armer, "and it looked like the bus was going backwards down the road. It was ludicrous, there were forty to fifty people on the soundstage and nobody noticed it and they printed it. The next day in the projection room, we watched it and everybody fell down. So we took the film and printed it backwards. We didn't use any dialogue with it and we didn't use it long enough so that anyone noticed the bus was going backwards. We rolled it backwards, at the beginning of the scene, maybe once in the middle, and once at the end, so the movements of the actors would not give away that the bus was going backwards."

• Although they divorced later, Bruce Dern and Diane Ladd were married when this episode was filmed. The union produced actress Laura Dern, who has starred in such movies as *Wild at Heart* (1990) and *Rambling Rose* (1991).

• Bruce Dern played E. J. Stocker on *Stoney Burke* on ABC from 1962–63. He used his television career as a springboard to movie stardom, in films like *The King of Marvin Gardens* (1972), *The Great Gatsby* (1974), *Black Sunday* (1977), *Tattoo* (1981), and countless others.

• Diane Ladd played the original Flo in the movie *Alice Doesn't Live Here Anymore* (1974) and then played waitress Belle Dupree in *Alice* on CBS from 1980–81. She also played opposite her daughter Laura in *Rambling Rose.* Ladd and Dern were the first real-life mother and daughter to be nominated for Oscars in the same year.

EPISODE 18:
"WHERE THE ACTION IS"
(1-28-64)

Written by: Harry Kronman
Directed by: James Sheldon

Guest Cast:

Dan Polichek	Telly Savalas
Mrs. Gaines	Maxine Stuart
Chris Polichek	Joanna Frank
Ben Haddock	Don Keefer
Hotel Proprietor	Connie Gilchrist
Stripper	Miss Beverly Hills

Employed as a pool man at a Reno, Nevada,

resort, Kimble gets in the middle of a dispute between a teenaged girl and her father, who owns the resort. With Kimble's help, the two settle their differences and family harmony is restored.

Note:
• Telly Savalas didn't start acting until he was in his mid-thirties but he was a familiar sight on television in the 1960s, appearing on shows like *The Untouchables* and *Burke's Law*. The bald actor hit the big time as Theo Kojak on *Kojak* on CBS from 1973–78 and on ABC from 1989–90.

EPISODE 19:
"SEARCH IN A WINDY CITY"
(2-4-64)

Written by: Stuart Jerome
Directed by: Jerry Hopper

Guest Cast:
Lt. Gerard . . . . Barry Morse
Decker . . . . Pat Hingle
Paula Decker . . . . Nan Martin
One-armed man . . . . Bill Raisch
Connelley . . . . Addison Richards
Cogen . . . . Lewis Charles
Sgt. DeSantis . . . . Paul Picerni
Wimpy . . . . Arthur Batanides

A Chicago columnist believes in Kimble's innocence and tries to help him catch the one-armed man. In the process, the writer destroys his career and Kimble is nearly caught.

Pat Hingle as Mike Decker with Janssen in "Search in a Windy City."

Notes:
• Pat Hingle played Chief Paulton on *Stone* on ABC in 1980 and has enjoyed a long career as one of television's best character actors.

EPISODE 20:
"BLOODLINE"
(2-11-64)

Teleplay by: Harry Kronman
Story by: John Hawkins and Harry Kronman
Directed by: John Erman

Guest Cast:
Max Bodin . . . . George Voskovec
Lee Burroughs . . . . Parley Baer
Johnny Bodin . . . . John Considine
Lt. Samson . . . . Dan Barton
Cora Bodin . . . . Nancy Malone

Working at a prestigious kennel, Kimble discovers a woman releasing a prized dog. When the dog is injured, Kimble is ordered to destroy the animal, but saves the dog, only to discover a dark secret that could ruin the family business. With Kimble's help, the kennel and the family are saved.

Warren Oates as Herbie with David Janssen in "Rat in a Corner."

EPISODE 21:
"RAT IN A CORNER"
(2-18-64)

Teleplay by: Sheldon Stark and
William Morwood
Directed by: Jerry Hopper

Guest Cast:
Herbie . . . . Warren Oates
Lorna . . . . Virginia Vincent
Sharp . . . . Glen Vernon
Ryan . . . . Tommy Farrell
Santelli . . . . Malachi Throne
Sergeant . . . . Stuart Bradley

Kimble becomes involved with a two-bit thief who robs a liquor store where Kimble is working. When the police arrest the robber, he suspects Kimble turned him in. After the man is freed, the police come after Kimble, who seeks refuge with the thief's sister.

Notes:
• Warren Oates got his start in television, demonstrating stunts for CBS' *Beat the Clock* in the 1950s. His career really developed in 1960s television westerns, when he played an assortment of grizzled villains. He also appeared in films like *The Wild Bunch* (1969) and *Dillinger* (1973).

EPISODE 22:
"ANGELS TRAVEL ON LONELY ROADS" PART ONE
(2-25-64)

Written by: Al C. Ward
Directed by: Walter Grauman

Guest Cast:
Sister Veronica . . . . Eileen Heckart
Janet . . . . Ruta Lee
Chuck . . . . Albert Salmi
Sherie . . . . Shary Marshall
Sheriff Morris . . . . Sandy Kenyon

Kimble catches a ride with Sister Veronica, a nun headed for Sacramento. As they drive over the mountains, a series of miracles hasten their journey. Kimble and Sister Veronica are both fugitives. He is running from the law, while she is on her way to renounce her vows.

Notes:
• " 'Angels Travel on Lonely Roads' was such a beautiful show," said producer Alan Armer. "It was originally written as a one-part show and it just kept getting richer and richer. Al C. Ward wrote it, and the poor guy, we worked his butt off. I think he or his agent complained to Quinn Martin, but it worked out okay, because it eventually became a two-parter and he got paid for two scripts. It was a lovely script and Heckie [Eileen Heckart] was wonderful, and it was the perfect show to display David's sense of humor. It was wonderful."
• Director Walter Grauman remembers one of his favorite scenes from this episode. "I found a shot in which two railroad tracks paralleled and then crossed. I put the camera and David between the two sets of tracks and found out when the trains were going to come east and west. I got two trains

going opposite directions and put the action between these two roaring trains. David said, 'You crazy bastard, what are you doing? You're going to get us all killed.' It was a wild effect with these two roaring trains going on both sides of us and the camera is panning around."

EPISODE 23:
"ANGELS TRAVEL ON LONELY ROADS" PART TWO
(3-3-64)

Written by: Al C. Ward
Directed by: Walter Grauman

Guest Cast:
Sister Veronica . . . . Eileen Heckart
Anderson. . . . . Lane Bradford
Chuck . . . . Albert Salmi
Lt. Craig . . . . Ken Lynch
Janet . . . . Ruta Lee
Friar. . . . . Jason Wingreen
Sheriff Morris . . . . Sandy Kenyon

The miracles continue as Kimble and Sister Veronica continue their journey. Sister Veronica finds out who Kimble really is and believes in his innocence. When they finally arrive in Sacramento, Kimble thanks Sister Veronica for reawakening his spiritual side, and she decides not to renounce her vows.

Notes:
• "There was a scene where these boys chase us," recalled Eileen Heckart. "I hated doing that scene because I had to hit this kid and the young man kept saying, 'Don't be frightened.' Wally Grauman, the director, said, 'Let this kid have it.' So I hit the kid so hard I knocked him flat on the ground and I started crying. Wally looked at me and said, 'Oh, there's so much violence pent up in you, no wonder you were afraid to show it.' I was scared to death I'd broken the kid's jaw."

• Eileen Heckart has been nominated for a Tony five times and an Oscar twice, winning for Best Supporting Actress in *Butterflies Are Free*. She also has won two Emmy Awards. The first in 1967 was for *Win Me a Place at Forest Lawn* and another in 1994 was for her guest appearance on *Love & War* on NBC. She has appeared in almost every imaginable TV show and is still going strong in her seventies.

EPISODE 24:
"FLIGHT FROM THE FINAL DEMON"
(3-10-64)

Written by: Philip Saltzman
Directed by: Jerry Hopper

Guest Cast:

Steve	Ed Nelson
Joey	Rudi Solari
Linda	Ellen Madison
Horton	Don Dubbins
Sheriff	Carroll O'Connor
Telegraph Clerk	Kathleen O'Malley

Working at a health club, Kimble unknowingly gives a massage to the town sheriff, who becomes suspicious and runs a check on him. Kimble flees with a co-worker who is also a fugitive from his past.

Notes:
• Carroll O'Connor starred as Archie Bunker on *All in the Family* on CBS from 1971-79, on *Archie Bunker's Place* on CBS from 1979-83, and is currently starring as Gillespie on *In The Heat of the Night* on CBS. He won four Emmys for his work on *All in the Family*.
• Ed Nelson played Dr. Michael Rossi on *Peyton Place* on ABC from 1964-69, Ward Fuller on *The Silent Force* on ABC from 1970-71 and Dr. Michael Wise on *Doctor's Private Lives* on ABC in 1979.

EPISODE 25:
"TAPS FOR A DEAD WAR"
(3-17-64)

Teleplay by: Harry Kronman
Story by: Harry Kronman and Merwin Gerard
Directed by: William A. Graham

Guest Cast:

Joe	Tim O'Connor
Millie	Lee Grant

Kenny	Flip Mark
Coates	Dave Armstrong
Keefer	Noam Pitlik
Russ	Nick Nicholson

Working as a roller-rink supervisor, Kimble becomes involved with a boy and his uncle, who was in Kimble's army unit. The man has a badly scarred face, blames Kimble for his predicament, and vows to get even. Overcoming the man's attempt to kill him, Kimble helps him put his life back together.

Lee Grant as Millie with Janssen in "Taps for a Dead War."

Notes:
• Lee Grant won an Emmy for her role as Stella Chernak on *Peyton Place* on ABC from 1965-66 and an Oscar for *Shampoo*. She has also won a Tony Award. Her only starring role in a TV series was as Fay Stewart on *Fay*, which aired on NBC from 1975-76.
• Noam Pitlik played Mr. Gianelli on *The Bob Newhart Show* on CBS from 1972-73 and Officer Swanhauser on *Sanford and Son* on NBC in 1972.

EPISODE 26:
"SOMEBODY TO REMEMBER"
(3-24-64)

Written by: Robert C. Dennis
Directed by: Jerry Hopper

Guest Cast:

Gus Priamos	Gilbert Roland
Capt. Carpenter	Paul Birch
Sophie	Madlyn Rhue
Lt. Gerard	Barry Morse
Nicky	Peter Coe

Pete . . . . Peter Mamakos
Detective . . . . Alan Baxter

Kimble befriends Gus Priamos, an older man who is terminally ill and has been given six months to live. Seeking to do "one great thing" before he dies, Priamos hatches a plan to help Kimble escape from Lieutenant Gerard forever. The man's girlfriend tips off Gerard but Kimble manages to escape as his benefactor dies.

Notes:
• Gilbert Roland dates all the way back to the silent screen era, when he played dashing leading men in the 1920s. The son of a Mexican bullfighter made the successful transition to movies and television.
• Madlyn Rhue played Marjorie Grant on *Bracken's World* on NBC from 1969–70 and Hilary Madison on *Executive Suite* on CBS from 1976–77.

EPISODE 27:
"NEVER STOP RUNNING"
(3-31-64)

Written by: Sheldon Stark
Directed by: William A. Graham

Claude Akins as Ralph in "Never Stop Running."

Guest Cast:
Ralph . . . . Claude Akins
Dave . . . . Wright King
Helen . . . . Joanna Moore
Jimmy . . . . Michael Petit

Kimble comes to the aid of a kidnapped boy who is a hemophiliac and is bleeding to death. The boy is the son of a pro football team owner and is being held for ransom by a disgruntled former player. When the boy is denied medical attention, Kimble helps him escape and takes him to a hospital as the kidnappers are arrested.

Notes:
• Claude Akins went from playing villains to good guys. He's best known on television as Sonny Pruitt on *Movin' On* which aired on NBC from 1974–76 and as Sheriff Lobo on *B.J. and the Bear* on NBC in 1979.
• Joanna Moore played Andy Taylor's girlfriend Peggy on *The Andy Griffith Show* on CBS in 1962.

EPISODE 28:
"THE HOMECOMING"
(4-7-64)

Written by: Peter Germano
Directed by: Jerry Hopper

Guest Cast:
Dorina Pruitt . . . . Gloria Grahame
Seth . . . . James Griffith
Janice Pruitt . . . . Shirley Knight
Sheriff Floyd . . . . Warren Kimble
Allan Pruitt . . . . Richard Carlson
Ellie Parker . . . . Mary Jackson
Judge Parker . . . . Walter Woolf King
Seth'S boy . . . . Eddie Rosson

Kimble becomes involved in a family struggle. The owner of a southern estate has recently remarried. His new wife is jealous of the man's daughter, who is returning from a sanitarium. The girl's mental problems developed because a boy whom she was baby-sitting was killed. Trying to drive the girl insane, the devious wife seeks to reenact the tragedy. Kimble gets caught in the struggle between the two women and exposes the woman's plan.

Notes:
• Richard Carlson starred as Herbert Philbrick in *I Led Three Lives,* a syndicated television show which aired from 1953–56, and played Colonel Ranald S. Mackenzie on *Mackenzie's Raiders,* another syndicated show, from 1958–59.
• Shirley Knight was a member of Quinn Martin's "repertory company," appearing in three episodes of *The Fugitive.* She later won an Emmy playing Hope Steadman's mother on *thirtysomething* on ABC.

EPISODE 29:
"STORM CENTER"
(4-14-64)

Written by: George Eckstein
Directed by: William A. Graham

Guest Cast:
Marcie . . . . Bethel Leslie
Montjoy . . . . Dennis Patrick

Despite an oncoming hurricane, a man and woman force Kimble into taking them by boat to the other side of an island. The two are on the run from the law. En route, the man is thrown overboard and drowns. Five years earlier, the woman came to Dr. Kimble seeking an abortion. When he refused, she went to an abortionist, whose surgery has prevented her from having children. She blames Kimble, seeks revenge, but then falls in love with him.

Notes:
•In "Storm Center" David Janssen had to pilot a small fishing boat through a hurricane and then, in a later scene, he was forced to rescue guest-star Bethel Leslie from the sea. Instead of using a model boat in a tank, as some shows would have done, *The Fugitive* employed a 700-gallon tank sunk beneath Stage 5 at the Goldwyn Studios. Rollers were used to agitate the water, wind machines blew up a 50-mile-per-hour gale, fire hoses sprayed water in front of the wind machines, and the boat was moved through the water using a system of cables. Finally, an apparatus called a "dump through" was employed, a tank with a false bottom, which dumped the whole 700 gallons of water into the "real" bottom of the tank, causing waves to pitch and roll, just as if the scene was being filmed in the middle of the ocean. It was one of the largest water scenes ever set up for television.

EPISODE 30:
"THE END GAME"
(4-21-64)

Written by: Stanford Whitmore
Directed by: Jerry Hopper

Guest Cast:
Lt. Gerard . . . . Barry Morse
Lt. Spencer . . . . Joe Campanella
Devlin . . . . John McGiver
TV Newscaster . . . . Chick Hearn
Reed . . . . John Fiedler

Kimble escapes from a police roadblock and goes to a house occupied by two cantankerous old men, Devlin and Reed, who argue about everything, including Kimble's innocence. When Lieutenant Gerard arrives, Devlin tries to turn Kimble in, while Reed helps him escape.

Notes:
•"The End Game" was the last episode written by Stanford Whitmore. "One of the basic problems of *The Fugitive* was that you had a protagonist who did not want to get involved. His very nature said, 'I'm not going to get involved.' And yet you had to get him involved every week. It really sort of exhausted me after a while and I said, 'I can't write any more of these because I'm really reaching for it.' So I moved on to movies of the week and stuff like that. They were more rewarding than these 'grind 'em out' hour shows."
•John Fiedler played Mr. Peterson on *The Bob Newhart Show* on CBS from 1973–78, and was the voice of Piglet in Walt Disney's *Winnie the Pooh*. He also acted in a number of films including *Twelve Angry Men, Fitzwilly, The Odd Couple,* and *True Grit.*
•John McGiver was best known as Dr. Luther Quince on *The Jimmy Stewart Show* on NBC from 1971–72 and as the salesman at Tiffany's in the movie *Breakfast at Tiffany's.*
•Joseph Campanella played lawyer Brian Darrell on *The Bold Ones* on NBC from 1969–72, Hutch Corrigan on *The Colbys* on ABC from 1985–86, and Harper Deveraux on *Days of Our Lives* on NBC in 1987 and 1990.
•Basketball fans . . . look for long-time Los Angeles Lakers announcer Chick Hearn, who played a newscaster.

Second Season

EPISODE 31:
"MAN IN A CHARIOT"
(9-15-64)

Written by: George Eckstein
Directed by: Robert Butler

Guest Cast:
Professor G. Stanley Lazer . . Ed Begley
Lee Gould . . . . Robert Drivas
Nancy Gilman . . . . Kathleen Maguire
McNeil. . . . . Gene Lyons

G. Stanley Lazer, a former lawyer now confined to a wheelchair and teaching in a law school, believes in Kimble's innocence. Feeling he can destroy the circumstantial evidence that convicted Kimble, Lazer uses his law class to stage a mock trial. As it turns out, Lazer is on trial as much as Kimble.

Notes:
• Ed Begley was a veteran of radio, stage, television, and movies, who won an Oscar for *Sweet Bird of Youth* (1962). He guest starred in numerous series in the '50s, '60s, and '70s. Begley is the father of actor Ed Begley, Jr.

EPISODE 32:
"WORLD'S END"
(9-22-64)

Written by Stuart Jerome
Directed by: Robert Butler

Guest Cast:
Ellie Burton . . . . Suzanne Pleshette
Ada . . . . Carmen Mathews
Lt. Gerard . . . . Barry Morse
Capt. Carpenter . . . . Paul Birch
Keller . . . . Henry Beckman
Mr. Newlin . . . . Woodrow Parfrey
Sgt. Keith . . . . Dabney Coleman

Placing a newspaper personal ad, an old family friend contacts Kimble, saying she's found the one-armed man. When the woman finds out a one-armed man has been killed in a fire, she lies, telling Kimble it's the man he's searching for.

Desperately in love with Kimble, she wants to run away with him. As they prepare to leave for Brazil, she confesses her lie and Kimble's search resumes.

David Janssen and Suzanne Pleshette as Ellie Burton in "World's End."

Notes:
• Suzanne Pleshette began her television career right out of college, in the 1950s. She is best remembered as Emily Hartley, Bob Newhart's wife on *The Bob Newhart Show* on CBS from 1972–78. She has also appeared in numerous films and TV miniseries. Among her films is *Along Came a Spider* in 1970 in which she worked with *Fugitive* alums Alan Armer, Ed Nelson, Andrew Prine, and Richard Anderson.

EPISODE 33:
"MAN ON A STRING"
(9-29-64)

Written by: Barbara & Milton Merlin, and
Harry Kronman
Directed by: Sydney Pollack

Guest Cast:
Lucey Russell . . . . Lois Nettleton
Sheriff Mead . . . . Malcolm Atterbury
George Duncan. . . . . John Larch
Old Timer . . . . Cyril Delevanti
Amy Adams . . . . Patricia Smith
Doc Phillips . . . . Russell Collins

When Kimble helps a woman fix her broken-down car, he becomes involved in a murder investigation and a love triangle involving two women and the town deputy. When Kimble is asked to testify, one of the women threatens to expose him if he reveals the killer.

Notes:
• Lois Nettleton won an Emmy for *The American Woman: Portraits in Courage* in 1977 on ABC. She also played Sue Kramer on *Accidental Family* on NBC from 1967–68 and Maude Wendell in the epic television series *Centennial* on NBC from 1978–79.

EPISODE 34:
"WHEN THE BOUGH BREAKS"
(10-6-64)

Teleplay by: George Eckstein
Story by: James Griffith & George Eckstein
Directed by: Ralph Senensky

Guest Cast:
Carol Hollister . . . . Diana Hyland
Norma . . . . Marge Redmond
Laura . . . . June Vincent
Sgt. Barrett . . . . Robert Hogan
Preacher . . . . Royal Dano
Whit Pearson . . . . Don Briggs
Malleson . . . . Lin McCarthy
Ruth Fisher . . . . Sue Randall
Dr. Eison . . . . Alex Gerry
Mr. Flynn . . . . Robert Duggan

Diana Hyland as Carol Hollister in "When the Bough Breaks."

While hopping a freight train, Kimble encounters a young girl with a baby. She says she's en route to Fargo, North Dakota, to meet her husband, but Kimble discovers she's mentally ill and has kidnapped the child. With Kimble's help, the baby is returned to its real mother and the young woman is reunited with her parents.

Notes:
• Diana Hyland, like Carol Rossen and Shirley Knight, was part of Quinn Martin's "repertory company." She played Susan Winter on *Peyton Place* on ABC from 1968–69 and Joan Bradford on *Eight Is Enough* on ABC in 1977. After a long career in television, she won an Emmy Award for *The Boy in the Plastic Bubble* which aired on ABC in 1976. The award was given to her posthumously following her death from cancer.

EPISODE 35:
"NEMESIS"
(10-13-64)

Written by: Harry Kronman
Directed by: Jerry Hopper

David Janssen with Kurt Russell as Phil Gerard, Jr. in "Nemesis."

Guest Cast:
Lt. Gerard . . . . Barry Morse
Davis . . . . Bing Russell
Phil Jr. . . . . Kurt Russell
Corbin . . . . Slim Pickens

Sheriff Deebold . . . . John Doucette
Capt. Carpenter . . . . Paul Birch

Told Kimble has been spotted in the Wisconsin mountains, Lieutenant Gerard and his son Phil Jr. rush to the site. As Gerard and the sheriff pursue Kimble, Phil Jr. hides in the back of a car that Kimble steals, and their lives become intertwined. After Kimble explains his innocence, Phil Jr. helps him escape.

Notes:
• Slim Pickens was a former rodeo clown who acted in many western films in the '40s and then moved into western TV series in the '50s, appearing in *Wagon Train, Bonanza, Gunsmoke,* and others. One of his best roles was as Big Guy Beck on *Filthy Rich* on CBS in 1982.

EPISODE 36:
"TIGER LEFT, TIGER RIGHT"
(10-20-64)

Written by: William Link and Richard Levinson
Directed by: James Goldstone

Guest Cast:
Harold Cheyney . . . . Leslie Nielsen
Glen Pryor . . . . Tim Stafford
Irene Cheyney . . . . Carol Rossen
Laura Pryor . . . . Jeanne Bal
Michael Pryor . . . . John Lasell
Lt. Hess . . . . David Steiner
Dr. Garber . . . . William Keene
Doug Warren . . . . James Noah

While working on the Pryor estate, Kimble is mistaken for Mr. Pryor, and is kidnapped by a man and a woman intent on holding him for $100,000 ransom. When they find out Kimble is just the gardener, they lower their demands to $25,000. Eventually, Kimble escapes.

Notes:
• This episode was the first of five which Carol Rossen appeared in. Oddly, she would never watch *The Fugitive* before appearing in the show. "I always found as an actress that it was best not to know too much about the shows you were doing," said Rossen. "So I would watch a show only once, when it first came on the air, to find out basically what it was about. But not to recall it and not to remember it and never to become familiar with any of the series' ongoing roles. So when I would hit a set and get a script, I didn't

know who these other people were and I had no preconceptions about how to deal with them. I think it helped me. It made my work fresher and more spontaneous."

EPISODE 37:
"TUG OF WAR"
(10-27-64)

Written by: Dan Ullman
Directed by: Abner Biberman

Guest Cast:
Samuel Cole . . . . Arthur O'Connell
Art Mallet . . . . Harry Townes
Morgan Fallon . . . . Don Gordon
Al . . . . John Harmon
Patty Mallet . . . . Katie Sweet

As Kimble tries to run, he is tracked into the wilderness by both the town's former sheriff, Samuel Cole, and the current sheriff, Fallon. When the men catch Kimble, they vie over who will take him in.

EPISODE 38:
"DARK CORNER"
(11-10-64)

Written by: Harry Kronman
Directed by: Jerry Hopper

Guest Cast:
Mattie Braydon . . . . Tuesday Weld
Sam Braydon . . . . Crahan Denton
Clara Braydon . . . . Elizabeth MacRae
Sheriff . . . . John McLiam
Bob Mathers . . . . Paul Carr

Kimble runs to a farm, where he encounters a blind girl, Mattie Braydon, who convinces him to stay. Mattie is devious: She's had an affair with her sister's fiancé, has attempted to murder her sister, and succeeds in killing her father. When Kimble exposes her, Mattie is arrested.

Notes:
• Tuesday Weld was known more for her work in films but she frequently showed up on television shows of the '50s and '60s. She played Thalia Menninger on *The Many Loves of Dobie Gillis* on CBS from 1959-60.

EPISODE 39:
"ESCAPE INTO BLACK"
(11-17-64)

Written by: Larry Cohen
Directed by: Jerry Hopper

Guest Cast:
Lt. Gerard . . . . Barry Morse
Lasco . . . . Bernard Kats
Margaret Ruskin . . . . . . Betty Garrett
Marty . . . . Herb Vigran
Dr. Towne . . . . Ivan Dixon
The Checker . . . . Donald Barry
One-armed man . . . . . . Bill Raisch
Dr. Bloch . . . . Tom Troupe

Kimble goes into a cafe in Decatur, Illinois, looking for the one-armed man. A fire breaks out and Kimble is injured in a stove explosion. Waking up in a hospital, Kimble has amnesia. A social worker locates the one-armed man and a doctor helps Kimble regain his memory. When the doctor tells him he can use amnesia as a murder defense, Kimble decides to turn himself in to Lieutenant Gerard, but comes to his senses just in time.

Notes:
• Betty Garrett played Irene Lorenzo on *All in the Family* on CBS from 1973–75 and landlady Edna Babish on *Laverne & Shirley* on ABC from 1976–81.
• Ivan Dixon played Corporal James Kinchloe on *Hogan's Heroes* on CBS from 1965–70.

EPISODE 40:
"THE CAGE"
(11-24-64)

Written by: Sheldon Stark
Directed by: Walter Grauman

Guest Cast:
Carla . . . . Brenda Scott
Miguel . . . . Richard Evans
Vardez . . . . Joe DeSantis
Chrisman . . . . John Kellogg
Dr. Davis . . . . Tim O'Connor

While working in a fishing village, Kimble discovers a case of bubonic plague, and the docks are quarantined. A fisherman's daughter has a doctor fixation and latches on to Kimble. When Kimble brushes her off, she turns him in to the police. Later, the girl helps Kimble escape, but insists on going with him. He refuses to let her go and resumes his flight.

EPISODE 41:
"CRY UNCLE"
(12-1-64)

Written by: Philip Saltzman
Directed by: James Goldstone

Guest Cast:
Sean . . . . Donald Losby
Miss Edmonds . . . . Brett Somers
Gus . . . . Ronny Howard
Officer Hasbro . . . . Steve Ihnat
Kathy . . . . Dianne Ramey
Josh Kovaks . . . . Edward Binns

Kimble winds up at an orphanage and becomes involved in the lives of its residents. One of the boys forces Kimble to pose as his uncle. When the boy tries to run away, Kimble risks his safety and convinces the youth to return to the school.

Notes:
Brett Somers played Blanche, ex-wife of Oscar

Madison (Jack Klugman) on *The Odd Couple* on ABC from 1971–75. At the time, Somers was married to Klugman. Somers was also a regular on *Match Game* on CBS from 1973–79.

EPISODE 42:
"DETOUR ON A ROAD GOING NOWHERE"
(12-8-64)

Teleplay by: Philip Saltzman and
William D. Gordon
Story by: Philip Saltzman
Directed by: Ralph Senensky

Guest Cast:
Louanne	Elizabeth Allen
Enid Langer	Phyllis Thaxter
Ted Langer	Lee Bowman
Jesse Platt	Walter Brooke
Sandy Baird	Don Quine
Andy	Warren Vanders
Hornbeck	Frank Marth
The Doll	Lana Wood
Bus Driver	Barry Cahill

Working at a resort, Kimble is suspected of theft and flees aboard a bus full of diverse characters: a young woman with whom Kimble has had an argument, a man suffering from a mid-life crisis, the man's jealous wife, and a thief. When the passengers find out who Kimble is, they hold him at gunpoint. As Kimble explains his innocence, he wins over the young woman and she helps him escape.

Notes:
• Elizabeth Allen was the girl who shouted, "And away we go!" on *The Jackie Gleason Show* on CBS, 1954–55, 1956–57. She also played Laura Deane on *Bracken's World* on NBC from 1969–70, Martha Simms on *The Paul Lynde Show* on ABC from 1972–73, and Captain Quinlan on *C.P.O. Sharkey* on NBC from 1976–77.
• Lee Bowman played Ellery Queen on *Ellery Queen* on ABC from 1951–52 and was a member of the panel on *Masquerade Party* on CBS in 1958.

EPISODE 43:
"THE IRON MAIDEN"
(12-15-64)

Teleplay by: Paul Lucey and Harry Kronman
Story by: Peter R. Brooke and Paul Lucey
Directed by: Walter Grauman

Guest Cast:
Lt. Gerard	Barry Morse
Susan Lait	Christine White
Congresswoman Snell	Nan Martin
Jack Glennon	Stephen McNally
Colonel Lawrence	Richard Anderson

A stuffy congresswoman arrives to inspect a missile-launching silo under construction. When a cave-in occurs, she is trapped in a shaft along with Kimble and the rest of the workers. Kimble becomes a hero when he attends to the woman's injured ankle and risks his life to help restore the air supply. As word of Kimble's heroics spread, Lieutenant Gerard arrives. With the help of his co-workers and the congresswoman, Kimble escapes.

(L to R) David Janssen with Christine White and Nan Martin in "The Iron Maiden."

Notes:
• This was a milestone episode for Richard Anderson, who played an air force colonel. "I remember after the first day's work, I got a call from the front office saying, 'good work, keep it up.' Arthur Fellows [assistant to the executive producer] came down to meet me and said they had something in mind for me. It turned out to be *Dan August*." QM Productions cast Anderson

as Police Chief George Untermeyer in *Dan August*, part of a long career playing authoritative types like military officers, policemen, and government officials.

EPISODE 44:
"DEVIL'S CARNIVAL"
(12-22-64)

Written by: William D. Gordon
Directed by: James Goldstone

Guest Cast:
Hanes McClure . . . . Warren Oates
Sue Ann . . . . Ronnie Harran
Capt. Shafter . . . . Philip Abbott
Tad . . . . Dee Pollock
Marybeth . . . . Madeleine Sherwood
Potter . . . . Woodrow Parfrey
Shirky Saulter . . . . Strother Martin

Hitchhiking, Kimble is picked up by a local criminal, Hanes McClure, who is on his way to terrorize a small town. When McClure nearly runs down a boy named Tad Thompson, Kimble jerks the car's steering wheel, preventing an accident. After the sheriff arrests McClure and Kimble, Tad helps Kimble escape and McClure is killed in a shootout.

Notes:
• Philip Abbott played agent Arthur Ward on *The FBI*, Quinn Martin's successful show, which aired on ABC from 1965–74.
• Madeleine Sherwood played Mother Superior on *The Flying Nun* on ABC from 1967–70.
• Strother Martin, a grizzled character actor, is best remembered for his role as the camp captain in *Cool Hand Luke* (1967).

EPISODE 45:
"BALLAD FOR A GHOST"
(12-29-64)

Teleplay by: George Eckstein
Story by: Sidney Ellis and George Eckstein
Directed by: Walter Grauman

Guest Cast:
Hallie . . . . Janis Paige
Davey . . . . Noam Pitlik
Johnny . . . . Mark Richman
Nora . . . . Anne Helm
Dan Morgan . . . . Paul Fix

While working in an Ohio roadhouse, Kimble becomes obsessed with nightclub singer Hallie Martin, who looks exactly like his late wife Helen. Because her friends have told her of the resemblance, Hallie has studied the Kimble case and believes in Richard's innocence. When Kimble discovers Hallie is dying of a terminal illness, the two agree to share each other's secrets.

Janis Paige guest starred as Hallie Martin in "Ballad for a Ghost."

Notes:
• Janis Paige played singer Hallie Martin, but it took quite an effort to talk executive producer Quinn Martin into using her in this episode. "Quinn didn't want her," recalled John Conwell, "and George Eckstein and I wanted her. George said, 'Come on, John, do a number on Quinn, talk him into it.' So I really had to fight to get her and then Quinn said he didn't like her. I think he was pretending not to like her because he couldn't admit that he liked her, because we wanted her so badly. She was terrific. A neat lady, very talented."

Janis Paige starred in musicals of the '40's and '50s and became a major Broadway star in *The Pajama Game* in 1954. She played Janis Stewart in *It's Always Jan* on CBS from 1955–56. She occasionally made guest appearances on TV shows like *The Fugitive* but preferred to work in musical specials. She was married for many years to songwriter Ray Gilbert and didn't increase her TV work until after his death in 1976. Then she played Kate Lanigan on *Lanigan's Rabbi* on NBC in 1977 and Catherine Hackett on *Trapper John*,

M.D. on CBS from 1985–86.

The song which Janis Paige sings, "Just One Road I Travel," was written by the episode's co-writer, George Eckstein.

EPISODE 46:
"BRASS RING"
(1-5-65)

Written by: Leonard Kantor
Directed by: Abner Biberman

Guest Cast:
Norma Sessions . . . . Angie Dickinson
Lars . . . . John Ericson
Leslie Sessions . . . . Robert Duvall
Lt. Gavin . . . . Phillip Pine
Morgan . . . . Karl Swenson

A beautiful woman, Norma Sessions, hires Kimble to work with her brother Leslie, who's been crippled in an auto accident and is confined to a wheel chair. With Kimble's help, Leslie's rehabilitation is rapid, which threatens Norma's plan to bilk Leslie out of his money. Norma's boyfriend Lars kills Leslie, and Kimble is framed for the murder. Because she's falling in love with Kimble, Norma confesses the scheme. She and Lars are arrested and Kimble is freed.

Angie Dickinson as Norma Sessions with David Janssen in "Brass Ring."

Notes:
• Angie Dickinson became a television superstar playing Sgt. Suzanne "Pepper" Anderson in *Police Woman* on NBC from 1974–78 and also played Cassie Holland on *Cassie & Company* on NBC in 1982. She has appeared in numerous films and television shows and was married to composer Burt Bacharach from 1965–1980.
• John Ericson played Sam Bolt, sidekick of private eye Honey West on *Honey West* on ABC from 1965–66.

EPISODE 47:
"THE END IS BUT THE BEGINNING"
(1-12-65)

Teleplay by: George Fass and Arthur Weiss
Story by: George Fass
Directed by: Walter Grauman

Guest Cast:
Lt. Gerard . . . . Barry Morse
Harlan . . . . Andrew Duggan
Aiemee . . . . Barbara Barrie
Sam . . . . Robert Yuro
Garlock . . . . Frank Maxwell

Driving through the mountains, Kimble picks up a hitchhiker. When a car pulls in front of Kimble's truck, he swerves and crashes over a cliff. Kimble escapes but the hitchhiker is killed and burned beyond recognition. With the help of a woman, Kimble tries to convince Lieutenant Gerard that he was killed in the accident and that the lieutenant's search is over.

Notes:
• Barbara Barrie is best known as Elizabeth Miller, wife of Barney Miller, on ABC's *Barney Miller* from 1975–76. She also played the sensitive mother, Evelyn Stohler, in the film and TV versions of *Breaking Away*.
• Andrew Duggan, a leading man of the '50s and '60s, played Cal Calhoun on *Bourbon Street Beat* on ABC from 1959–60 and rancher Murdoch Lancer on *Lancer* on CBS from 1968–71.

EPISODE 48:
"NICEST FELLA YOU'D EVER WANT TO MEET"
(1-19-65)

Written by: Jack Turley
Directed by: Sutton Roley

Guest Cast:
Marshal Joe Bob Simms . Pat Hingle
Thelma . . . . Mary Murphy
Floyd . . . . Dabney Coleman
Mr. Hollister . . . . Curt Conway

Neely Hollister . . . . Tom Skerritt
Charley . . . . Burt Mustin
Mayor Duncan . . . . Dabbs Greer

Arrested for hitchhiking, Kimble is thrown into a cell with Neely Hollister, a young man who hates the marshal, Joe Bob Simms. Later, Kimble sees the marshal kill Hollister. Although Simms maintains the death was accidental, the coroner schedules a hearing. Fearing Kimble's testimony, Simms tries to run him out of town. Before he goes, Kimble tells Hollister's family that Simms killed Neely. As the marshal tries to murder Kimble, Simms', deputy, Floyd, comes to the rescue. In a shootout, Simms is killed and Kimble escapes.

Tom Skerritt as Neely Hollister in "Nicest Fella You'd Ever Want to Meet."

Notes:
• Tom Skerritt has enjoyed a long television and film career. He played Dr. Thomas Ryan in *Ryan's Four* on ABC in 1983 and is currently enjoying TV stardom on ABC's *Picket Fences.*

EPISODE 49:
"FUN AND GAMES AND PARTY FAVORS"
(1-26-65)

Written by: Arthur Weiss
Directed by: Abner Biberman

Guest Cast:
Dan Holt . . . . Mark Goddard
Phil Andrews . . . . Anthony Call
Joanne Craig . . . . Katherine Crawford
Charles Craig . . . . Tom Palmer
Maude Craig . . . . Joan Tompkins
Buzzy . . . . Peter E. Deuel

When a domineering mother tries to force her daughter into a relationship with a society blue blood, the girl decides to elope with someone else, and Kimble becomes a marriage counselor. Kimble also chaperons the girl's party but finds a party crasher is a crime buff who knows who he is.

Katherine Crawford as Joanne Craig in "Fun and Games and Party Favors."

Notes:
• Katherine Crawford is the daughter of *The Fugitive*'s creator Roy Huggins. Using her grandmother's name, she acted in many television shows of that era. Because Huggins didn't watch the show, he didn't learn of his daughter's appearance until years later. "It was so unimportant, she didn't even tell me," said Huggins, "and I still see my daughter every week. She could have mentioned it at the time, but I probably said, 'Oh yeah . . . great.' "
• Peter Deuel launched his career in shows like *Combat, Twelve O'Clock High,* and *The Big Valley.* He played Hannibal Heyes in *Alias Smith and Jones* on ABC in 1971. Then, on December 31, 1971, Deuel, age thirty-one, was found shot to death in his Hollywood Hills home, an apparent suicide.

EPISODE 50:
"SCAPEGOAT"
(2-2-65)

Teleplay by: William D. Gordon
Story by: Larry Cohen
Directed by: Alexander Singer

Guest Cast:

Janice Cummings	Dianne Foster
Roy Briggs	David Macklin
Justin Briggs	John Anderson
Vin Briggs	Don Quine
Gibson	Whit Bissell

Kimble learns that an innocent man has been convicted of murder and the victim is supposedly Kimble. Returning to a small town where he once worked, Kimble tries to save the accused man, but he's too late. The man was killed trying to escape. The man's two sons are bitter and one of them tries to kill Kimble and the woman whose testimony helped convict his father.

EPISODE 51:
"CORNER OF HELL"
(2-9-65)

Teleplay by: Jo Heims and
Francis Irby Gwaltney
Story by: Jo Heims and Zahrini Machadah
Directed by: Robert Butler

Guest Cast:

Lt. Gerard	Barry Morse
Elvie	Sharon Farrell
Tully	R. G. Armstrong
Kyle	Sandy Kenyon
Cody	Bruce Dern
Sheriff	Dabbs Greer
Roy	Edward Faulkner

Lieutenant Gerard chases Kimble into an area inhabited by moonshiners. When Kimble aids an injured man, the moonshiners call him "Doc" and protect him. When Gerard arrives and is wrongly accused of attacking a girl, he is put on trial, and is forced to ask Kimble for help. Kimble uncovers the truth and both he and Gerard are freed.

EPISODE 52:
"MOON CHILD"
(2-16-65)
Written by: Dan Ullman
Directed by: Alexander Singer

Guest Cast:

Joanne	June Harding
Alma	Virginia Christine
Starling	Murray Hamilton
Johnny	Burt Douglas
Sheriff Mack	David Sheiner

Being pursued by a sheriff and vigilantes who think he's been killing women in the area, Kimble encounters a special young girl who hides him. When the real killer attacks the girl, Kimble rescues her. The sheriff shoots the killer and Kimble escapes.

Notes:
• Murray Hamilton played Steve Baker on *Love & Marriage* on NBC from 1959-60, Colonel Jack Forbes on *The Man Who Never Was* on ABC from 1966-67, Rutherford T. Grant on *B.J. and the Bear* on NBC from 1979-81, and General Sam Cotton on *Hail to the Chief* on ABC in 1985.
• June Harding was a regular on *The Richard Boone Show* on NBC from 1963-64 and played Ann on *Matt Lincoln* on ABC from 1970-71.

EPISODE 53:
"THE SURVIVORS"
(3-2-65)

Written by: George Eckstein
Directed by: Don Medford

Guest Cast:

Terry Waverly	Louise Sorel
Ed Waverly	Lloyd Gough
Edith Waverly	Ruth White
Phil Corbin	Burt Metcalfe

When Kimble discovers that his late wife's family is having financial problems, he returns to Indiana to help. There, he finds a mother-in-law who hates him and a sister-in-law who loves him. He attempts to straighten out the family's problems before resuming his flight.

EPISODE 54:
"EVERYBODY GETS HIT IN THE MOUTH SOMETIMES"
(3-9-65)

Written by: Jack Turley
Directed by: Alexander Singer

Guest Cast:

Hendricks	Jack Klugman
Jimmy	Jimmy Stiles
Lucia	Geraldine Brooks
Ernie	Michael Constantine
Logan	G. B. Atwater
Lucy	Tracy Stratford

Working as a trucking company dispatcher,

Kimble becomes involved with the owner and a devious woman who's trying to squeeze money out of him. Desperate to pay her off, the man agrees to cooperate in a truck hijacking. Kimble tries to save his boss but is too late. The man is killed in a truck accident and the woman winds up empty-handed.

Notes:
• Michael Constantine won an Emmy playing principal Seymour Kaufman on *Room 2220* on ABC from 1969–74 and played Matthew J. Sirota on *Sirota's Court* on NBC from 1976–77.

EPISODE 55:
"MAY GOD HAVE MERCY"
(3-16-65)

Written by: Don Brinkley
Directed by: Don Medford

Guest Cast:

Lt. Gerard	Barry Morse
Gloria	Abigail Shelton
Victor Leonetti	Telly Savalas
Lt. Germak	Norman Fell
Anne Leonetti	Carol Rossen
Toby Weems	Jud Taylor
Nurse Oberhansly	Mary Jackson
Nurse Stockwell	Maggie Pierce

Kimble comes face-to-face with Anne and Victor Leonetti, an Indiana couple whose daughter was once Dr. Kimble's patient. Blaming him for their daughter's death, Leonetti turns Kimble in to the police. When Leonetti realizes his error, he tries to take Kimble's place, confessing to the murder of Helen Kimble.

Notes:
• Carol Rossen remembers a scene in which Telly Savalas was supposed to slap her: "Telly's a very macho guy and all, but one of the things that was not part of his ethnic background was beating up girls. He was just starting out as an actor and he didn't know how to hit somebody without hurting them. I said, 'Telly, you don't have to hit me in the face, you can hit me on the neck and it will look like the face,' but it took a good deal of twisting Telly's arm to get him to beat me up. But I finally won and the scene went very well."
• Norman Fell played Stanley Roper on *Three's Company* on ABC from 1977–79 and on the spinoff *The Ropers* on ABC from 1979–80.

EPISODE 56:
"MASQUERADE"
(3-23-65)

Written by: Philip Saltzman
Directed by: Abner Biberman

Guest Cast:

Leonard Hull	John Milford
Pinto	H. M. Wynant
Mrs. Hull	Norma Crane
Jenkins	Rayford Barnes
Sheriff Mayhew	Edward Asner
Grub	Wayne Heffley

Thinking that Kimble is Leonard Hull, a witness who has returned to town to testify against his former boss, the police take the fugitive into protective custody. When Kimble meets Mrs. Hull, the witness' wife, she plays along with the ruse. Fearing for her life, Mrs. Hull asks for Kimble's help as a killer stalks them both.

EPISODE 57:
"RUNNER IN THE DARK"
(3-30-65)

Written by: Robert Guy Barrows
Directed by: Alexander Singer

Guest Cast:

Dan Brady	Ed Begley
Mrs. Ferguson	Nellie Burt
Mayor Penfield	Vaughn Taylor
Vilattic	Richard Anderson
Claire Whittaker	Diana Van Der Vlis
Sterne	Peter Haskell

With the police chasing him, Kimble seeks refuge in a home for the blind. One of the home's residents is Dan Brady, the town's former police chief, who has been put out to pasture. Brady resents his successor, Chief Vilattic, and sees Kimble as a prized trophy that will help him regain his lost stature.

EPISODE 58:
"A.P.B."
(4-6-65)

Written by: Dan Ullman
Directed by: William D. Gordon

Guest Cast:

Pinkerton	Paul Richards
Smiley	Jim Nusser
Mooney	Lou Antonio
Mona	Shirley Knight
Mrs. Ross	Virginia Gregg
Lt. Peterson	Fred Beir

Kimble hops a freight train but discovers three other passengers aboard, one of them dead. The men have escaped from prison, and the two live ones, Neil Pinkerton and Matt Mooney, take Kimble with them. When the fugitives hide in a nearby house, the residents, Mrs. Ross and her daughter Mona, treat them like celebrities.

EPISODE 59:
"THE OLD MAN PICKED A LEMON"
(4-13-65)

Written by: Jack Turley
Directed by: Alexander Singer

Guest Cast:

Flo	Celeste Holm
Lisa	Jean Hale
Blaine Hagerman	Ben Piazza
Lois	Jan Shutan
Carlos	Rico Alaniz
Leland	Byron Morrow

When Lee Hagerman, the beloved owner of a lemon orchard, dies, he asks Kimble to take care of his arrogant son Blaine. The migrant workers hate Blaine, feeling he killed a Mexican girl whom he'd gotten pregnant. Kimble becomes involved in a bitter dispute between Blaine and his mother, which ends in Blaine's death and Kimble's escape.

Notes:
• Celeste Holm hit it big in the original Broadway production of *Oklahoma* in 1943. She played Celeste Anders in *Honestly Celeste* on CBS in 1954, Abigail Townsend on *Nancy* on NBC from 1970-71, and Anna Rossini on *Falcon Crest* on CBS in 1985. In 1982 President Reagan named her to a six-year term as a member of the National Arts Council.

EPISODE 60:
"LAST SECOND OF A BIG DREAM"
(4-20-65)

Teleplay by: George Eckstein
Story by: John Eastman
Directed by: Robert Butler

Guest Cast:

Lt. Gerard	Barry Morse
Sheriff Ralls	Robert Karnes
Harry Craft	Steve Forrest
Al	Marlowe Jensen
Alan Fielding	Laurence Naismith
Bert	James Sikking
Lou Cartwright	Milton Selzer

Kimble is working for a wild animal circus on the verge of bankruptcy. When Lieutenant Gerard arrives looking for Kimble, the circus' owner sees Kimble as the attraction that can save his business. Although a prized tiger is killed, Kimble manages to get away.

Notes:
• "We used to receive scripts from little old ladies in Kentucky and people who were working in a grocery store in Nebraska," said *The Fugitive*'s producer, Alan Armer. "One show, 'Last Second of a Big Dream,' came from a guy, John Eastman, who worked for an advertising agency in Michigan. We had him come out, we liked the idea, did some rewrites, and that was one of the few shows that came from the outside."
• This episode was filmed in part at Jungleland, an animal park in Thousand Oaks, California.
• Steve Forrest played SWAT commander Lt. Dan "Hondo" Harrelson on *SWAT* on ABC from 1975-76 and Wes Parmalee on *Dallas* on CBS in 1986.

Third Season

EPISODE 61:
"WINGS OF AN ANGEL"
(9-14-65)

Teleplay by: Don Brinkley
Story by: Don Brinkley and Otto King
Directed by: William A. Graham

Guest Cast:

Warden Maddox . . . . Lin McCarthy
Janet . . . . Lane Bradbury
Mickey Deming . . . . Greg Morris
Troy . . . . Ned Glass
Dr. Willis . . . . Harold Gould
Kulik . . . . Val Avery
Mrs. Thompson . . . . Sue Randall

When an escaped convict attempts to kill a young woman, Kimble comes to the rescue but is stabbed. Taken to a nearby prison hospital, Kimble is recognized by an inmate, who threatens to turn him in unless he helps steal morphine from the prison hospital. When an innocent hospital attendant is arrested, Kimble risks his safety to clear the man.

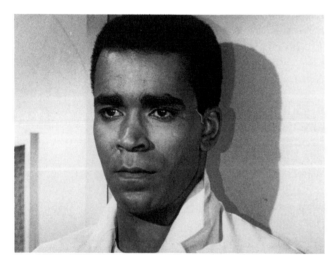

Greg Morris as Mickey Deming in "Wings of an Angel."

Notes:
• Greg Morris rose to stardom as Barney Collier on *Mission: Impossible* on CBS from 1966–73. He also played Lt. David Nelson on *Vega$* on ABC from 1979–81.
• Harold Gould played Martin Morgenstern on

Rhoda on CBS from 1974–78 and made numerous guest appearances on television shows. He also appeared in several movies including *Love and Death* (1975) and *Birch Street Gym* (1991).

EPISODE 62:
"MIDDLE OF THE HEAT WAVE"
(9-21-65)

Written by: Robert Hamner
Directed by: Alexander Singer

Guest Cast:

Laurel . . . . Carol Rossen
Officer Collison . . . . J. D. Cannon
Sheila . . . . Sarah Marshall
Frank . . . . John Lassello
Doctor . . . . James Doohan

When a young woman is attacked, Kimble is arrested and jailed. The attacker was actually the girl's brother-in-law, but she's had an emotional blackout and is unable to clear Kimble. Finally, she admits to having encouraged the assault, and Kimble is freed.

Notes:
• Carol Rossen loved to work on *The Fugitive* because she enjoyed her relationship with David Janssen. "David was really a wonderful human being and a wonderful actor. He was committed

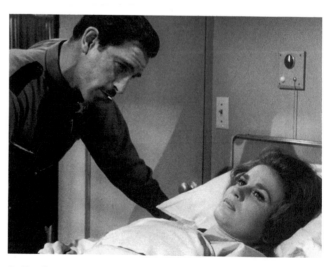

J. D. Cannon as Officer Collison with Carol Rossen as Laurel in "Middle of the Heat Wave."

to the work and he never gave me any trouble about rehearsing. Often when you worked with series' leads, at least fifty percent of the time, you couldn't get them to rehearse with you. But David was always there for me and I really loved him. I loved him as a person too and he loved me. We were good friends and we had respect for each other and for the work. It was a very sweet relationship. It was a fun set."

• J. D. Cannon spent many lean years in the '50s and '60s working the New York stage and appearing in television shows like *The Fugitive, The Defenders,* and *Profiles in Courage.* He finally found financial security playing Peter B. Clifford, McCloud's boss, on *McCloud* on NBC from 1970–77.

EPISODE 63:
"CRACK IN A CRYSTAL BALL"
(9-28-65)

Written by: William Link and Richard Levinson
Directed by: Walter Grauman

Guest Cast:
Sal Mitchell . . . . Larry Blyden
Wilcox . . . . Walter Brooke
Mrs. Mitchell . . . . Joanna Moore
Mr. McBride . . . . J. Pat O'Malley
Lt. Bliss . . . . Frank Maxwell
Mrs. Daniels . . . . Nellie Burt

Nightclub psychic Sal Mitchell spots Kimble and decides he wants to use his act to turn the fugitive over to the police. When the psychic tells the police Kimble is in a park, they close in, but Kimble miraculously escapes.

Notes:
• Larry Blyden did a little of everything on television in the '50s, '60s, and '70s. He played Joe Sparton on *Joe and Mabel* on CBS in 1956, Harry Burns on *Harry's Girls* on NBC from 1963–64, and was a game show host on *Personality, You're Putting Me On, The Movie Game,* and *What's My Line.* On the stage, he was three times nominated for a Tony Award, winning in 1972 for *A Funny Thing Happened on the Way to the Forum.*

EPISODE 64:
"TRIAL BY FIRE"
(10–5–65)

Written by: Philip Saltzman
Directed by: Alexander Singer

Guest Cast:
Lt. Gerard . . . . Barry Morse
Donna . . . . Jacqueline Scott
Capt. Eckhardt . . . . Charles Aidman
Burton Green . . . . Frank Aletter
J.J. . . . . Tommy Rettig
Marian Eckhardt . . . . . . Marion Ross
Sgt. Rainey . . . . Ed Deemer

During a telephone conversation with his sister Donna, Kimble learns there was a witness the night his wife was murdered. An army man, Captain Eckhardt, saw a one-armed man running from the Kimbles' house and is willing to testify. As Kimble prepares to turn himself in, the witness is discredited, and Kimble is forced to run.

Notes:
• Tommy Rettig is best known as Jeff Miller on *Lassie* on CBS from 1954–57. During the '60s he appeared on a number of shows like *The Fugitive, Lawman,* and *Mr. Novak.*

EPISODE 65:
"CONSPIRACY OF SILENCE"
(10-12-65)

Written by: William D. Gordon
Directed by: Jerry Hopper

Guest Cast:
David Jones . . . . Malachi Throne
Avery . . . . Bill Gunn
Pickett . . . . Robert Cornthwaite
Murchison . . . . Mort Mills
Berger . . . . Dick Wilson
Price . . . . Wesley Addy

Kimble is working in an Arizona resort when government officials arrive to test a top secret chemical. When a disaster occurs, Kimble is caught in the middle.

EPISODE 66:
"THREE CHEERS FOR LITTLE BOY BLUE"
(10-19-65)

Teleplay by: Chester Krumholz and
Harry Kronman
Story by: Chester Krumholz
Directed by: Walter Grauman

Guest Cast:
George Forster . . . . Richard Anderson
Arvin Keel . . . . Vaughn Taylor
Roy Malinek . . . . Edward Asner
Nora Keel . . . . Fay Spain
Willoughby . . . . Milton Selzer

Employed as a chauffeur, Kimble drives successful industrialist George Forster to his homecoming. Some of Forster's old classmates resent his success, an old girlfriend laments her lost love, and an old high school friend wants to kill him.

Richard Anderson and Edward Asner in "Three Cheers for Little Boy Blue."

Notes:
•It was déjà vu for Richard Anderson when he attended a class reunion in 1993. "I was student body president. I saw a lot of my old friends and my old high school coach. We had a good experience but I couldn't help notice a long look or someone saying, 'He's still the same weight.' It brought 'Three Cheers for Little Boy Blue' to mind."
•Ed Asner played Roy Malinek, a former high school football star who limped from a knee injury resulting from George Forster's negligence. Malinek blamed Forster for costing him a pro football career and when Forster returned home,

Malinek tried to kill him. "I felt that Richard Anderson was always too pretty," recalled Asner, "so the thought of putting a bullet in him was delectable to me. Malinek's limp took a lot of concentration and energy and was a pain in the ass. Most of my roles on *The Fugitive* didn't thrill me. The football player was one of the few good ones. I enjoyed working with Walter Grauman [director]. He's a delightful son of a bitch. He's up and he's totally approachable and I did some of my best work for Walter."

EPISODE 67:
"ALL THE SCARED RABBITS"
(10-26-65)

Teleplay by: William Bast and Norman Lessing
Story by: William Bast
Directed by: Robert Butler

Guest Cast:
Peggy Franklin . . . . Suzanne Pleshette
Ann . . . . Nancy Rennick
Nancy . . . . Debi Storm
Mrs. White . . . . Meg Wyllie
Dean . . . . Liam Sullivan
Mona . . . . Susan Davis
Matt . . . . R. G. Armstrong

Peggy Franklin, a recently divorced woman, hires Kimble to help her drive from Iowa to California. They pick up her daughter, who steals a rabbit from a laboratory where her father is working. The rabbit is carrying a deadly form of meningitis and the girl becomes ill. Kimble is forced to result to desperate measures to save her.

Notes:
•"I recently saw 'All the Scared Rabbits,' " said Suzanne Pleshette, "and I thought it was damned good. It holds up well. Usually when I see material with that kind of age on it, it seems dated. The styles of acting and writing are more modern, and I thought that episode was intelligent and very well done."

EPISODE 68:
"AN APPLE A DAY"
(11-2-65)

Written by: Dan Ullman
Directed by: Ralph Senensky

Guest Cast:

Josephus Adams	Arthur O'Connell
Sheriff	Gene Dardler
Marianne Adams	Sheree North
Dr. Olney	Bill Quinn
Sharon	Kim Darby
Mrs. Crandall	Amzie Stickland
Dr. Olney	Bill Quinn

Kimble is injured and is taken to a quack doctor who believes in honey and herbs rather than X rays and drugs. When the doctor's niece is injured and lapses into a coma, Kimble spirits her away for more conventional medical treatment.

Notes:

• Arthur O'Connell played Mr. Hansen on *Mr. Peepers* on NBC from 1953-54 and Edwin Carpenter on *The Second Hundred Years* on ABC from 1967-68.

• Kim Darby played Virginia Calderwood on *Rich Man, Poor Man, Book I* on ABC from 1976-77 and Ann Rowan on T*he Last Convertible* on NBC in 1981.

• Sheree North, a former '50s film actress, wound up on television playing Honey Smith on *Big Eddie* on CBS in 1975, Edie McKendrick on *I'm a Big Girl Now* on ABC from 1980-81, and Lynn Holtz on *The Bay City Blues* on NBC in 1983. She also played Marilyn Monroe's mother in the TV movie *Marilyn: The Untold Story* in 1980.

EPISODE 69:
"LANDSCAPE WITH RUNNING FIGURES"
PART ONE (11-16-65)

Written by: Anthony Wilson
Directed by: Walter Grauman

Guest Cast:

Lt. Gerard	Barry Morse
Sergeant	William Zuckert
Marie Gerard	Barbara Rush
Luis Bota	Rodolfo Hoyos
Capt. Ames	Herschel Bernardi

Gerard's wife has had enough of her husband's obsession with Richard Kimble. But when she tries to leave town, she unknowingly winds up on the same bus with Kimble. After she's blinded in an accident, Mrs. Gerard is forced to rely on Kimble for help.

Notes:

• " 'Landscape with Running Figures,' was one of

Barbara Rush as Marie Gerard with David Janssen in "Landscape with Running Figures."

my favorite scripts," said producer Alan Armer, "but I thought the show should have been much better. I had the concept of: would it ever be possible to bring Kimble into some kind of relationship with Gerard's wife? When Tony Wilson came in to see me about writing a *Fugitive* script, I threw that thought at him. He came back in two days with essentially the story that is the two-parter. I said, 'Tony, that's marvelous, let's do it.' About three weeks later, Tony came back with a marvelous script but it was something like eighty-seven pages and we'd been shooting scripts that were fifty-three or fifty-four pages long. I said, 'Quinn [Martin], what are we going to do? We could knock the script down, but it's so good. I hate to do that.' And Quinn said, 'Let's make it a two-parter.' David [Janssen] was always good-naturedly grousing to us that we never put beautiful women in his shows, that we always gave him actresses with Coke-bottle glasses. So Quinn said, 'All right, David, you pick the actress to play Mrs. Gerard.' So Barbara Rush was totally David's choice. The director, Walter Grauman, who is one of my close personal friends, let her cry all the way through the goddamned thing. It just ruined the character. This was not a cry-baby, wimpy woman. And I just felt that her concept, the concept that she and Walter worked out for Gerard's wife, was faulty and bad. I just felt they really blew it on the character of Mrs. Gerard.

• Herschel Bernardi played Lt. Jacoby on *Peter Gunn* on NBC from 1958-60 and Arnie Nuvo on *Arnie* on CBS from 1970-72. He also starred on Broadway in *Fiddler on the Roof* and voiced commercials as Charlie the Tuna and the Jolly Green Giant.

• William Zuckert played General Cross on *The Wackiest Ship in the Army* on NBC from 1965–66 and Chief Sagal on *Captain Nice* on NBC in 1967.

EPISODE 70:
"LANDSCAPE WITH RUNNING FIGURES"
PART TWO (11-23-65)

Written by: Anthony Wilson
Directed by: Walter Grauman

Guest Cast:

Lt. Gerard	Barry Morse
Tommy	Robert Doyle
Marie Gerard	Barbara Rush
Rainey	Jud Taylor
Capt. Ames	Herschel Bernardi
Joanie	Judith Morton
Jarvis	John Clarke
Beavo	Robert Biheller

As Kimble drives Mrs. Gerard to a hospital, they are terrorized by juvenile delinquents and forced to hide in an abandoned town. Blinded and scared, Mrs. Gerard asks Kimble probing questions about his life, and eventually realizes who he is. With Lieutenant Gerard on the way, she frantically tries to keep Kimble there. When Mrs. Gerard is taken away in an ambulance, Kimble magically escapes, and Gerard's obsession continues.

EPISODE 71:
"SET FIRE TO A STRAW MAN"
(11-30-65)

Written by: Jack Turley
Directed by: Don Medford

Guest Cast:

Stella	Diana Hyland
Mickey	Barbara Baldavin
George	Edward Binns
Ginny	Shelley Morrison
Jesse	Joseph Campanella
Max	Lewis Charles
Johnny	Clint Howard

Despite the warnings of his boss, George Savano, Kimble becomes involved with Savano's disturbed sister Stella. Stella and Jesse Stansel have had an affair which produced an illegitimate child

named Johnny, who lives with his father. Stella wants to abduct her son and enlists Kimble's help, jeopardizing his safety.

EPISODE 72:
"STRANGER IN THE MIRROR"
(12-7-65)

Written by: Don Brinkley
Directed by: Joseph Sargent

Guest Cast:

Tony Burrell	William Shatner
Berger	Jeff Burton
Carole Burrell	Julie Sommars
Sgt. McKay	Paul Bryar
Lt. Green	Norman Fell
Benny Bycek	Tony Face

Kimble takes a job at a youth center run by former policeman Tony Burrell and his wife Carole. Burrell was discharged from the police force because of psychological problems. When three policemen are murdered, Kimble becomes a suspect, but the real killer is Burrell. When Burrell is cornered, he confesses to the murders, but panics and begins shooting. Carole is forced to kill him.

Notes:
• William Shatner starred as Captain Kirk on *Star Trek* on NBC from 1966–69 and 1973–75 and as T. J. Hooker on ABC from 1982–85. Barry Morse gave Shatner his first job in the Canadian theater in the early '50s.
• Julie Sommars played J. J. Drinkwater on *The Governor & J.J.* on CBS from 1969–72 and Julie March on *Matlock* on NBC from 1987–92.

EPISODE 73:
"THE GOOD GUYS AND THE BAD GUYS"
(12-14-65)

Written by: Don Brinkley
Directed by: Alexander Singer

Guest Cast:

Lt. Gerard	Barry Morse
Laura	Collin Wilcox
Sheriff Judd	Earl Holliman
Roy	Michael Witney
Hank	Bruce Dern
Wally	Erik Holland

In Drover City, Montana, the annual "Vigilante Roundup" is in full swing. Anyone not wearing western garb is "arrested." An unsuspecting Kimble is not properly attired and is pinched. As Lieutenant Gerard arrives, the town marshal figures there must be a reward for Kimble. He decides to hide Kimble until Gerard leaves and then collect the reward himself.

Notes:
• Earl Holliman is best known as Lieutenant Bill Crowley, Angie Dickinson's sidekick, on *Police Woman* on NBC from 1974–78.

EPISODE 74:
"END OF THE LINE"
(12-21-65)

Written by: James Menzies
Directed by: William A. Graham

Guest Cast:

Betty Jo	Barbara Dana
R. T. Unger	Crahan Denton
Neil	Andrew Prine
Glen	Richard Roat
Kress	Len Wayland
Edward Hee	James Hong
Sammy	James McCallion

Penniless, Kimble steals a man's wallet to buy a train ticket. Attempting to pay back the money, Kimble follows the man, whom he learns is R. T. Unger, who is bringing his pregnant, unmarried daughter Betty Jo, back to town. Betty Jo's boyfriend, Neil Hollis, is being paroled, and Unger wants to pay him off and get rid of him. When Unger and Neil end up in an argument, Neil kills the older man but Kimble is arrested. After exposing the real murderer, Kimble escapes.

EPISODE 75:
"WHEN THE WIND BLOWS"
(12-28-65)

Written by: Betty Langdon
Directed by: Ralph Senensky

Guest Cast:

Lois Carter	Georgann Johnson
Jake Wilkins	Don Hanmer
Steve Jackson	Larry Ward
Russ Atkins	Harry Townes
Kenny Carter	Johnny Jensen

In Wyoming, Kimble takes a job helping Lois Carter run a motel. Her son Kenny has been labeled "a problem child," but Kimble befriends the boy and convinces Mrs. Carter there is nothing wrong with her son. When the police spot Kimble, he runs and Kenny hides in his truck. When Kimble discovers the youngster, he convinces him to return home, and the fugitive continues to run.

EPISODE 76:
"NOT WITHOUT A WHIMPER"
(1-4-66)

Written by: Norman Lessing
Directed by: Alexander Singer

Guest Cast:

McAllister	Laurence Naismith
Teacher	Marcelle Hebert
Willis	Lee Meriwether
Joey	Jimmy Stiles
Lieutenant	Jack Dodson
Joey's mother	Jane Barclay

Kimble returns to visit his old mentor, Dr. McAllister, an anti-smog crusader who is dying of heart problems. Before he goes, McAllister wants to land "one more knockout punch," and plants a bomb in a factory. When a fifth-grade class visits the factory, Kimble comes to the rescue.

Lee Meriwether as Willis with David Janssen in "Not Without a Whimper."

Notes:
• Lee Meriwether, Miss America of 1955, is best known as Betty Jones on *Barnaby Jones* on CBS from 1973–78.

EPISODE 77:
"WIFE KILLER"
(1-11-66)

Written by: Dan Ullman
Directed by: Richard Donner

Guest Cast:
Lt. Gerard . . . . Barry Morse
Chief Blaney . . . . Stephen Roberts
Barbara Webb . . . . Janice Rule
Herb Malone . . . . Kevin McCarthy
Fred Johnson . . . . Bill Raisch
Ed Warren . . . . Lloyd Haynes

When the one-armed man, Fred Johnson, is arrested, both Kimble and Lieutenant Gerard head to the scene. Johnson escapes but is injured in an auto accident. Kimble and a reporter, Barbara Webb, take Johnson to a nearby girls' camp, where he confesses to the murder of Helen Kimble but passes out before he can sign the confession. Badly needing a story, Webb forges Johnson's signature, but Kimble knows the confession is now useless. Although Webb tells Gerard the one-armed man confessed, the lieutenant says Johnson is guilty only of car theft.

Notes:
• Kevin McCarthy has been in show business since 1938, playing mostly shady authoritarian figures like Claude Weldon on *Flamingo Road* on NBC from 1981–82. He is the brother of writer Mary McCarthy.

EPISODE 78:
"THIS'LL KILL YOU"
(1-18-66)

Written by: George Eckstein
Directed by: Alex March

Guest Cast:
Charlie . . . . Mickey Rooney
Sgt. Thorpe . . . . George Tyne
Paula . . . . Nita Talbot
Mrs. Belson . . . . Joan Allen
Pete . . . . Phillip Pine
Harrison . . . . Henry Scott

Kimble gets involved with Charlie Paris, a night-club comic turned bookmaker. Paris is trying to patch things up with his old girlfriend, Paula Jellison, who sells him out to the mob. When Paula tells Charlie that Kimble hit on her, he calls the police. After discovering that Paula is lying, Charlie tries to save Kimble but is gunned down by a hit man.

Notes:
• Mickey Rooney has been working since he began in his parents' vaudeville act in the 1920s. He has starred in all aspects of show business and won an Emmy for *Bill* on CBS in 1981.

EPISODE 79:
"ECHO OF A NIGHTMARE
(1-25-66)

Teleplay by: John Kneubuhl
Story by: Robert Lewin
Directed by: James Sheldon

Guest Cast:
Jane Washburn . . . . Shirley Knight
Lt. Wynn . . . . Ford Rainey
Wes . . . . Dennis Joel
Jackson . . . . Arch Johnson
Harry . . . . Harry Millard
Perry . . . . Kevin O'Neal
Wes's Dad . . . . John Lasell

David Janssen with Shelley Knight as Jane Washburn in "Echo of a Nightmare."

When Kimble is beaten up and robbed, a policewoman takes an interest in him. Suspecting he's wanted, she handcuffs herself to Kimble, who drags her with him in his escape. During their flight, the woman reveals deep psychological scars resulting from a childhood kidnapping. Both she and Kimble are chained to their pasts. When Kimble's life is jeopardized, she rescues him.

EPISODE 80:
"STROKE OF GENIUS"
(2-1-66)

Written by: John Kneubuhl
Directed by: Robert Butler

Guest Cast:

Lt. Gerard . . . . Barry Morse
Sheriff Bilson . . . . Malcolm Atterbury
Gary Keller . . . . Beau Bridges
Mrs. Barlow . . . . Ellen Corby
Steve Keller . . . . Telly Savalas

While playing with a rifle, a teenage boy, Gary Keller, accidentally kills Reverend Barlow, who was driving a car in which Richard Kimble was riding. Although Gary wants to confess to the crime, his father won't let him, knowing it will jeopardize his son's bright future. Knowing that Kimble has witnessed the shooting, Keller warns him not to implicate Gary. Then, wracked by guilt, Gary confesses and Keller helps Kimble escape.

Notes:
• "I had been casting director on *The Untouchables*," recalled associate producer George Eckstein, "and I remember not being able to sell them on Telly Savalas. I had been a major fan of his off a show he'd done in New York called *Trial*. We tried for two years to sell him to the 'powers that be' on *The Untouchables*, so I was delighted whenever we were able to use him on *The Fugitive*."
• Beau Bridges, son of Lloyd Bridges, appeared in his father's TV shows *(Sea Hunt, The Lloyd Bridges Show, The Loner)* when he was in his teens. He eventually appeared as Seaman Howard

Spicer in *Ensign O'Toole* on NBC from 1962–63 and Richard Chapin on *United States* on NBC in 1989. Beau's main success, like that of his brother Jeff, has been in movies. The two teamed up in *The Fabulous Baker Boys* in 1989.
• "I loved Beau Bridges," recalled John Conwell. "Both he and Jeff worked for me. Jeff and my son went to school together. They were professional, wonderful, terrific people. That's a terrific family, they're not the typical Hollywood family. Those boys were brought up great."

EPISODE 81:
"SHADOW OF THE SWAN"
(2-8-66)

Written by: Anthony Lawrence
Directed by: James Sheldon

Guest Cast:

Tina . . . . Joanna Pettet
Mrs. Carny . . . . Carole Kane
Harry Anderson . . . . Andrew Duggan
Carny . . . . Don Quine
Dr. Motter . . . . Monroe Arnold
Jacobs . . . . David Sheiner

At a carnival, Kimble meets a young woman, Tina Anderson, who becomes obsessed with him. Tina takes him home to meet her uncle Harry, a retired policeman who recognizes Kimble and tries to arrest him. When Tina tries to run away with Kimble, he brushes her off. In anger, she starts a fire, and when her uncle tries to arrest her, she's accidentally killed.

EPISODE 82:
"RUNNING SCARED"
(2-22-66)

Written by: Don Brinkley
Directed by: James Sheldon

Guest Cast:

Lt. Gerard . . . . Barry Morse
Penny . . . . Wright King
Donna . . . . Jacqueline Scott
Leonard Taft . . . . Lin McCarthy
Ballinger . . . . James Daly
Sgt. Burns . . . . Frank Maxwell

After learning that his father has died, Richard Kimble risks his life to see his sister Donna in his old hometown. When he becomes aware that

Lieutenant Gerard will stake out her house, Kimble plans to meet Donna elsewhere. However, the wife of an ambitious politician spots them and alerts Lieutenant Gerard.

Notes:
• James Daly played Michael Powers on *Foreign Intrigue* on NBC in 1953 and Dr. Paul Lochner on *Medical Center* on CBS from 1969–76. He won an Emmy for Best Supporting Actor in a Drama for *The Hallmark Hall of Fame* production "Eagle in a Cage" in 1966.

EPISODE 83:
"THE CHINESE SUNSET"
(3-1-66)

Written by: Leonard Kantor
Directed by: James Sheldon

Guest Cast:
Penelope Dufour ...... Laura Devon
Orin .... Sheldon Allman
Eddie Slade .... Paul Richards
Rita .... Mary Gregory
Frankie .... Sandra Warner
Mrs. Ball .... Connie Sawyer
Woody .... Melville Ruick
Bragin .... Wanye Rogers
Buddy .... Karl Held
Sam .... Ned Glass

Penelope Dufour, a beautiful but naive blonde, and her hoodlum boyfriend Eddie Slade check in at the Chinese Sunset Motel, where Kimble is a bellman. As Kimble improves Penelope's speech and manners, Slade becomes jealous. When Slade tries to swindle the other motel guests, Penelope puts Kimble's lessons to use in exposing the scam.

Notes:
• Wayne Rogers played Trapper John on *M*A*S*H* on CBS from 1972–75 and Dr. Charley Michaels on *House Calls* on CBS from 1979–82.

EPISODE 84:
"ILL WIND"
(3-8-66)

Written by: Al C. Ward
Directed by: Joseph Sargent

Guest Cast:
Lt. Gerard .... Barry Morse
Sheriff .... Lew Brown
Lester .... John McIntire
Deputy No. 1 .... Mel Gallagher
Naomi .... Jeanette Nolan
Deputy No. 2 .... Bill Hart
Jonesie .... Tim McIntire
Mrs. Herrera .... Renata Vanni
Jock Sims .... Lonny Chapman
Josephina .... Silvia Marino

Lieutenant Gerard locates Kimble working with field workers and arrests him. Heading toward town, the two men run into a storm and are forced to take cover with Kimble's co-workers, who will do anything to free him. When Gerard is injured and needs a transfusion, a young girl reluctantly offers her blood. Then Kimble's friends form a human shield, allowing him to escape.

Notes:
• John McIntire played wagon master Christopher Hale on *Wagon Train* on NBC from 1961–62 and Clay Grainger on *The Virginian* on NBC 1967–68.
• Tim McIntire, son of John McIntire and actress Jeanette Nolan, played Bob Younger on *The Legend of Jesse James* on ABC from 1965–66 and Brad Knight on *Rich Man, Poor Man, Book I* on ABC from 1976–77.
• The song "Ballad for a Bitter Land – The Running Man" was written by producer George Eckstein.

EPISODE 85:
"WITH STRINGS ATTACHED"
(3-15-66)

Written by: John Kneubuhl
Directed by: Leonard Horn

Guest Cast:
Max .... Donald Pleasence
Stage Manager........ Paul Pepper
Ellen .... Carol Rossen
Watchman............. Jason Johnson
Geoffrey .... Rex Thompson
Officer.............. Jim Raymond
Lyman .... Bill Quinn

Kimble takes a job as chauffeur with a gifted but disturbed young violinist, Geoffrey Martin. Geoffrey is seeking to break away from his tyrannical teacher, Max Pfeiffer, and will do anything to gain his freedom. When Geoffrey decides to murder Max, Kimble risks his safety and intercedes.

Notes:

• Today, Carol Rossen looks back on her work with great fondness. "It was a sweet time and I think of it fondly and with sadness because I'm really, really sorry David Janssen isn't with us anymore. And I'm sorry that Quinn Martin isn't with us. I don't know that Quinn could function in the business as it exists today. I don't know that he would be allowed to be the producer he is, because there is not enough respect for the talent. The power resides too definitively in the institutions, the networks, and you can't do shows that way. Quinn was autonomous and it was a time in television history when the shows were as good as they were because they came from the passion of the producers and therefore the writers and directors were brought into that vision."

• Donald Pleasence, a longtime movie bad guy, appeared on TV as Prince John on *The Adventures of Robin Hood* on CBS from 1955–58 and as Salomon Van der Merwe on *Master of the Game* on CBS in 1987. He also frequently appeared in TV movies and miniseries and was nominated for an Emmy for *The Defection of Simas Kudirka* on CBS in 1978.

EPISODE 86:
"THE WHITE KNIGHT"
(3-22-66)

Written by: Dan Ullman
Directed by: Robert Gist

Guest Cast:

Glenn Madison . . . . Steven Hill
Russ Haynes . . . . James Callahan
Pat Haynes . . . . Jessica Walter
Claire Madison . . . . Nancy Wickwire
Lt. Mooney . . . . Ted Knight
Sgt. Evers. . . . . Bob Doqui

When Kimble pulls a politician, Glenn Madison, and his girlfriend, Pat Haynes, from a plane crash, he becomes a reluctant hero. Madison is married, but is having an affair with Pat, who is married to Madison's aid, Russ Haynes. When Madison's wife Claire finds out about the affair, she threatens to ruin her husband's political career. When the Madisons fight, Claire is killed, and Madison tries to pin the blame on Kimble.

Notes:

• Steven Hill played Daniel Briggs, the first leader of the Impossible Missions Force on *Mission:*

Impossible on CBS from 1966–67. An Orthodox Jew, Hill left the show when the shooting schedule conflicted with his sabbath.

• Ted Knight appeared in many TV shows of the '50s and '60s before striking TV gold as Ted Baxter on *The Mary Tyler Moore Show* on CBS from 1970–77. He also played Roger Dennis on *The Ted Knight Show* on CBS in 1978 and Henry Rush on *Too Close for Comfort* on ABC from 1980–83.

• Jessica Walter won an Emmy playing police chief Amy Prentiss on *Amy Prentiss* on NBC from 1974–75. She is also well remembered for playing the beautiful psychotic who stalks Clint Eastwood in *Play Misty for Me* in 1971.

EPISODE 87:
"THE 2130"
(3-29-66)

Written by: Dan Ullman
Directed by: Leonard Horn

Guest Cast:

Lt. Gerard . . . . Barry Morse
Millie Oates . . . . June Dayton
Mark Ryder . . . . Melvyn Douglas
Allan Oates . . . . Kevin Burchett
Laurie Ryder . . . . Susan Albert
Bonnie Oates . . . . Jamie Russell
Donald Bassett . . . . Jason Wingreen
Charlie Oates . . . . James Bracken

Melvyn Douglas as Mark Ryder in "The 2130."

Detective Wallace	Harlan Wade
Homer	Hampton Fancher
Tim Oates	Bill Bramley
Richardson	Stuart Nisbet

A young woman, Laurie Ryder, is involved in an auto accident. Afraid of her father, Dr. Ryder, she asks the family chauffeur, Kimble, to take the blame. When the police arrive and Kimble runs, Dr. Ryder discovers who he is and uses a computer, "the 2130," to track the fugitive's every move.

Notes:
• The distinguished actor Melvyn Douglas played Dr. Ryder. In his sixty-year career, Douglas won two Oscars, an Emmy, and a Tony Award. "Melvyn was wonderful," said Producer Alan Armer. "He knew his lines, hit his marks, and was a really wonderful guy. We were lucky to have such quality performers and it gave the show a certain degree of quality."
• Jason Wingreen played Harry Snowden on *All in the Family* on CBS from 1977–79 and on *Archie Bunker's Place* on CBS from 1979–83.

EPISODE 88:
"A TASTE OF TOMORROW"
(4-12-66)

Teleplay by: John Kneubuhl
Story by: Mann Rubin
Directed by: Leonard Horn

Guest Cast:

Joe Tucker	Fritz Weaver
Dave	Robert Ivers
Ben Wyckoff	Michael Constantine
Charlie Fletcher	Dabbs Greer
Sarah Tucker	Brenda Scott
Carolyn Fletcher	Mary Jackson
Shep	Paul Sorenson
Truck Driver	Bill Hickman

On the run, Kimble sneaks into a house where he finds Joe Tucker, another fugitive. Tucker has been mistakenly accused of embezzling $200,000 and is searching for the real thief, Charlie Fletcher. Kimble risks his safety to prove Tucker's innocence and prevent him from murdering Fletcher.

Notes:
• Dabbs Greer played Reverend Alden on *Little House on the Prairie* on NBC from 1974–83.

EPISODE 89:
"IN A PLAIN PAPER WRAPPER"
(4-19-66)

Teleplay by: John Kneubuhl
Story by: Jackson Gillis and Glen A. Larson
Directed by: Richard Donner

Guest Cast:

Susan Cartwright	Lois Nettleton
Joe	Mark Dymally
Shaw	Michael Strong
Hoffman	Wolfe Barzell
Eddie	Kurt Russell
1st Officer	Bing Russell
Gary	Pat Cardi
Landlady	Kay Riehl
Rick	Michael Shea
Swanzie	Arthur Malet

Kimble is involved with Susan Cartwright, a waitress whose nephew, Gary Reed, has just come to live with her. Gary has lived in Stafford, Indiana, and knows her aunt's boyfriend is a convicted murderer. With Gary's help, a group of teenagers send away for a mail order gun, intending to use it to capture Kimble. When Gary learns of Kimble's innocence, he tries to stop them and is shot.

EPISODE 90:
CORALEE"
(4-26-66)

Written by: Joy Dexter
Directed by: Jerry Hopper

Guest Cast:

Joe Steelman	Murray Hamilton
Pete	James Frawley
Coralee Reynolds	Antoinette Bower
Milt Carr	Joe Maross
Lucille Steelman	Patricia Smith
Frank Reynolds	Rusty Lane
George Graham	Dabney Coleman

While working on a boat, Kimble witnesses the death of a diver named Johnny. Although the boat captain, Joe Steelman, blames Johnny's death on the "town jinx," Coralee Reynolds, Kimble knows better. Kimble becomes involved with Coralee and convinces her she's not a bad luck charm. He also knows Steelman killed Johnny and risks his life to prove it.

Eddie, played by Kurt Russell, holds a mail order gun in "In a Plain Paper Wrapper."

Fourth Season

EPISODE 91:
"THE LAST OASIS"
(9-13-66)

Written by: Barry Oringer
Directed by: Gerald Mayer

Guest Cast:

Annie Johnson	Hope Lange
Deputy O'Hara	Lew Brown
Deputy Steel	Mark Richman
Mexican guard	Eugene Iglesias
Sam	Jamie Sanchez
Sheriff Prycer	Arch Johnson
Deputy Kelton	John McLiam
Roger	Vincent Arias
American guard	Don Ross
Nellie	Silvia Marino

When a relentless deputy wounds Kimble and tracks him into the desert, the fugitive takes refuge in a nearby Indian school. After the school's teacher, Annie Johnson, treats his wounds, Kimble remains as her assistant, finding work and friendship. Kimble's bliss is destroyed when the deputy locates him. When Kimble is forced to run, Annie risks her life to help him escape.

Notes:
• Hope Lange, a former dancer on *The Jackie Gleason Show,* played Mrs. Carolyn Muir on *The Ghost and Mrs. Muir* on NBC from 1968–69 and Jenny Preston on *The New Dick Van Dyke Show* on CBS from 1971–74.
• Mark Richman, now known as Peter Mark Richman, appeared in hundreds of TV series from the 1950s to the 1980s. He played Nick Cain on *Cain's Hundred* on NBC from 1961–62, Duke Paige on Longstreet on ABC from 1971–1972, and lawyer Andrew Laird on Dynasty on ABC from 1981–84.

EPISODE 92:
"DEATH IS THE DOOR PRIZE"
(9-20-66)

Written by: Oliver Crawford
Directed by: Don Medford

Guest Cast:

Marcia Stone	Lois Nettleton
Mr. Lee	John Lasell
Pete Dawes	Howard Da Silva
Gary	Kevin O'Neal
Johnny Gaines	Ossie Davis
Mrs. Lee	June Vincent
Boles	Len Wayland

While being pursued by security guards at a hi-fi exposition, Kimble hides in a basement room. One of the guards, Pete Dawes, follows him and discovers a group of boys stealing hi-fi equipment. Kimble sees Dawes shoot and kill one of the boys in self-defense. Later, when Dawes is about to be charged with murder, Kimble is forced to testify to clear the man.

Notes:
• Howard Da Silva won an Emmy for PBS's *Great Performances'* "Verna: U.S.O. Girl" in 1978.
• Ossie Davis has played Burt Reynolds's sidekick in two series. He played Oz Jackson on *B. L. Stryker* on ABC from 1989–90 and Ponder Blue on *Evening Shade* on CBS from 1990–93. He is also a veteran of many TV movies and miniseries.

EPISODE 93:
"A CLEAN AND QUIET TOWN"
(2-27-66)

Written by: Howard Browne
Directed by: Mark Rydell

Guest Cast:

Cramer	Bill Raisch
Hamp	Alan Emerson
Cora Reed	Carol Rossen
Tailor	Peter Brocco
Ollie Enright	Michael Strong
Ralph	Ed Deemer
Luchek	Eduardo Cianelli
Miss Moretti	Susan Davis
Cab Driver	George Brenlin
Lynch	Bill Bramley
Officer	Lloyd Haynes
Stripper	Wanda Barbre
Sgt.	Ted Gehring

When the one-armed man makes repeated attempts on his life, Kimble goes to a local mobster for protection. Kimble eventually catches the one-armed man and takes him to the police. But the police are tied in with the mob and Kimble and the one-armed man are taken to the estate of a MAFIA don, who warns them both to leave town.

Notes:
• "This was the first television show that Mark Rydell ever directed," recalled Carol Rossen. "Mark had been an actor and I remember rehearsing, David, Mark, and myself. It was fun because Mark had respect for the process and he was good with actors. I knew he would do well as a director.
• Eduardo Cianelli was a busy supporting actor in the '50s and '60s. He had just one starring role himself, as restaurant owner Waldo on *Johnny Staccato* on NBC and ABC from 1959–60.

EPISODE 94:
"THE SHARP EDGE OF CHIVALRY"
(10-4-66)

Written by: Sam Ross
Directed by: Gerald Mayer

Guest Cast:
Lt. Gerard	Barry Morse
Boyfriend	Walter Gregg
Roger Roland	Robert Drivas
Plainclothesman	Sy Prescott
Edward Roland	Eduard Franz
Fingerprintman	Ralph Montgomery
Liz Roland	Madlyn Rhue
Policeman	Paul Kent
Mrs. Turney	Rosemary Murphy
Policeman	Henry Scott
Mrs. Murdock	Ellen Corby
Woman	Ruth Packard
Lt. Sloan	Richard Anderson
Sergeant	Peter Madsen
Policeman	Robert Duggan
Millie	Judith Morton
Man	Bobby Johnson

When a psychotic Roger Roland murders a girl, he hides the murder weapon in Kimble's apartment. When a witness says the murderer had black hair, Kimble becomes a suspect. Hearing about the case, Lieutenant Gerard heads to the scene. Finally, Kimble convinces the boy's father that his son is the killer and the boy is turned over to the police.

Notes:
• Ellen Corby won three Emmy Awards as Grandma Esther Walton on *The Waltons* on CBS from 1972–79.

EPISODE 95:
"TEN THOUSAND PIECES OF SILVER"
(10-11-66)

Teleplay by: E. Arthur Kean and Wilton Schiller
Story by: E. Arthur Kean
Directed by: James Nielson

Guest Cast:
Lt. Philip Gerard	Barry Morse
Deputy Marsh	James Sikking
Jacob Lawrence	Lin McCarthy
Oliver Corman	Ford Rainey
Sheriff Mel Bailey	Joe Maross
Martin Pierce	Simon Scott
Ella Lawrence	Bonnie Beecher
Jack Burmas	Paul Mantee
Cathy Lawrence	June Harding

In a small town where Kimble is working, a killer named Burmas is on the loose. When the editor of the Stafford, Indiana, paper puts Kimble's picture on the front page, with an offer of a $10,000 reward, the police began to search for two fugitives. When Burmas jumps in the back of Kimble's truck, their lives become intertwined and Kimble is nearly killed. With the help of a young girl, Kimble manages to escape.

EPISODE 96:
"JOSHUA'S KINGDOM"
(10-18-66)

Written by: Lee Loeb
Directed by: Gerd Oswald

Guest Cast:
Joshua Simmons	Harry Townes
Sheriff	John Milford
Ruth	Kim Darby
Feeney	Vaughn Taylor
Pete	Tom Skerritt
Deputy	Mark Russell
Doc Martin	Walter Burke

Working as a veterinarian's assistant, Kimble goes to a farm to attend to a sick horse and discovers a baby who is quite ill. Kimble suggests medical attention, but the family's religious beliefs and Joshua Simmons won't allow it. When the baby lapses into a coma, Kimble risks his life to save the child.

EPISODE 97:
"SECOND SIGHT"
(10-25-66)

Written by: Dan Ullman
Directed by: Robert Douglas

Guest Cast:
Fred Johnson .... Bill Raisch
Detective............ James Noah
Howie Keever........ Tim Considine
Doctor.............. Glenn Sipes
Albert .... Ned Glass
Nurse 1 .... Janet MacLachlan
George .... Crahan Denton
Bartender .... Sidney Clute
Sgt. Denny .... Bill Sargent
Macklin .... Richard O'Brien
Dr. Rains .... Ted Knight
Driver .... Charles McDaniel
Wingo .... Stuart Lancaster
Foreman .... Byron Keith

Kimble finds a photo of Fred Johnson, and with the help of photographer Howie Keever, he confronts the one-armed man. Kimble is blinded in an explosion and is hospitalized. Johnson turns him in to the police and although he can't see, Kimble is forced to run, and is eventually arrested. With Howie's help, Kimble escapes and regains his sight.

Tim Considine as Howie Keever with David Janssen in "Second Sight."

Notes:
• Tim Considine played Marty in "Spin and Marty," on *The Mickey Mouse Club* on ABC from 1956–59 and then played the oldest son, Mike, on *My Three Sons* on ABC from 1960–65 and on CBS in 1965.

EPISODE 98:
"WINE IS A TRAITOR"
(11-1-66)

Written by: Arthur Dales
Directed by: Gerd Oswald

Guest Cast:
Carl Crandall .... Roy Thinnes
Felipe .... Martin Garralaga
Elena .... Pilar Seurat
Morales .... Carlos Romero
Pete Crandall......... James Gregory
Thomas .... Dabbs Greer

Kimble is riding with two Mexican workers, when a sniper kills the driver. When the wrong man, Morales, is accused of the murder, Kimble exposes the real killer, Carl Crandall, son of a wealthy winery owner. In a shootout at the winery, Crandall fires at Kimble but is killed by his father. Morales is cleared and Kimble escapes.

Notes:
• Roy Thinnes starred as David Vincent on another QM show, *The Invaders* on ABC from 1967–68, and played Nick Hogan on *Falcon Crest* on CBS from 1982–83. Today, Thinnes plays Sloan Carpenter on the daytime soap opera *One Life to Live* on ABC.

EPISODE 99:
"APPROACH WITH CARE"
(11-15-66)

Written by: Lee Loeb
Directed by: William Hale

Guest Cast:
Willie Turner .... Denny Miller
Steve .... Dabney Coleman
Marv .... Collin Wilcox
Hogan .... Michael Conrad
Sheriff .... Malcolm Atterbury
Old Man .... E. J. Andre
Matt .... Nick Colasanto

While working at a carnival, Kimble befriends Willie Turner, a retarded young man who has escaped from an institution. When a hospital attendant arrives to take Willie away, he recognizes Kimble and calls the police. Kimble and Willie escape together, but eventually Willie is killed and Kimble continues to run.

Notes:
• Nick Colasanto played "Coach" Pantusso on *Cheers* on NBC from 1982–85.
• Michael Conrad, a supporting actor from the 1950s, 1960s, and 1970s, is best remembered as Sergeant Phil Esterhaus, "And hey, let's be careful out there," on *Hill Street Blues* on NBC from 1981–84. He also played Lt. Macavan on *Delvecchio* on CBS from 1976–77.

EPISODE 100:
"NOBODY LOSES ALL THE TIME"
(11-22-66)

Written by: E. Arthur Kean
Directed by: Lawrence Dobkin

Guest Cast:
Lt. Philip Gerard . . . . Barry Morse
McCaffrey . . . . Don Dubbins
Maggie Tibbett . . . . Barbara Baxley
Fred Johnson . . . . Bill Raisch
Bianchi . . . . Joanna Moore
Hallet. . . . . Herb Ellis
Rowan. . . . . Phillip Pine
Ferguson . . . . Ben Wright

While working as a bartender, Kimble sees the one-armed man during a televised report of a factory explosion. Kimble rushes to the scene and finds Fred Johnson with his girlfriend, Maggie Tibbett. As Johnson runs, Maggie is hit by a car. Because of a doctor shortage at the hospital, Kimble saves Maggie's life and is offered a job as a doctor. However, the one-armed man forces Maggie to betray Kimble, which draws Lieutenant Gerard to the scene.

Notes:
Barbara Baxley was a regular on *Search for Tomorrow* on CBS in 1962 and 1969 and in *Where the Heart Is* on CBS from 1969–73.

EPISODE 101:
"RIGHT IN THE MIDDLE OF THE SEASON"
(11-29-66)

Written by: Sam Ross
Directed by: Chris Nyby

Guest Cast:
Tony Donovan . . . . Dean Jagger
Morgan . . . . James Seay
Nedda Donovan . . . . . . Nancy Malone
Fisherman . . . . Charles Wagenheim
Joe Donovan . . . . James Callahan
Boatswain's mate . . . . . Ron Stokes
Lt. Irwin . . . . Douglas Henderson
Fingerprint man . . . . . . John Mayo

Working on a fishing boat owned by Tony Donovan, Kimble becomes embroiled in a dock strike, and is arrested and fingerprinted. When the police discover who Kimble is, Tony agrees to help him escape. As the men head to sea, they discover a stowaway, Tony's daughter, Nedda, who's sweet on Kimble. When Tony suffers a heart attack, Kimble attends to him until the Coast Guard arrives. As Nedda and Tony are rescued, Kimble swims safely to shore.

Notes:
• Dean Jagger played principal Albert Vane on *Mr. Novak* on NBC from 1963–65 and won an Emmy for "Independence and 76" on the religious drama *This Is the Life* in 1980.

Dean Jagger as Tony Donovan with David Janssen in "Right in the Middle of the Season."

EPISODE 102:
"THE DEVIL'S DISCIPLES"
(12-6-66)

Teleplay by: Jerry Emmett and
Steven W. Carabatsos
Story by: Robert Dillon and
Steven W. Carabatsos
Directed by: Jud Taylor

Guest Cast:

Don . . . . Lou Antonio
Chino . . . . Robert Viharo
Hutch . . . . Bruce Dern
Curly . . . . Robert Sorrells
Penny . . . . Diana Hyland
Benson . . . . Crahan Denton
Hendricks . . . . Frank Marth
Andy . . . . Hal Lynch
Pilot . . . . William Wintersole
Dr.Crossland . . . . Harry Ellerbe

Lou Antonio, Diana Hyland and Bruce Dern in "The Devil's Disciples."

Kimble is picked up by a motorcycle gang on their way to avenge the death of a member, Tommy Joe, who was arrested following a gas station robbery. Given the choice of jail or the army, he enlisted, was sent to Vietnam, and was killed. The gang's leader, Hutch, plans to kill a "Mr. Benson," who, Hutch claims, turned Tommy Joe in. But Hutch is lying, and Benson turns out to be Tommy Joe's father. Kimble saves Benson and escapes.

EPISODE 103:
"THE BLESSINGS OF LIBERTY"
(12-20-66)

Written by: Dan Ullman
Directed by: Joseph Pevney

Guest Cast:

Josef Karac . . . . Ludwig Donath
Jim Macklin . . . . Noam Pitlik
Carla Karac . . . . Julie Sommars
Sgt. Charney . . . . George Tyne
Magda Karac . . . . Arlene Martel
Stark . . . . Edwin Max
Jan Karac . . . . Jan Merlin

Judge . . . . Nolan Leary
Billy . . . . Tony Musante
Detective . . . . Chuck Courtney

Kimble is taken in by a family of immigrants who work with him at a furniture factory. The family patriarch, Josef, is, like Kimble, a doctor hiding from his past. Josef had tried to help a girl injured in an abortion attempt. Since the girl died, Josef thinks he may be wanted for murder. When a killer holds the family at gunpoint, a shootout ensues and a policeman is injured. The two doctors, Kimble and Josef, save the man's life.

Notes:
•Tony Musante played undercover cop Dave Toma on *Toma* on ABC from 1973–74.

EPISODE 104:
"THE EVIL MEN DO"
(12-27-66)

Written by: Walter Brough
Directed by: Jesse Hibbs

Guest Cast:

Lt. Gerard . . . . Barry Morse
Waitress . . . . Jhean Burton
Arthur Brame . . . . James Daly
Clark . . . . William Zuckert
Sharon . . . . Elizabeth Allen
Sgt. Endicot . . . . Barry Russo
Officer Robinson . . . . . . David Sheiner
Mechanic . . . . Tom Signorelli
Delaney . . . . James McCallion

Kimble is working on a Pennsylvania horse farm, when the owner, Arthur Brame, is nearly stomped to death by a horse. Brame is a retired gangster who tries to repay Kimble by taking out a contract on Lieutenant Gerard. Brame lures Gerard to a Pittsburgh plant and tries to kill him. Kimble saves Gerard and Brame is killed in a shootout.

EPISODE 105:
"RUN THE MAN DOWN"
(1-3-67)

Teleplay by: Barry Oringer
Story by: Fred Freiberger
Directed by: James Sheldon

Guest Cast:

Owen Troop	James Broderick
Kenny	John D. Chandler
Bantam	Edward Asner
Runnels	Sam Melville
Laura Craig	Georgann Johnson
Lt. Hodges	Roy Engle
Larry	Robert Doyle
Ossie	Stuart Nisbet
Ross	Val Avery

Running from the police, Kimble finds a wounded man lying on the ground. The man has been shot in a bank robbery and forces Kimble to take him to a mountain cabin. The cabin is inhabited by a woman who has just broken up with her boyfriend, the town sheriff. Eventually, the bank robber's accomplices arrive, looking for the money. When the sheriff shows up, a shootout ensues.

Notes:

• "We shot that episode at Running Springs [California], up in the mountains," recalled Ed Asner. "It rained most of the time up there. It was bleak and cold. My ears hurt because of the altitude, and it was not a joyful shoot."

• James Broderick labored for years in television before becoming a star as Doug Lawrence on *Family* on ABC from 1976–80. He is the father of actor Matthew Broderick.

EPISODE 106:
"THE OTHER SIDE OF THE COIN"
(1-10-67)

Written by: Sam Ross
Directed by: Lewis Allen

Guest Cast:

Ben Corby	John Larch
Nancy	Barbara Baldavin
Harry Banner	Joseph Campanella
Sears	Pitt Herbert
Larry Corby	Beau Bridges
Associate Deputy	Glenn Sipes
Ellen Tolan	Melinda Plowman
Officer	Buck Young
Al Cooney	Parley Baer
Another Deputy	Don Eitner
Mrs. Blake	Claudia Bryar

Kimble and Larry Corby work together in a small-town market. Planning to elope with his girlfriend, Larry needs money. Donning a ski mask, the boy robs the market, but is shot trying to escape. Larry is arrested by Sheriff Corby, his father. When the sheriff discovers the robber is his son, he hides him. As Larry's condition worsens, he needs medical attention. When the sheriff discovers who Kimble is, he offers the doctor a deal: save Larry and go free.

EPISODE 107:
"THE ONE THAT GOT AWAY"
(1-17-67)

Written by: Philip Saltzman and Harry Kronman
Directed by: Leo Penn

Guest Cast:

Felice	Anne Francis
Mitchell	Harlan Wade
Oliver Greer	Charles Drake
Calderone	Pepe Callahan
Ralph Schuyler	Charles Bronson
Hodges	David Fresco
Brooks	Vince Howard
Girlfriend	Thordis Brandt
Guillermo	David Renard
Perez	Rico Alaniz

An undercover policeman, Ralph Schuyler, poses as a ship's captain on a boat chartered by Mrs. Greer, wife of embezzler Oliver Greer. During a ship's fire, Schuyler is injured and the deckhand, Kimble, rescues him. Kimble discovers Greer is planning to dump his wife, take the money, and run off with his secretary. When Greer comes aboard, Kimble exposes his plan. A fight breaks out, the Greers are arrested and Kimble escapes.

Anne Francis guest starred as Felice in "The One That Got Away."

Notes:

• Anne Francis has been in show business since childhood. On TV she played a female James Bond in *Honey West* on ABC from 1965–66, Terri Dowling on *My Three Sons* on CBS from 197–72, Arliss Cooper on *Dallas* on CBS in 1981, and Mama Jo on *Riptide* on NBC in 1984.

• Charles Bronson became a major movie star, but in the '50s and '60s, he guest-starred on a number of series. He also played Mike Kovac on *Man with a Camera* on ABC from 1958-60, Paul Moreno on *Empire* on NBC in 1963, and Linc Murdock on *The Travels of Jaimie McPheeters* on ABC from 1963–64.

EPISODE 108:
"CONCRETE EVIDENCE"
(1-24-67)

Teleplay by: Jeri Emmett and Jack Turley
Story by: Jack Turley
Directed by: Murray Golden

Guest Cast:

Pat Patton	Jack Warden
Sheriff	Ray Kellog
Pearl	Celeste Holm
Townsman	Ed Garrett
Nebbs	Jason Wingreen
Townswoman	Jane Barclay
Crailer	Harold Gould
Roughneck	E.A. Nicholson
Pete	Billy Snyder
Deputy	Jim Crowell
Charlie	Larry Blake

David Janssen with Jack Warden as Pat Patton in "Concrete Evidence."

Pat Patton is dying. He hires Dr. Richard Kimble to keep him alive until he can finish building a children's hospital. It is Patton's way of repaying a debt to the city of Coleman. Years earlier, a

theater Patton built collapsed. Three children were killed and Pat's daughter suffered irreparable mental damage. Since the accident, Pat and his partner-wife, Pearl, have lived a bitter existence.

Notes:

• Jack Warden has been a television mainstay for almost forty years and has been a regular on eight different series. He played Detective Lieutenant Mike Haines on *N.Y.P.D.* on ABC from 1967–69, John St. John on *Jigsaw John* on NBC in 1976, Morris Buttermaker on *The Bad News Bears* on CBS from 1979–80, Harry Fox on *Crazy Like a Fox* on CBS from 1984–86, and Hank Knight on *Knight & Dave* on NBC in 1989. He won an Emmy for *Brian's Song* on ABC in 1971.

EPISODE 109:
"THE BREAKING OF THE HABIT"
(1-31-67)

Written by: John Meredyth Lucas
Directed by: John Meredyth Lucas

Guest Cast:

Sister Veronica	Eileen Heckart
Policeman Landers	Clay Sister
Angelica	Antoinette Bower
Policeman No. 2	Paul Hahn
Father Taylor	Linden Chiles
Policeman No. 3	John Newton
Vicky	Brooke Bundy
Attendant	Peter Marko
Policeman	Dallas Mitchell
Counterman	Bill Erwin
Traffic Policeman	Pat Patterson
Marie	Heather North

In a sequel to "Angels Travel on Lonely Roads," (Numbers 22 and 23), Kimble goes to Sacramento to ask Sister Veronica to help him find the one-armed man. Now running a girls' school, the nun is preoccupied with wayward girls. She is also dying of a brain tumor. Although she eventually helps Kimble, the one-armed man escapes, and Kimble and Sister Veronica bid an emotional farewell.

Notes:

• "I remember the first day on the set," said Eileen Heckart. "Here I am again with my cigarette holder and I had a white mink coat over the nun's habit. *The Flying Nun* was popular then and the crew saw me and yelled, 'Here she comes, our swinging nun.'"

EPISODE 110
"THERE GOES THE BALLGAME"
(2-7-67)

Written by: Oliver Crawford
Directed by: Gerald Mayer

Guest Cast:

Andrew Newmark	Martin Balsam
Nadine Newmark	Lynda Day
Phil	Jonathan Lippe
Chester	Gabriel Dell
Vicki	Susan Seaforth
Gibbs	Vincent Gardenia
Joe	Sidney Clute
Rose	Joan Tomkins
Jerry	John Ward
Aggie	Barbara Dodd
Al	Jon Kowal
Guard	Michael Harris

While watching a baseball game, Richard Kimble witnesses the kidnapping of Nadine Newmark, daughter of powerful newspaperman Andrew Newmark. When Kimble describes the kidnapper to Newmark, he is placed in immediate jeopardy. Newmark will stop at nothing to insure his daughter's safe return and Kimble is caught in the middle.

EPISODE 111:
"THE IVY MAZE"
(2-21-67)

Written by: Edward C. Hume
Directed by: John Meredyth Lucas

Guest Cast:

Lt. Gerard	Barry Morse
Ken	Don Mitchell
Fritz Simpson	William Windom
Coed	Jill Janssen
Caroline Simpson	Geraldine Brooks
Coed	Iris Ratner
Fred Johnson	Bill Raisch
Assistant	Carl Reindel
Sally	Lorri Scott
Policeman	James Farley
Chief Terry	Bill Quinn
Policeman	Mark Russell
Landlady	Dani Nolan
Bus Driver	Perry Cook

Richard Kimble isn't the only one obsessed with the murder of his wife. Kimble's old college classmate, Professor Fritz Simpson, was once engaged to Helen and still carries a torch for her. Simpson tricks Fred Johnson into participating in a sleep-deprivation experiment, during which the one-armed man confesses to the murder. But when Simpson's wife alerts Lieutenant Gerard, the professor's plan to trap Johnson is ruined.

Notes:

• William Windom has worked steadily on television since the early '60s. He played Congressman Glen Morley on *The Farmer's Daughter* on ABC from 1963–66, cartoonist John Monroe on *My World and Welcome to It* on NBC from 1969–70, and Dr. Seth Hazlitt on *Murder, She Wrote* on CBS from 1985–90.

• Jill Janssen, David's half sister, had a small part as a coed.

EPISODE 112:
"GOODBYE MY LOVE"
(2-28-67)

Written by: Lee Loeb
Directed by: Lewis Allen

Guest Cast:

Alan Bartlett	Jack Lord
Charles	Jack Raine
Gayle Martin	Marlyn Mason
Policeman	Hal Riddle
Norma Bartlett	Pat Smith
Detective	Ivan Bonar
Paul	James Lanphier

Alan Bartlett and his fortune-hunting girlfriend Gayle Martin plot to kill Bartlett's rich wife,

Jack Lord as Alan Bartlett with Patricia Smith as Norma Bartlett in "Goodbye My Love."

Norma. When they discover who Kimble is, they set him up to take the fall. But with Norma's help, Kimble foils the plan and Bartlett and Martin are arrested.

Notes:
• Jack Lord is best known as Steve "Book 'em, Dano" McGarrett on *Hawaii Five-O* on CBS from 1968–80. He also starred in *Stoney Burke* on ABC from 1962–63.

EPISODE 113:
"PASSAGE TO HELENA"
(3-7-67)

Written by: Barry Oringer
Directed by: Richard Benedict

Guest Cast:

Rafe Carter	James Farentino
Sheriff Dalton	Percy Rodriguez
Lockett	Gene Kirkwood
Kline	Michael Mikler
Thornton	Russ Conway
Webster	Garry Walberg
Laura	Phyllis Love
Prewitt	Orville Sherman

In Wyler City, Montana, Kimble is stopped for questioning in connection with an auto theft. He runs, but is caught and booked. On a hunch that Kimble is wanted for "something big," Sheriff Dalton decides to take him to nearby Helena for investigation. Dalton is also transporting a young racist, convicted murderer Rafe Carter, for execution in Helena. However, they must all pass through Carter's home territory.

Notes:
James Farentino played lawyer Neil Darrell on *The Bold Ones* on NBC from 1969–72, adventurer Jefferson Keyes on *Cool Million* on NBC from 1972–73 and Frank DeMarco on *Mary* on CBS from 1985–86.

EPISODE 114:
"THE SAVAGE STREET"
(3-14-67)

Teleplay by: Jerri Emmett and Mario Alcalde
Story by: Mario Alcalde
Directed by: Gerald Mayer

Guest Cast:

Jose Anza	Gilbert Roland
Ollie	Bobby Diamond
Jimmy Anza	Tom Nardini
Mercedes	Miriam Colon
Miguel Anza	Michael Ansara
Harrigon	Barney Phillips
Benton	Ross Hagen
Compadre	Frank Puglia
Banks	Kevin Coughlin
Policeman	Ralph Montgomery
Cotton	David Macklin

Kimble befriends Jimmy Anza, a young boy with a domineering father. When the police pursue Kimble and wound him, Jimmy overcomes his father and a group of bullies to hide the fugitive and help him escape.

Notes:
• Michael Ansara played Cochise on *Broken Arrow* on ABC from 1956–58, a role that led to his playing Indians for the next twenty years. He also played Sam Buckhart on *Law of the Plainsman* on NBC from 1959–60 and Kane on *Buck Rogers in the 25th Century*.
• Bobby Diamond played Joey on *Fury* on NBC from 1955–60 and Duncan Gillis on *The Many Loves of Dobie Gillis* on CBS from 1962–63.

EPISODE 115:
"DEATH IS A VERY SMALL KILLER"
(3-21-67)

Written by: Barry Oringer
Directed by: John Meredyth Lucas

Guest Cast:

Dr. Howell	Arthur Hill
Sailor	Bard Stevens
Reina Morales	Carol Lawrence
Man	Robert Hernandez
Sgt. Rodriguez	Carlos Romero
Arenas	Raoul Perez
Capt. Gomez	Valentin De Vargas
Nurse	Stella Garcia
Sancho	Rodolfo Hoyos
Delivery man	Natividad Vacio
Diego	Roberto Contreras
Attendant	Mike Abelar
Captain	Sam Gillman
Officer	George Lymburn

In Mexico, Kimble becomes ill and is taken to a nearby clinic run by Dr. Howell. Recognizing

Kimble, Howell blackmails him into helping with experiments to find a cure for meningitis. Kimble discovers Howell is using humans as guinea pigs, and against the doctor's wishes gives the ailing patients badly needed serum. Kimble also falls in love with Howell's assistant, Reina Morales. When Howell contracts meningitis, the experiments end and Kimble flees.

Carol Lawrence as Reina Morales with David Janssen in "Death is a Very Small Killer."

Notes:

• Arthur Hill played Owen Marshall in *Owen Marshall, Counselor at Law* on ABC from 1971–74, Carl Palmer on *Hagen* on CBS in 1980, and Charles Hardwick on *Glitter* on ABC from 1984–85.

• Carol Lawrence is an actress and singer who has been seen on Television since the 1950s. She appeared in the Broadway production of *West Side Story* and on numerous series and variety shows.

EPISODE 116:
"DOSSIER ON A DIPLOMAT"
(3-28-67)

Teleplay by: J. T. Gollard and Jeri Emmett
Story by: J. T. Gollard
Directed by: Gerald Mayer

Guest Cast:

Lt. Gerard . . . . Barry Morse
Cabbie . . . . K. L. Smith
Mr. Unawa . . . . Ivan Dixon
Policeman . . . . Vince Howard
Davala Unawa . . . . Diana Sands
Detective. . . . . William Hudson
Ell Priestly . . . . Diana Hyland
2nd Detective . . . . Marlowe Jensen
Hobar . . . . Lloyd Gough
Mover . . . . Don Kennedy

In Washington, D.C., Kimble meets Ambassador Unawa, an African diplomat who believes in his innocence and offers him asylum until he can get a new trial. Unawa is suffering from an inoperable brain tumor and the diplomat's wife thinks Kimble is endangering his health. When her husband collapses, Mrs. Unawa moves the family out of the embassy, allowing the police to try to capture Kimble.

EPISODE 117:
"THE WALLS OF NIGHT"
(4-4-67)

Written by: Lawrence Louis Goldman
Directed by: John Meredyth Lucas

Guest Cast:

Barbara Wells . . . . Janice Rule
Lt. Gould . . . . Martin Brooks
Meredith . . . . Steve Ihnat
Manager . . . . Jean Wood
Leonard. . . . . Tige Andrews
Landlady . . . . Marcelle Fortier
Willy . . . . Sheree North

Working for an Oregon trucking company, Kimble becomes involved with the dispatcher, Barbara Wells. Unaware that she's a prisoner out on a work-release program, Kimble invites Barbara to spend the weekend with him. Barbara risks her freedom and joins Kimble at a country inn, touching off a manhunt that almost lands Kimble in jail.

EPISODE 118:
"THE SHATTERED SILENCE"
(4-11-67)

Teleplay by: Barry Oringer
Story by: Ralph Goodman
Directed by: Barry Morse

Guest Cast:

Andrea Cross. . . . . Antoinette Bower
Second Deputy . . . . Jack Demave
John Mallory . . . . Laurence Naismith
Howe . . . . Paul Mantee
Jensen . . . . Dabbs Greer

While running from the police, Kimble is wounded and is taken in by Mallory, an old hermit, who insists he doesn't like people but forces Kimble to stay. When Kimble discovers

Mallory is ill, he deceives the old man and risking his safety, goes for medical supplies. After treating the hermit, Kimble escapes.

EPISODE 119:
"THE JUDGMENT" PART ONE
(8-22-67)

Written by: George Eckstein and Michael Zagor
Directed by: Don Medford

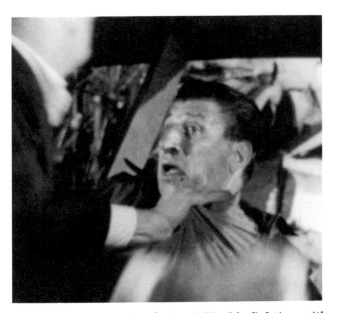

David Janssen as Dr. Richard Kimble fighting with Bill Raisch (the one-armed man) in the final episode, "The Judgment."

Guest Cast:

Lt. Gerard	Barry Morse
Fred Johnson	Bill Raisch
Jean Carlisle	Diane Baker
Policeman No. 3	Michael Harris
Howe	Michael Constantine
Trucker	Mark Allen
Capt. Lee	Joseph Campanella
Attendant	Perry Cook
Nat Harris	Skip Ward
Cabbie	Seymour Cassell
Policeman No. 1	Dort Clark
Plainclothesman	Paul Hahn
Dispatcher	Paul Sorensen
Officer No. 1	Paul Comi
Newscaster	Don Lamond
Detective Franks	Lloyd Haynes
Driver	James Nolan

Devlin	Walter Brooke
Policeman No. 2	Arch Whiting

The arrest of a one-armed man lures Kimble to Los Angeles. Jean Carlisle, a former resident of Stafford, Indiana, recognizes Lieutenant Gerard and saves Kimble from the police. Taking Kimble to her home, she and the fugitive begin to fall in love. After verifying that the prisoner is Fred Johnson, Kimble decides to turn himself in. As Kimble arrives at the police station, Johnson is released to a bail bondsman, and Jean rescues Kimble again. Before killing the bondsman, Johnson learns that "Leonard Taft" bailed him out. "Taft" is Kimble's brother-in-law. Gerard arrests Kimble and they board a train for Stafford. Johnson is on another train headed for the same destination.

EPISODE 120:
"THE JUDGMENT" PART TWO
(8-29-67)

Written by: George Eckstein and Michael Zagor
Directed by: Don Medford

Guest Cast:

Lt. Gerard	Barry Morse
Helen Kimble	Diane Brewster
Jean Carlisle	Diane Baker
Bobby Taft	Johnny Jensen
Lloyd Chandler	J. D. Cannon
Reporter No. 1	Richie Adams
Betsy Chandler	Louise Latham
Reporter No. 2	Al Dunlap
Fred Johnson	Bill Raisch

In Stafford, Gerard gives Kimble twenty-four hours to find the one-armed man. Lloyd Chandler, a former neighbor of Kimble's, witnessed Johnson killing Helen Kimble but remained silent. Having bailed Johnson out of jail, Chandler decides to atone for his cowardice by killing the one-armed man. At an old amusement park, Chandler and Johnson shoot it out as Kimble and Gerard arrive. When Johnson wounds Gerard, the lieutenant gives Kimble his gun and tells him to get the one-armed man. In a climactic fight scene on a tower, Johnson admits killing Helen and tries to murder Kimble. Gerard shoots the one-armed man, who falls to his death. Chandler's testimony clears Kimble and he and Jean Carlisle begin a new life together.

Production Credits 1963-67

Executive Producer: Quinn Martin
Created by: Roy Huggins
Producers: Alan A. Armer, Wilton Schiller
Co-Producers: John Meredyth Lucas, George Eckstein
Associate Producers: Arthur Weiss, William B. Gordon, George Eckstein
Assistant to the Executive Producer: Arthur Fellows, John Conwell
In Charge of Production: Arthur Fellows, Adrian Samish
Production Manager: Fred Ahern
Directors of Photography: Lloyd Ahern, Carl Guthrie, Fred Mendl, Meredith Nicholson, Robert Hoffman
Music: Peter Rugolo
Production Design: Claudio Guzman
Assistant to the Producer: John Conwell
Post-Production Supervisor: John Elizalde
Location Manager: Bud Brill
Film Editors: Larry Heath, Walter Hannemann, Jerry Young, Marston Fay, James D. Ballas, Richard H. Calhoun, Jodie Copelan, John Post, Robert L. Swanson
Art Directors: Serge Krizman, James Vance, James Hulsey
Assistant Directors: Maxwell Henry, Paul Wurtzel, Lloyd Allen, James E. Newcomb, William Shanks, Read Kilgore, Wes McAfee, David L. Salven, Jack Barry, Lou Place, Robert Rubin, Russ Haverick, Phil Cook
Property Managers: Don Smith, Irving Sindler
Chief Electricians: Lester Miller, Robert Farmer, James Potevin, Vaughn Ashen

2nd Cameramen: Roger C. Sherman, Joe August Jr., Richard A. Kelley, Edward Nugent
Special Photographic Effects: Howard Anderson
Special Effects: Si Simonson
Music Supervisors: John Elizalde, Ken Wilhoit
Music Editor: Ted Roberts
Set Decorators: Charles Thompson, Sandy Grace
Makeup Artists: Walter Schenck, Jack Wilson
Costume Supervisors: Bob Wolfe, Elmer Ellsworth, Edward McDermott
Costumers: George Harrington, Stephen Lodge, Karlice Hinson
Hair Stylists: Lavaughn Speer, Lynn Burke, Carol Meikle, Jean Austin
Key Grip: Ray Rich
Assistant Film Editors: Tom Neff Jr., John Shouse, John Post, Carl Mahakian, Harry Kaye, Anthony Friedman, Martin Fox, Orven Schanzer, O. Nicholas Brown
Script Supervisors: Billy Vernon, Duane Toler, Frances McDowell, Richard Chaffee, Kenneth Gilbert
Editorial Consultant/2nd Unit Director: Carl Barth
Sound: The Goldwyn Studio
Casting: Kerwin Coughlin, Meryl Abeles O'Laughlin
Production Mixers: John Kean, Barry Thomas
Sound Editors: Chuck Overhulser, Chuck Perry, Eddie Campbell
Re-recording: Clem Portman

A QM Production
In Association with United Artists
Television, Inc.

The Fugitive's *Original Sponsors*

Brown and Williamson Tobacco Company

Minnesota Mining and Manufacturing

Mobil Oil Company

The Procter and Gamble Company

Standard Brands Incorporated

Block Drug Company

Clairol Incorporated

E. I. Dupont De Nemours and Company

Max Factor and Company

Lincoln-Mercury Division Ford Motor Company

Menley and James Labs

The Norwich Pharmacal Company

Polaroid Company

Remington Rand Electric Shaver and Portable Typewriter

Division Sperry Rand Corporation

Chapter 14

Where Are They Now?

Alan Armer, who produced the first ninety episodes of *The Fugitive* is currently a college professor, teaching screenwriting full-time at California State University–Northridge. In addition to *The Fugitive,* Armer also worked on *The Invaders, Cannon, The Name of the Game,* and the TV movie *Birds of Prey,* starring David Janssen. Armer is also the author of two books about television directing and screenwriting. *The Fugitive's* Emmy sits proudly in Armer's den in Southern California.

John Conwell, *The Fugitive's* casting director and eventually vice president of QM Productions, retired in the late 1980s. After QM Productions was sold, Conwell freelanced as a casting director, working on various feature films and TV movies. The last job he did was a movie of the week with Katharine Hepburn in 1985. During retirement Conwell spent his time painting abstracts. "I've been very successful," said Conwell. "Nobody is more surprised than I am though. It's been very rewarding and I do it to fulfill the creative need. To sell the paintings is gravy." In November 1994 Conwell died from cancer.

George Eckstein, *The Fugitive's* associate producer and a writer of many episodes, is still active in the television-film industry. Eckstein has written for other shows including *The Untouchables, Gunsmoke, Dr.Kildare,* and *Perry Mason,* and has produced many series and movies for television. He lives in Studio City, California.

Walter Grauman, who directed *The Fugitive's* pilot and other episodes, is also still working in television. Grauman also directed the pilot episodes for *Most Wanted, Barnaby Jones,* and *Manhunter,* and worked with David Janssen on several TV movies including the acclaimed *Golden Gate Murders.* He is still quite active as a principal director on *Murder, She Wrote.* Grauman lives in Los Angeles.

Roy Huggins, who created *The Fugitive,* has worked in television and film for almost fifty years, as writer, director, producer, executive producer, and head of three television studios. After his graduate school hiatus, Huggins returned to television in 1962. His additional credits include the creation and/or production of shows like *Alias Smith and Jones, Toma, Baretta, The Rockford Files, City of Angels,* and *Hunter.* Huggins served as an executive producer on *The Fugitive,* the movie, and is now hard at work on his show business memoirs. Huggins lives in Los Angeles.

Berniece Janssen, David Janssen's 83-year old mother, occasionally worked as an extra on her son's television shows, *The Fugitive, O'Hara: United States Treasury,* and *Harry O.* She continues to work as an extra on shows including *Cheers,* and made a cameo appearance as a court reporter in *The Fugitive,* the movie. She lives in Tarzana, California.

Dani Janssen, the second wife of David Janssen, still lives in the Century City town house she shared with the actor. Following Janssen's death, she married stuntman-director Hal Needham. Now divorced, Dani spends her time managing her investments and traveling. She numbers among her friends Joan Collins and Linda Evans.

Ellie Janssen, the actor's first wife, has recently moved to Portland, Oregon. After a recent bout with health problems, Ellie plans on resuming work on her book about David Janssen.

Don Medford, who directed *The Fugitive's* two-part conclusion, "The Judgment," first started in television directing James Dean and Rod Steiger in early shows like *Tales of Tomorrow.* Medford directed feature films such as *The Organization* and *The Hunting Party,* and has since turned to producing. "I have one of the hottest writers in the country, James Lee Burke," said Medford in 1993. "I have optioned a property of his, *The Electric Mist of the Confederate Dead,* for the big screen." Medford lives in Southern California.

Carol Rossen, who guest-starred in five episodes of *The Fugitive,* has developed a dual career as an actress and author. In addition to appearing in over one hundred television shows including *East Side/West Side, Naked City, Dr. Kildare, Harry O,* and *The Streets of San Francisco,* she has worked on the New York stage, and has written her first work of nonfiction, *Counterpunch.* She has just completed a screenplay of the book and is currently working on her second book. She lives in both New York and Los Angeles.

Stanford Whitmore, who wrote *The Fugitive's* pilot, "Fear in a Desert City," and several other episodes, continues a productive career in television and film writing. Besides working on shows like *McLeod* and *The D.A.,* Whitmore has written screenplays for films including *Baby Blue Marine, The Dark, Hammersmith is Out,* and *Your Cheatin' Heart,* the story of singer Hank Williams. A screenplay Whitmore wrote twelve years ago has been turned into a movie, *Alicia's Book.*

Appendix 1

Roy Huggins's Original Treatment of The Fugitive

What follows is Roy Huggins's original treatment for *The Fugitive,* written in 1960. Huggins used this treatment in making his presentation to ABC in 1962. With Huggins' permission, the treatment is being reprinted in its original form.

THE FUGITIVE
A Series Format
September 19, 1960
Roy Huggins

FADE IN:

LONG SHOT - TRAIN   NIGHT

A passenger train, its enormous headlight glowing in the
distance, is racing TOWARD CAMERA through dark and lonely
country. The RHYTHMIC SOUND of the train RISES SWIFTLY as
it approaches and PASSES CAMERA, the HEAVY, CADENCED SOUND
reaching a climax which breaks off abruptly as we go into:

INT. PASSENGER CAR - (PROCESS)   NIGHT

The RHYTHMIC SOUND of the train continues in a lower key.

BIG CLOSE ON RICHARD KIMBLE

He is a prematurely grey-haired man in his mid thirties. His
eyes are turned toward the dark window where broad farmland,
with its occasional solitary glow of light, swiftly passes.
But we sense from his inward air that he is seeing little of
this, that whatever beauty there may be in the swift passage
of quiet, moonlit countryside has no meaning for him. From
the beginning of this CLOSE SHOT we have HEARD the off stage
voice of a NARRATOR, a voice suggesting an infinite detachment,
which gives it the authority of a disinterested, omniscient
observer.

                    NARRATOR
          This man is known by a number:
          565-9880. His name is Richard
          Kimble. Once a doctor: specialty,
          pediatrics.

The CAMERA has DRAWN BACK over this to reveal the MAN next to
Kimble and two MEN in the seat immediately behind him. These
men are all members of the State's Attorney's office, and in
their varying ways they suggest precisely what they are.
They look neither grim nor watchful. They are doing their
jobs, thinking their private thoughts.

                    NARRATOR
                 (continuing)
          He is returning from his fourth
          and final appeal from a conviction
          on a charge of murder in the first
          degree. The victim: Helen Kimble,
          his wife.

2.

TWO SHOT - KIMBLE AND OFFICER

The police officer beside him, using his left hand, offers a
cigarette to Kimble and takes one himself. He lights both
cigarettes with a lighter, using the same left hand. During
this action we may notice a light topcoat covering Kimble's
left forearm and the officer's right forearm. The Camera
does not single this out because the action itself suggests
that the unseen wrists are joined by handcuffs.

                NARRATOR
          (continuing)
      Richard Kimble had offered only this
      defense: He had caught one brief
      glimpse of the actual criminal, a
      gaunt and redhaired man.
         (brief pause)
      This was the simple but unprovable
      truth. The provable truth was that
      Helen and Richard Kimble were childless,
      and bitterly estranged by his determination
      to change that condition through adoption.

BIG CLOSE ON KIMBLE

                NARRATOR
          (continuing)
      Crimes without plan, motive or
      evidence are not only insoluble,
      they often victimize the innocent.
      Richard Kimble is returning to
      Death Row, State Prison. Execution
      date: 10:00 A.M., July 18. No further
      appeals are possible.

EXT. THE TRAIN

It passes CAMERA, the SOUND almost deafening once again. As
the train roars AWAY FROM CAMERA the whistle SOUNDS, an eerie,
fading wail.

                NARRATOR
          (continuing)
      But this train is the Capitol Limited,
      and this is the tragic night of
      July 2 ...

3.

CLOSE SHOT - A RAILROAD SWITCH

CLOSE SHOT

The engine of the Capitol Limited. The whistle SOUNDS again.

CLOSE SHOT

A division in the track, showing the rails set for a 15^0
turn onto a spur line.

INT. THE TRAIN - THE FOUR MEN

silent, utterly unaware of what awaits them.

EXT. THE TRAIN

It is still travelling at headlong speed.

ANOTHER ANGLE

as the train takes the unintended turn onto the spur.

THE WRECK

We HOLD only for the first, shocking impact and go into an
EFFECT DISSOLVE.

EXT. EMPTY COUNTRYSIDE   NIGHT

We DISSOLVE INTO A SHOT designed for the MAXIMUM EFFECT of
tranquility. The night sounds are distant, undisturbed.

INTO SHOT the figure of a man stumbles, and as the figure
comes into a

CLOSE SHOT

we recognize Richard Kimble. Breathless, he stops. We see
his face clearly in the moonlight. He is bewildered, emerging
from shock. He stands for a moment, listening. And as full
realization of what has happened rises in him, he turns as if
expecting to find the wreckage of the train behind him. We
see nothing. We hear nothing but the sounds of the crickets
and an occasional night bird.

4.

CLOSER ON KIMBLE

As we see him face the almost terrifying fact of freedom. He glances quickly around him, then begins to run. The CAMERA HOLDS and the MUSIC BEGINS. As his figure recedes we see an odd configuration in the distance into which he is vanishing. This jagged configuration begins to move toward us swiftly as the MUSIC RISES. The configuration becomes two sharply, violently formed words which finally fill the screen:

THE
FUGITIVE

We HOLD for the musical climax and

FADE OUT.

The foregoing is the cinematic signature of a proposed new hour-long series, THE FUGITIVE. Each week this 70 second introduction will excitingly restate the premise and reset the mood of the series.

Each episode will deal with a week, a month, a day, or an hour in the life of Richard Kimble as a fugitive, a life which involves flight, search, moral dilemma, friendship, love, laughter, all underlain with unfulfillment, danger and tragedy. In a heightened and imaginative sense Kimble's life as a fugitive will relate to deep and responsive drives, needs and fantasies in the American audience, not the least of which is that Kimble lives with alienation and anxiety, but in his case they are real and can be dealt with. At the heart of the series is the preoccupation with guilt and salvation which has been called the American Theme. Kimble is pursued, and in the eyes of the law he is guilty. But no American of any persuasion will find him so. The idea of natural law is too deeply embedded in the American spirit for anyone to question Kimble's right, after all recourse to law has been exhausted, to preserve his own life. Even Hobbes, the great philosopher of authoritarianism, acknowledged one circumstance in which a man has a right to resist Leviathan: when an attempt is made to take his life on mistaken grounds.

In the summer of 1960 it became abundantly clear that the Western on television was about to undergo an eclipse. I had given much thought to the broad and durable appeal of the Western, and I concluded that the essence of that appeal lay solely in the character and mode of life of the Western hero.

5.

That hero is a man without roots, without obligations, without fixed goals, without anxiety about his place in the order of things. He not only avoids commitment to one locale, one occupation, or one woman, he actually seems compelled to change his dwelling place, his occupation, his human attachments. This implicit factor of willed irresponsibility without a concomitant sense of guilt is the element of basic appeal in the Western. The good-vs-evil formula, the omnipotence of the hero, these elements are found in contemporary melodrama. But not the element of absolute freedom that the traditional Western contains. SHANE is the great example of the tradition in its most faithful and successful form, and strangely enough, SHANE also contained the element of pursuit. Early in SHANE we realize that he is in flight, but we are never told from what. At the end of the picture Shane moves on, still pursued, but by what we are not told.

THE FUGITIVE was a long time in gestation. My aim was to capture the essence of the Western in a contemporary setting. My confidence in the basic theory was boundless, but a truly workable solution did not come easily. In these regimented and conformist times, the protagonist had to be unregimented, apart from society, rootless, immune to permanent human commitment, and ever on the move. And we had to understand precisely why this was so and to accept it with no uneasy sense of guilt; otherwise there would be a rejection of the protagonist and the concept.

THE FUGITIVE met all these needs and more. Richard Kimble is guilty by act of law, but innocent in fact. As a fugitive he is compelled to live in a drifting, alienated way, and the specifics will be spelled out dramatically from episode to episode. Here they are:

1) He must change his appearance, and he does. This purposeful loss of identity is one of our most deep-seated fantasies. It is found in countless children's stories and in equally countless sophisticated novels (The Moon & Sixpence, The Art of Lewellyn Jones, The Count of Monte Cristo, ad infinitum).

2) He must keep moving. To stay in one place over long is to multiply geometrically the dangers of recognition and apprehension. He finally adopts an arbitrary rule against staying in any given locale for more than six weeks.

3) He must stay in this country. Here he is one American among nearly 200 million Americans. Outside our borders passports are required, questions are asked; he is the conspicuous stranger.

6.

4) He can take only unusual, no-questions-asked
   jobs. An ordinary job requires letters of
   recommendation, a social security number, often
   even a finger-print check. This necessity of
   course opens the door in a natural and credible
   way to a vast store of exciting and fresh story
   material.

5) He cannot make friendships that are not ended,
   or fall in love without heartbreak. In terms
   of the needs of a weekly series, the story-telling
   advantages in this are obvious and infinite.

Because the thematic base of the series is so explicit and yet
so much a part of the unconscious yearnings of the broadest
possible spectrum of the audience, the actual story content
of each episode can and should be on the most sophisticated
level possible in television. Implicit in each episode is
the ultimate in sympathy for the protagonist, and the never
ending presence of jeopardy; therefore the wpisodes can be
built around character and premise.

This brief presentation has left a multitude of questions
unanswered, but not because they are unanswerable. For
example: Is he being searched for? Yes. One man in the
State's Attorney's office has been assigned that task, and at
least one episode, and probably more than one, will deal with
the pursuit itself. The story of Jean Valjean and his Javert
has not remained a classic for insignificant reasons, and the
best will be distilled from those reasons. Does he ever meet
anyone who recognizes him? Yes, and at least one episode
will be built around it. Questions of this kind all lend
themselves to answers in terms of dramatic treatment.

An element that will be used in the series, but only in the
most limited way, is the faint, almost unacknowledged hope
in Richard Kimble that he might one day come face to face
with the gaunt, red-haired man he had so briefly seen on the
night of his wife's death. The reason for this is obvious.
This will be a series which will be brought to a planned
conclusion, that conclusion being of course Richard Kimble's
release from his predicament and the ultimate salvation of
justice.

Appendix 2

The Twenty Highest-Rated Shows of All Time

THE TWENTY HIGHEST-RATED SHOWS OF ALL TIME

Rank	Program	Date	Network	Average Audience (percentage)	Share
1	M*A*S*H Special	2/28/83	CBS	60.2	77
2	Dallas	11/21/80	CBS	53.3	76
3	Roots, Part VII	1/30/77	ABC	51.1	71
4	Super Bowl XVI	1/24/82	CBS	49.1	73
5	Super Bowl XVII	1/30/83	NBC	48.6	69
6	Super Bowl XX	1/26/86	NBC	48.3	70
7	Gone With The Wind (Part I)	11/7/76	NBC	47.7	65
8	Gone With The Wind (Part II)	11/8/76	NBC	47.4	64
9	Super Bowl XII	1/15/78	CBS	47.2	67
10	Super Bowl XIII	1/21/79	NBC	47.1	74
11	Bob Hope Christmas Show	1/15/70	NBC	46.6	64
12	Super Bowl XVIII	1/22/84	CBS	46.4	71
12	Super Bowl XIX	1/20/85	ABC	46.4	63
14	Super Bowl XIV	1/20/80	CBS	46.3	67
15	ABC Theater (The Day After)	11/20/83	ABC	46.0	62
16	Roots, Part VI	1/28/77	ABC	45.9	66
16	**The Fugitive**	**8/29/67**	**ABC**	**45.9**	**72**
18	Super Bowl XXI	1/25/87	CBS	45.8	66
19	Roots, Part V	1/27/77	ABC	45.7	71
20	Cheers	5/20/93	NBC	45.5	64

Rating – percent of all TV households

Share – percent of all TV households with sets in use

Information provided by Nielsen Media Research
Based on reports July 1960–August 1993

Appendix 3

Richard Kimble's Aliases

RICHARD KIMBLE'S ALIASES

Allen, Pete
Anderson, Jack
Anderson, Tom
Baker, Carl
Barlow, Frank
Barrett, Thomas (twice)
Beaumont, Paul
Beckett, Douglas
Benson, Chris
Benton, David
Blake, George
Broderick, Pete
Browning, George
Burns, Tom
Carson, Harry
Carter, Bill
Carter, Eddie
Carter, Frank
Carter, Tony
Carver, Steve
Clark, Richard
Cooper, Jeff
Corbin, Jim
Crowley, Dan
Curtis, Ed
Davies, Bob
Davis, Frank
Davis, Jack
Dexter, Al
Dexter, Steve
Douglas, Bill
Dyson, Stan
Egan, George
Evans, John
Farrell (No first name)
Fickett, Jack

Fleming, Al
Fowler, Jim
Frye, Eddie
Garrison, Bill
Glenn, Pete
Gordon, Dan
Grant, Bob
Hayes, Bill
Horton, Ben
Hull, Leonard
Hunter, Paul
Johnson, Mike
Jordan, Frank
Jordan, Russell
Keller, Paul
Kelly (No first name)
Lewis, Ben
Lincoln, Jim
Lindsey, Dick
Livingston, Dave
Manning, Stuart
March, Bill
Marlowe, Tom
Martin, Bill
Maxwell, Tony
McGuire, Jim
Mead, Phil
Miller, David
Miller, Paul
Miller, Ray
Mitchell, Alan
Morris, Ed
Mossman, Bob
Nash, Tom
Owen, Jim
Parker (No first name)

Parker, Jeff
Parker, Jim
Peters, Nick
Phelps, Larry
Phillips, Nick
Porter, George
Reynolds, Harry
Robinson, Dr. Harry
Rogers, Ben
Russell, Ben
Russell, Jim
Sanders, Ed
Sanford (No first name)
Shelton, Jerry
Sherman, Johnny
Sinclair, Jerry
Smith, Jack
Smith, William
Spaulding, Richard
Stoddard, Bob
Taft, Joe
Talman, Larry
Tate, Fred
Taylor (No first name)
Taylor, Richard
Thomas, Pat
Tyler, Gene
Walker, Joe
Walker, Joseph
Walker, Nick
Wallace, Jim
Warren, Joe
Watkins, Bill
Whistler, Frank
Younger, Steve

Appendix 4

List of Episodes

LIST OF EPISODES

First Season

1. "Fear in a Desert City" (9-17-63)
2. "The Witch" (9-24-63)
3. "The Other Side of the Mountain" (10-1-63)
4. "Never Wave Goodbye" (Part One) (10-8-63)
5. "Never Wave Goodbye" (Part Two) (10-15-63)
6. "Decision in the Ring" (10-22-63)
7. "Smoke Screenl' (10-29-63)
8. "See Hollywood and Die" (11-5-63)
9. "Ticket to Alaska" (11-12-63)
10. "Fatso" (11-19-63)
11. "Nightmare at Northoak" (11-26-63)
12. "The Glass Tightrope" (12-3-63)
13. "Terror at High Point" ~12-17-63)
14. "The Girl from Little Egypt" (12-24-63)
15. "Home Is the Hunted" (1-7-64)
16. "The Garden House" (1-14-64)
17. "Come Watch Me Die" (1-21-64)
18. "Where the Action Is" (1-28-64)
19. "Search in a Windy City" ((2-4-64)
20. "Bloodline" (2-11-64)
21. "Rat in a Corner" (2-18-64)
22. "Angels Travel on Lonely Roads" (Part One) (2-25-64)
23. "Angels Travel on Lonely Roads" (Part Two) (3-3-64)
24. "Flight from the Final Demon" (3-10-64)
25. "Taps for a Dead War" (3-17-64)
26. "Somebody to Remember" (3-24-64)
27. "Never Stop Running" (3-31-64)
28. "The Homecoming" (4-7-64)
29. "Storm Center" (4-14-64)
30. "The End Game" (4-21-64)

Second Season

31. "Man in a Chariotll (9-15-64)
32. "World's End" (9-22-64)
33. "Man on a String" (9-29-64)
34. "When the Bough Breaks'l (10-6-64)
35. "Nemesis" (10-13-64)
36. "Tiger Left, Tiger Right" (10-20-64)
37. "Tug-of-War" (10-27-64)
38. "Dark Corner" (11-10-64)
39. "Escape into Black" (11-17-64)
40. "The Cage" (11-24-64)
41. "Cry Uncle" (12-1-64)
42. "Detour on a Road Going Nowhere" (12-8-64)
43. "The Iron Maiden" (12-15-64)
44. "Devil's Carnival" (12-22-64)
45. "Ballad for a Ghost" (12-29-64)
46. "Brass Ring" (1-5-65)
47. "The End Is But the Beginning" (1-12-65)
48. "Nicest Fella You'd Ever Want to Meet" (1-19-65)
49. "Fun and Games and Party Favors" (1-26-65)
50. "Scapegoat" (2-2-65)
51. "Corner of Hell" (2-9-65)
52. "Moon Child" (2-16-65)
53. "The Survivors" (3-2-65)
54. "Everybody Gets Hit in the Mouth Some-time" (3-9-65)
55. "May God Have Mercy" (3-16-65)
56. "Masquerade" (3-23-65)
57. "Runner in the Dark" (3-30-65)
58. "A.P.B." (4-6-65)
59. "The Old Man Picked a Lemon" (4-13-65)
60. "Last Second of a Big Dream" (4-20-65)

Third Season

61. "Wings of an Angel" (9-14-65)
62. "Middle of a Heat Wave" (9-21-65)
63. "Crack in a Crystal Ball" (9-28-65)
64. "Trial by Fire" (10-5-65)
65. "Conspiracy of Silence" (10-12-65)
66. "Three Cheers for Little Boy Blue" (10-19-65)
67. "All the Scared Rabbits" (10-26-65)
68. "An Apple a Day" (11-2-65)
69. "Landscape with Running Figures" (Part One) (11-16-65)
70. "Landscape with Running Figures" (Part Two) (11-23-65)
71. "Set Fire to a Straw Man" (11-30-65)
72. "Stranger in the Mirror" (12-7-65)
73. "The Good Guys and the Bad Guys" (12-14-65)
74. "End of the Line" (12-21-65)
75. "When the Wind Blows" (12-28-65)
76. "Not with a Whimper" (1-4-66)
77. "Wife Killer" (1-11-66)
78. "This'll Kill You" (1-18-66)
79. "Echo of a Nightmare" (1-25-66)
80. "Stroke of Genius" (2-1-66)
81. "Shadow of the Swan" (2-8-66)
82. "Running Scared" (2-22-66)
83. "The Chinese Sunset" (3-1-66)
84. "Ill Wind" (3-8-66)
85. "With Strings Attached" (3-15-66)
86. "The White Knight" (3-22-66)
87. "The 2130" (3-29-66)
88. "A Taste of Tomorrow" (4-12-66)
89. "In a Plain Paper Wrapper" (4-19-66)
90. "Coralee" (4-26-66)

Fourth Season

91. "The Last Oasis" (9-13-66)
92. "Death Is the Door Prize" (9-20-66)
93. "A Clean and Quiet Town" (9-27-66)
94. "The Sharp Edge of Chivalry" (10-4-66)
95. "Ten Thousand Pieces of Silver" (10-11-66)
96. "Joshua's Kingdom" (10-18-66)
97. "Second Sight" (10-25-66)
98. "Wine Is a Traitor" (11-1-66)
99. "Approach with Care" (11-15-66)
100. "Nobody Loses All the Time" (11-22-66)
101. "Right in the Middle of the Season" (11-29-66)
102. "The Devil's Disciples" (12-6-66)
103. "The Blessings of Liberty" (12-20-66)
104. "The Evil Men Do" (12-27-66)
105. "Run the Man Down" (1-3-67)
106. "The Other Side of the Coin" (1-10-67)
107. "The One That Got Away" (1-17-67)
108. "Concrete Evidence" (1-24-67)
109. "The Breaking of the Habit" (1-31-67)
110. "There Goes the Ball Game" (2-7-67)
111. "The Ivy Maze" (2-21-67)
112. "Goodbye My Love" (2-28-67)
113. "Passage to Helena" (3-7-67)
114. "The Savage Street" (3-14-67)
115. "Death Is a Very Small Killer" (3-21-67)
116. "Dossier on a Diplomat" (3-28-67)
117. "The Walls of Night" (4-4-67)
118. "The Shattered Silence" (4-11-67)
119. "The Judgment" (Part One) (8-22-67)
120. "The Judgment" (Part Two) (8-29-67)

Appendix 5

Index of
The Fugitive*'s*
Actors, Actresses,
Directors, and Writers

ACTORS AND ACTRESSES WHO APPEARED IN *THE FUGITIVE*
The entries listed below are all indexed by episode number.

Abbott, Philip, 44

Abelar, Mike, 115

Adams, Richie, 120

Addy, Wesley, 65

Adler, Jay, 12

Aidman, Charles, 64

Akins, Claude, 27

Alaniz, Rico 59, 107

Albert, Susan, 87

Aletter, Frank, 64

Allen, Elizabeth, 13, 42, 104

Allen, Joan, 78

Allen, Mark, 119

Allman, Sheldon, 83

Ames, Rachael, 4

Anderson, John, 17, 50

Anderson, Richard, 43, 57, 66, 94, 120

Andre, E.J.,.99

Andrews, Tige, 117

Ansara, Michael, 114

Antonio, Lou, 8, 58, 102

Armstrong, Dave, 25

Armstrong, R.G., 3, 51, 67

Arnold, Monroe, 81

Asner, Edward, 56, 66, 105

Atterbury, Malcolm, 33, 80, 99

Atwater, G.B., 54

Avery, Val, 61, 105

Baer, Parley, 20, 106

Baker, Diane, 119, 120

Bal, Jeanne, 36

Baldavin, Barbara, 71, 106

Balsam, Martin, 110

Barbre, Wanda, 93

Barclay, Jane, 76, 108

Barnes, Rayford, 56

Barrie, Barbara, 47

Barry, Donald, 39

Bartlett, Martine, 30

Barton, Dan, 20

Barzell, Wolfe, 89

Batonides, Arthur, 19

Baxley, Barbara, 100

Baxter, Allen, 26

Beckman, Henry, 32

Beecher, Bonnie, 84,95

Begley, Ed, 31, 57

Beir, Fred, 58

Bernardi, Herschel, 69,70

Best, James, 13

Beverly Hills, Miss, 18

Biheller, Robert, 70

Binns, Edward, 12,41,71

Birch, Paul, 1, 3, 4, 7, 10, 11, 15, 26, 32, 35, 39, 47, 51

Bisell, Whit, 50

Blake, Larry, 108

Blyden, Larry, 63

Bonar, Ivan, 112

Boone, Randy, 17

Bower, Antoinette, 90, 109, 118

Bowman, Lee, 42

Bracken, James, 87

Bradbury, Lane, 61

Bradford, Lane, 8, 23

Bradley, Stuart, 21

Bramley, Bill, 87, 93

Brandt, Thordis, 107

Brenlin, George, 93

Brewster, Diane, 14, 120

Bridges, Beau, 80, 106

Briggs, Don, 34

Brinckerhoff, Burt, 10

Brocco, Peter, 93

Broderick, James, 105

Bronson, Charles, 107

Brooke, Walter, 42, 63, 119

Brooker, Martin, 117

Brooks, Geraldine, 9, 54, 111

Brown, Lew, 84, 91

Bryar, Claudia, 2, 58, 106

Bryar, Paul, 72

Bundy, Brooke, 109

Burchett, Kevin, 87

Burke, Walter, 96

Burt, Nellie, 57, 63

Burton, Jeff, 72

Burton, Jhean, 104

Cahill, Barry, 42

Calder, King, 10

Call, Anthony, 49

Callahan, James, 86, 101

Callahan, Pepe, 107

Campanella, Joseph, 30, 71, 106, 119

Cannon, J.D., 62, 120

Cardi, Pat, 89

Carlson, Richard, 28

Carr, Paul, 9, 11, 38

Cassell, Seymour, 119

Challee, William, 8

Chandler, John D., 3, 105

Chapman, Lonnie, 84

Charles, Lewis, 19, 71

Chiles, Linden, 109

Christie, Audrey, 76

Christine, Virginia, 17, 52

Cianelli, Eduardo, 92

Clark, Dort, 119

Clarke, John, 70

Clute, Sidney, 97

Coe, Peter, 26

Colasanto, Nicholas, 99

Coleman, Dabney, 32, 48, 90, 99

Collins, Russell, 17, 33

Colon, Miriam, 114

Comi, Paul, 27, 62, 119

Conrad, Michael, 99

Considine, John, 20

Considine, Tim, 97

Constantine, Michael, 54, 88, 119

Contreras, Roberto, 115

THE FUGITIVE'S DIRECTORS

THE FUGITIVE'S WRITERS

Alcalde, Mario, 114

Barrows, Robert Guy, 57

Bast, William, 67

Black, John D.F., 7

Bleecker, Perry, 17

Brinkley, Don, 55, 61, 72, 73, 82

Brooke, Peter R., 43

Brough, Walter, 104

Browne, Howard, 93

Caillou, Alan, 3

Carabatsos, Steven W., 102

Cohen, Larry, 39, 50

Crawford, Oliver, 9, 92, 110

Dales, Arthur, 98

Dennis, Robert C., 12, 26

Dexter, Joy, 90

Dillon, Robert, 102

Eastman, John, 60

Eckstein, George, 8, 29, 31, 34, 45, 53, 60, 78, 119, 120

Ellis, Sidney, 45

Emmett, Jeri, 102, 108, 116

Fass, George, 47

Freibeger, Fred, 105

Gerard, Merwin, 25

Germano, Peter, 13, 28

Gillis, Jackson, 89

Goldman, Lawrence Louis, 117

Gollard, J.T., 116

Goodman, Ralph, 118

Gordon, William D., 2, 42, 44, 50, 65

Griffith, James, 34

Gwaltney, Francis Irby, 51

Hamner, Robert, 62

Hawkins, John, 20

Heims, Jo, 51

Hume, Edward C., 111

Jerome, Stuart, 11, 19, 32

Kantor, Leonard, 46, 83

Kean, E. Arthur, 95, 100

King, Otto, 61

Kneubuhl, John, 79, 80, 85, 88, 89

Kronman, Harry, 3, 13, 18, 20, 25, 33, 35, 38, 43, 66, 107

Krumholz, Chester, 66

Langdon, Betty, 75

Larson, Glen A., 89

Lawrence, Anthony, 81

Lessing, Norman, 67, 76

Lewin, Robert, 79

Link, William/Levinson, Richard, 36, 63

Loeb, Lee, 96, 99, 112

Lucas, John Meredyth, 109

Lucey, Paul, 43

Macadah, Zahrini, 51

Menzies, James, 74

Merlin, Barbara/Milton, 33

Morwood, William, 21

Oringer, Barry, 91, 105, 113, 115, 118

Pirosh, Robert, 10

Ross, Sam, 94, 101, 106

Rubin, Mann, 88

Saltzman, Philip, 24, 41, 42, 56, 64, 107

Schiller, Wilton, 95

Searls, Hank, 4, 5

Stark, Sheldon, 16, 21, 27, 40

Trivers, Barry, 12

Turley, Jack, 48, 54, 59, 71, 108

Ullman, Dan, 37, 52, 58, 68, 77, 86, 87, 97, 103

Ward, Al C., 22, 23, 84

Weiss, Arthur, 6, 15, 47, 49

Whitmore, Stanford, 1, 14, 17, 30

Wilson, Anthony, 69, 70

Zagor, Michael, 119, 120

Selected
Bibliography

BOOKS

Armer, Alan A. *Writing the Screenplay.* Belmont, California: Wadsworth Publishing, 1988.

Brooks, Tim. *The Complete Directory to Prime Time TV Stars,* New York: Ballantine Books, 1987.

Brooks, Tim and Earle Marsh. *The Complete Directory to Prime Time Network TV Shows, 1946–Present.* 5th edition. New York: Ballantine Books, 1992.

Brown, Les, *Les Brown's Encyclopedia of Television.* New York: New York Zoetrope, 1982.

Castleman, Harry and Walter J. Podrazik. *Harry and Wally's Favorite TV Shows.* New York: Prentice-Halll 1989.

Current Biography Yearbook, H.W. Wilson, various editions.

Goldenson, Leonard H., with Martin J. Wolf. *Beating the Odds.* New York: Scribners, 1991.

Halliwell, Leslie, *Halliwell's Filmgoer's Companion,* 8th edition, New York: Scribners, 1985.

Inman, David, *The TV Encyclopedia,* New York: Pedigree Books, 1991.

Maltin, Leonard. *Movie and Video Guide 1993.* New York: Penguin Books, 1993.

McNeil, Alex, *Total Television,* New York: Penguin Books, 1991 .

O'Neil, Thomas, *The Emmys,* New York: Penguin Books, 1992.

Rossen, Carol, *Counterpunch,* New York: E.P. Dutton, 1988.

Variety Who's Who in Show Business. New York: R.R. Bowker, 1989, revised edition.

ARTICLES

From TV Guide:

Amory, Cleveland. Review of *The Fuqitive.* January 11, 1964.

"Catching Up with the One-Armed Man," April 10, 1965.

Dern, Marian. "Ever Want to Run Away From It All? The Fugitive does this every week, and herein lies the secret of the show's success," February 22, 1964.

Hano, Arnold. "David's Drooping . . . Success Has Left Fugitive David Janssen Tired, Tense and Physically Ailing," March 6, 1965.

Hobson, Dick. "Eyeball to Eyeball with David Janssen: If He Knows Who He Is, He Isn't Saying," January 29, 1972.

"S.O.S. . . . Which Means, in the Case of *The Fugitive,* Storm on Schedule," June 6, 1964.

Whitney, Dwight. "He Never Did Much Running," November 2, 1963.

Whitney, Dwight. "He's the Long Arm of the Law Who Always Ends Up a Little Short: The most frustrating role in television is played by a Canadian actor who is happy about it all." September 12, 1964.

Whitney, Dwight. "Sometimes He Just Sits in the Bathtub: Quinn Martin is a Hot TV Producer, and Here's How He Works," October 23, 1965.

"The End of a Long Run: After four years, the climax of *The Fugitive* is at hand," August 19, 1967.

Others

Armstrong, Lois. "What David Is Really a Fugitive From is Contentment: Everyone Accepts Him But Himself," *People*, November 13, 1978.

Braithwaite, Dennis. "Mirror Image," *Toronto Globe*, June 2,

Brooks, Angela. "David Janssen Is Drinking Himself to Death," *National Enquirer*, September 4, 1979.

Chesis, Jane. "The Last Interview," *The Globe*, March 3, 1980.

Coyle, Paul Robert. "Great Shows: *The Fugitive*," *Emmy Magazine*, November-December, 1982.

Dangaard, Colin. "Fugitive No More," *Chicago Sun Times*, September 25, 1977.

Deeb, Gary. "David Janssen's Harry O is No O'Hara," *Chicago Tribune*, June 6, 1974

Grunberg, Abe. "Voice of Hollywood," *Hollywood Citizen-News*. 1968.

Grunberg, Abe, "End of the Road," *Newsweek*, August 28, 1967.

Haber, Joyce. "David Janssen Talks of His Steady, His Wife and His Work," *Los Angeles Times Calendar*, May 3, 1970.

Haber, Joyce. "Fact, Fiction in the Janssen Case," *Los Angeles Times*, December 17, 1973.

Haber, Joyce. "Hollywood Fugitive: The Tormented Life and Strange Death of David Janssen," *The Star*, May 5, 1988.

Haber, Joyce. "How David Janssen Became a Prisoner of His Mom's Ambition," *The Star*, May 17, 1988.

Lardine, Bob. "We Solve a Mystery!" *The New York Sunday Times*, February 16, 1964.

Latta, John. "David Janssen's Widow Slams Mom's Threat to Fight Will," *The Star*, May 29, 1980.

McCarthy, Todd. "David Janssen Dies of an Apparent Heart Attack," *Los Angeles Times*, February 14, 1980.

O'Connor, John J. "'A Sensitive, Passionate Man' Deals Effectively with Problems of Alcoholism," *The New York Times*, June 6, 1977.

Ragan, David, "TV's Fated Fugitive," *The Globe*, March 4, 1980.

Reilly, Sue. "Songwriter Carol Connors Is Gonna Keep On Flying with a Little Help from Her Friends," *People*, July 20, 1979.

Smith, Cecil. "David Janssen: A Final Haven for a Fugitive," *Los Angeles Times*, February 2, 1980.

Smith, Cecil. "The Will That Shocked Hollywood," *The Star*, May 24, 1988.

Thorburn, David, "Is TV Acting a Distinctive Art Form?" *The New York Times*, August 14, 1977.

Wilk, Stuart. "David Janssen's Sudden Death — the Untold Story," *National Enquirer*, March 4, 1980.

ABOUT THE AUTHOR

Mel Proctor is currently in his eleventh year as play-by-play announcer for the Baltimore Orioles baseball team and the Washington Bullets basketball team on HTS, Home Team Sports, a regional cable network based in Bethesda, Maryland. He has been named Maryland Sportscaster of the Year, three times in the last four years. Proctor has also broadcast college basketball for CBS, NFL football for NBC, and college football, boxing and pro basketball for TBS and TNT.

In his twenty years as a television and radio sportscaster, Proctor has also handled broadcasts for New Jersey Nets basketball and Texas Rangers baseball. Proctor also served as sports director for WTOP radio in Washington, D.C., and KGMB radio-TV in Honolulu, Hawaii.

Following graduation from Colorado College, Proctor worked for three and a half years in the film industry as producer-director for NFL Films.

Proctor has also worked as an actor in television and films. Over the past three years, he has played television reporter Grant Bessor on Barry Levinson's *Homicide: Life on the Street* on NBC and has appeared in numerous films and television shows.

Proctor, his wife Julie, and children, Billy and Maile, live in Ellicott City, Maryland.

If you enjoyed this Longmeadow Press Edition
you may want to add the following titles
to your collection:

ITEM No.	TITLE	PRICE
0-681-00525-4	New Eves SCIENCE FICTION ABOUT THE EXTRAORDINARY WOMEN OF TODAY AND TOMORROW	14.95
0-681-00693-5	Bloodlines	19.95
0-681-00725-7	The Works of Jack London	19.95
0-681-00687-0	The Works of Nathaniel Hawthorne	19.95
0-681-00729-X	The Works of H. G. Wells	19.95
0-681-00795-8	The Works of Henry David Thoreau	19.95
0-681-00753-2	Silver Screams: Murder Goes Hollywood	8.95

Ordering is easy and convenient.
Order by phone with Visa, MasterCard, American Express or Discover:
☎ **1-800-322-2000,** Dept. 706
or send your order to:
Longmeadow Press, Order/Dept. 706,
P.O. Box 305188, Nashville, TN 37230-5188

Name _____

Address _____

City _____ State _____ Zip _____

Item No.	Title	Qty	Total

Check or Money Order enclosed Payable to Longmeadow Press	Subtotal	
Charge: ❑ MasterCard ❑ VISA ❑ American Express ❑ Discover	Tax	
Account Number	Shipping	2.95
	Total	

Card Expires

Signaure _____ Date _____

Please add your applicable sales tax: AK, DE, MT, OR, 0.0%—CO, 3.8%—AL, HI, LA, MI, WY, 4.0%—VA. 4.5%—GA, IA, ID, IN, MA, MD, ME, OH, SC, SD, VT, WI, 5.0%—AR, AZ, 5.5%—MO, 5.725%—KS, 5.9%—CT, DC, FL, KY, NC, ND, NE, NJ, PA, WV, 6.0%—IL, MN, UT, 6.25%—MN, 6.5%—MS, NV, NY, RI, 7.0%—CA, TX, 7.25%—OK, 7.5%—WA. 7.8%—TN, 8.25%